The Poetic Hooligan

Richard Haldenby

RICHARD HALDENBY

A CIP catalogue record for this book is
available from the British Library

ISBN 978-1-9164 294-5-1

Design and Production by Riverhead Books,
Telephone: 07890 170063
email: mike.riverheadbooks@gmail.com

Printed by: Fisk Printers, Hull

CONTENTS

RICHARD HALDENBY

ACKNOWLEDGEMENTS
Special thanks to the following for their hard work, help
and support in the preparation of this book:
Linda Ellerby, Tony Rose, my son Jonathan
and Mike Sterriker at Riverhead

DEDICATION

I would like to dedicate this book to my ex-wife Jackie, our three wonderful children: Sarah, Lisa and Jonathan, and our beautiful grandaughters Lydia and Evie.

Jonathan and his wife Becki are expecting their first baby in May 2021 and the book is also for them and the generations to come. I hope it will be of interest to them.
It has taken me over ten years to write 'The Poetic Hooligan' but after looking back at over four generations and photographs up to 120 years old, I finally have the satisfaction of seeing it completed.

I would also like to thank Jackie for the forty-three years we spent together.
I met Jackie in 1971 whilst going out with her younger sister Avril at school. She said, 'Do you want to come and see my sister's baby Sarah?"
I was fifteen, Avril was sixteen and Jackie was seventeen.
Eighteen months went by and I bumped into Jackie in 1973 on The Arctic Ranger public house' opening night.
I started going out with her and we were married three years later when I officially adopted Sarah.
Even though Sarah is not mine biologically I love her the same as Lisa and Jonathan and treat her and my grandaughters Lydia and Evie all the same.
Lisa was born seven years later and we thought that we would have no more as we couldn't afford it. However, Jonathan arrived twelve years later. Twenty years between Sarah and Jonathan, for an explanation, read on...

Please sir, I want some more.
Me with a bowl down Lockwood Terrace
with Jeff and Pete Marshal.

CHAPTER ONE
GROWING UP IN LOCKWOOD STREET

Whenever I see black and white photos or TV footage of 1956 it looks like the dark ages, however when I think back to these times it all seems so colourful. Days were longer, summer was hotter, winter was colder with lots of snow and we seemed to have four seasons. I have photos of my brothers and sister sat outside on our living room window sill at Easter in our little red blazers with silver buttons on a hot Easter Sunday, before going to church. How many hot Easters do we have now?

Summer seemed to start at Easter with vivid memories of all the neighbours sat outside in Lockwood Terrace until late at night. We would be sent to bed early and sneak a look out of my Mam and Dad's front bedroom window into the terrace to watch the adults have a cuppa sat on chairs, chewing the fat as my old mate Maurice would say. We were envious of some of our friends like the Marshals who would be allowed to sit out with their parents. If we asked my Mam why we couldn't stay up with them she would reply, "You do as I say not as I do," never daring to ask my Dad. If he saw us looking out the window he'd shout up for us to get into bed or he'd come up and go through us like a dose of salts, which he never did but just the raised voice was enough. He never did lay a finger on us, as I never have my kids.

There were no barbecues, cheap cases of beer or bottles of wine from Aldi back then, only the continentals or upper class drank wine in those days. I

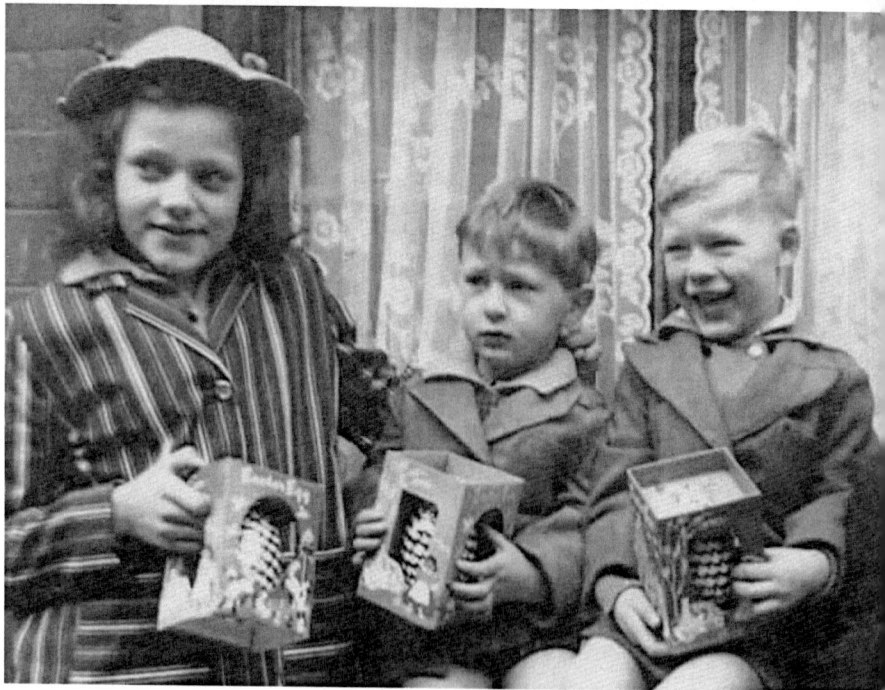

Top: Karen, Gary and Me at Easter
Below: L - R Dave Field. Mike Shipley, Me, and our Gary

don't suppose many of our parents had drunk much wine, as they didn't start to venture abroad on package holidays until the seventies. Their tipple was a pint of Hull Brewery mild for my Dad and a brandy and babycham for me Mam. If my Dad did see us and tell us off, we would then go to the back bedroom window and talk to the Fields next door, Graham, Dave and Steve, or Mike Shipley across the back passage who lived on Lockwood Street front.

It seemed to stay light until nearly midnight and you certainly appreciated the hot nights sleeping with no blankets on as opposed to the layer upon layer of itchy woolly blankets and candle wick covers, topped off with my Dad and Grandad's army trench coats in winter. When winter came, boy did it get cold and snow. Or did it? I'm sure every Christmas was white in a picture postcard kind of way, and every summer melted the tar between the cobbled streets, well that's how I seem to remember it through my rose tinted glasses. Yet in reality life was much harsher, wages were low and luxury comforts were few.

I was born on March 4th 1956 in a two-up, two-down terraced house at 5, Lockwood Terrace, off Lockwood Street, Hull, which was situated in the town centre. Looking back I suppose it can only be described as a slum area, with no hot water and only basic electricity. We had one single light in the living room dangling on a wire that was covered in dark brown netting and the same in the kitchen, each room had only one socket. We had no bathroom, inside toilet or hot running water. Our toilet was a tiny six-foot by two foot six inch outbuilding with a planked door which had a gap at the top and bottom, which is where we get the saying 'built like a brick shithouse'.

Our bum wipes came in the shape of newspaper squares hung on the back of the toilet door by a piece of

Patti Forth and me in 1958 on Lockwood Street.

The tin bath and outside toilet

string. One of the worst things about the loo though apart from the snow blowing through the gaps in the door was the spiders, I don't think my arse barely touched the seat whenever there was a spider there, usually a daddy-longlegs. Our garden, or should I say back yard was a ten foot square of concrete with a six foot wall adjoining the back passage, Coronation Street style, that looked into other backyards not more than three foot away, or should I say a metre. My Grannie and Grandad lived only a few doors away at the end of the passage.

Our Gary used to run down the passage to my Gran and Grandad's when he was about two if he was in trouble and shout to my Grandad Laurie, 'Let me in, I'm leaving home.' Wonderful days. It still makes me laugh when I think of it.

I know these squalid conditions must have been written about a thousand times by people who were brought up in the same conditions. Most people talk of the outside loo and the tin bath, but not only did the Izal toilet paper and newspaper squares leave a mark on your undies they also left a mental scar on your memory.

Nobody had bathrooms back then and our only method of bathing was in the traditional galvanised tin bath, which apart from bath night hung on a nail in the backyard. This was brought into the living room on a Saturday night and filled up with kettles and pans full of hot water in front of the open coal fire. We used to start off with our Gary who was the youngest up to Karen, then my Mam and Dad who would probably have to scoop the scum off the top before topping up as we used to get into some right states. For the rest of the week we would have a strip down wash in the kitchen sink, the big white ceramic Belfast sink that you now see for sale in garden centres today.

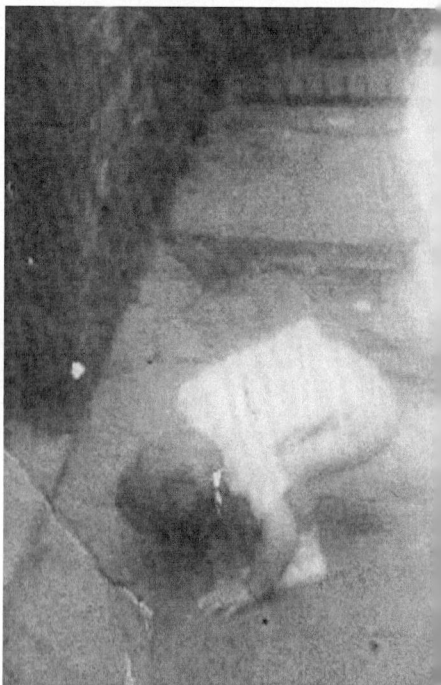

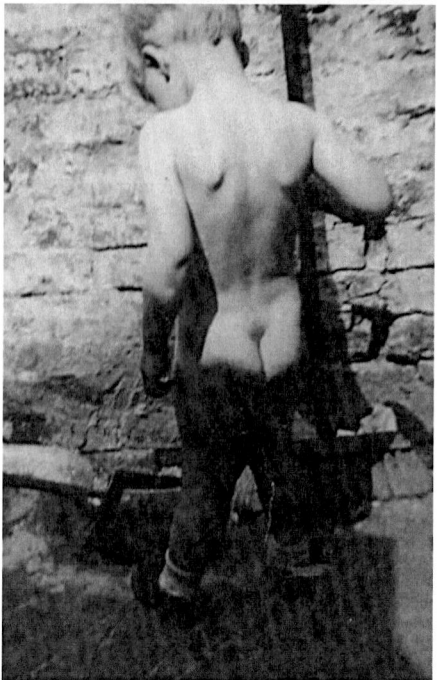

Clockwise from top left:
Gary on wall

Gary shouting under Grandad's gate

Gary having a pee in the sink

THE POETIC HOOLIGAN

The open fire was protected by a fine wire mesh guard to stop sparks flying out and burning you or your best bit of lino, but when my Mam or Dad weren't there, we would move it away to get warmer as the mesh reduced the heat. The fireguard also acted as a good clothes dryer by hanging your clothes over - that was until someone forgot and scorched them. I bet a lot of clothes had a yellow tinge to them from the fire or the shape of an iron from the unregulated irons, the irons then were either cast iron that you put in your Yorkie fireplace to heat up or electric irons that were hot or not. I remember turning them on and then spitting on the bottom to see how hot it was, if you wanted to steam iron something you would sprinkle water on your clothes and then cover them in brown paper to stop it scorching. As a friend of mine Arthur 'Bushybrows' once said to me, "Back in them days, nobody had out and the fost up was the best dressed."

If you wanted a pee in the middle of the night there were no en suites or upstairs toilets, we had to pee in a two gallon galvanised bucket with disinfectant in. What a struggle the everyday chores must have been for our parents and grandparents that we all take for granted now but I suppose those basics were luxuries to what their parents and grandparents had, and who knows what our grandchildren will think of how we live now. Even though my Mam Christina, nee Cox, would work hard to keep the house clean in-between being a cleaner at the Hull College of Further Education at Queens's gardens early mornings and afternoons, she could do nothing to stop the invasion of black clocks that came up through the floor boards and fireplace every night. Black clocks to those of you who don't know are a type of cockroach.

This was due to living in the middle of an industrial area with Barmston drain less than one hundred yards

My Mam Christina

My Dad Ralph

away. My worst memories of living there was having to come down in the middle of the night after waking up yet again and telling my Mam I felt like a loaf of bread, I used to feel completely numb. We laugh about it still but at the time it was bloody awful.

We would turn the light on and have to stand on the stairs until the beetles disappeared, the floor would part like a pair of black curtains. Them along with the terrible smells that used to come up from the hundred year old drains that run under our houses were some of the less romantic memories of the good old days, and yet we were lucky as a lot of the other families had a lot more children, in some houses they had up to ten kids and you could trust each and every one of them. Our doors were never locked but if you did want to lock the door and anyone wanted to be in they would just put their hand through the letter box and pull the key up that was tied to the end of a piece of string. It was obviously a close knit society and to this day we are still good friends with some of our then neighbours.

We left Lockwood Terrace on December 1st 1967 when our ages ranged from Gary who was the youngest at nine to Karen who was 17. We shared the same bedroom with Karen having her own bed as we got older, but when we were younger we top and tailed in a double bed.

My own children could not imagine life in such cramped conditions when you look at all the high tech equipment they've grown up with such as X Boxes, Playstations and lap tops it gives you a reality check on how far we've come in fifty years. The nearest we had to high-tech was to lift the arm on our record player and let Elvis play over and over. Then when it got crackly, we would pop down to Sydney Scarborough and buy a new stylus (needle) which you had to turn over from 45 for a single to 33 for an LP. If you played it the wrong

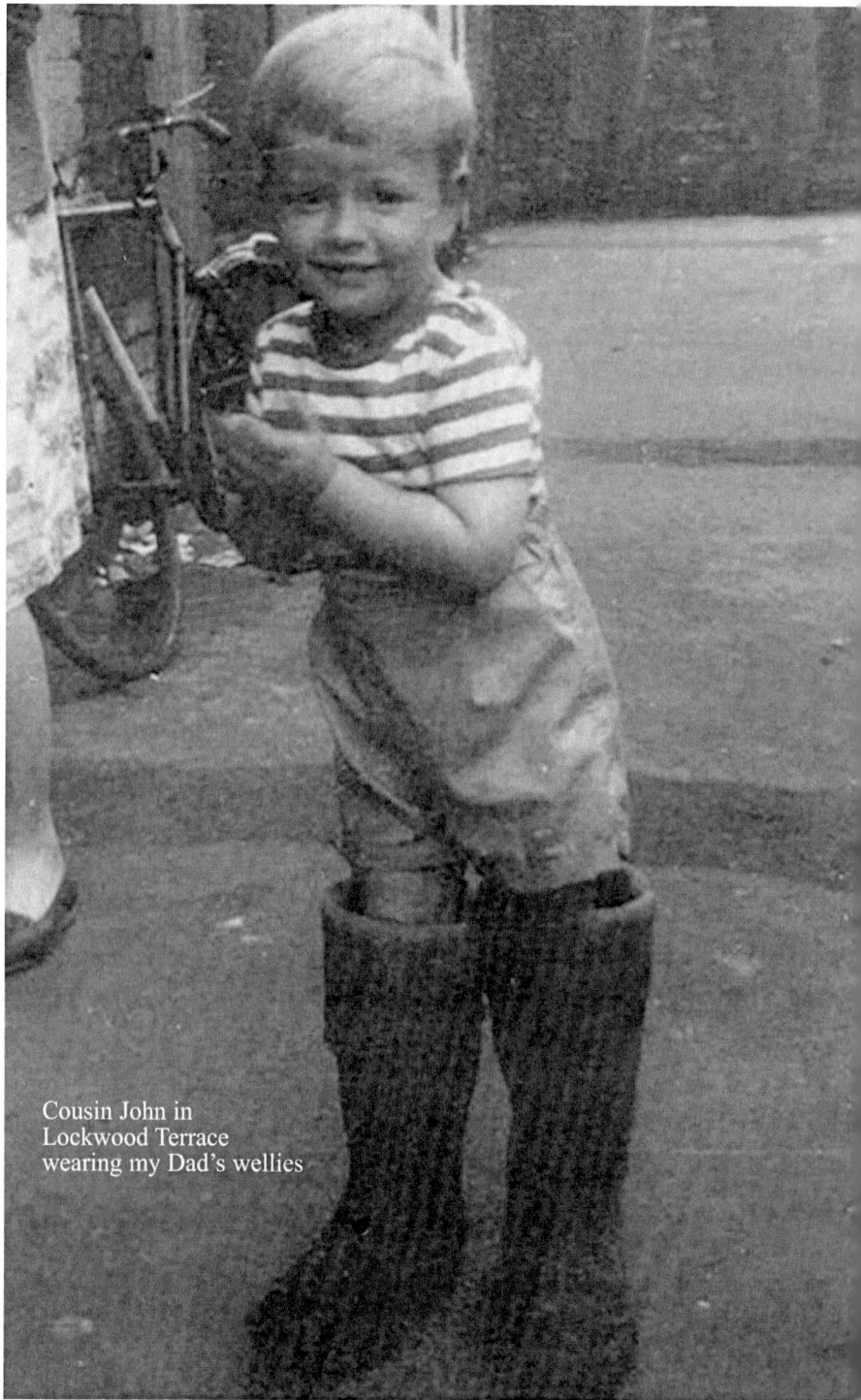

Cousin John in
Lockwood Terrace
wearing my Dad's wellies

way round it sounded slow like you were in a bad dream or fast like Pinky and Perky. So the correct side of the needle had to be placed on the record, hence the saying, 'Get in the groove'.

If there was such a thing as time travel as portrayed in TV series such as 'Goodnight Sweetheart' or 'Life on Mars' where they can go back in time, our kids would think they were having a nightmare. No central heating or double-glazing and ice on the inside of the windows in winter. But no matter how tough we had it in those days I feel lucky to have been born when I was. I not only avoided the war years just eleven years earlier but also experienced all the new revolutionary inventions, which are now taken for granted by our children and grandchildren.

The swinging sixties must have been the most exciting decade of all time with stockings, suspenders and miniskirts being normal fashion wear... WOW!

This was a transitional period from the dark near Edwardian times of the fifties and through the sixties and leading into the bright and vibrant Glamrock days of the seventies. When you look at our brightly-lit homes now with LED lighting that runs at a fraction of the cost and fibre optic cable or remote operated electrical items we've come a long way in a short time. When you think it was only 1969 that Neil Armstrong walked on the moon and the space ship Apollo 11 that took him only had the same computing ability of a 1980's calculator, it makes you wonder how they managed to travel that distance and back. In comparison to today's computers that are one and a half million times more powerful and even our mobile phones are considerably more powerful then Apollo eleven's computers.

When we used to watch 'Tomorrow's World' with the futuristic inventions that were supposed to be coming

Me and our Gary,
Dave, Graham and Maxine Field

Me in my pram in 1956
at six months old

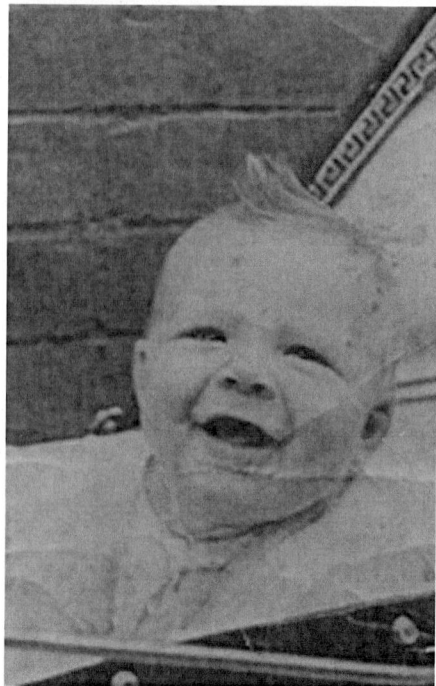

our way, I don't suppose anyone anticipated a telephone you could carry in your pocket that could send photos, videos, written text and even do your banking on. Even a watch that tells your blood pressure, use as a phone and receive emails. When I got my first phone in 1991 people would look at you and call me a poser because I had a mobile, albeit a big Motorola the size of a brick.

All thanks to Martin Cooper who invented the Motorola mobile phone on the 4/3/73. Same day as my birthday. We were also blessed with colour TV in 1967 and the jet engine took a giant leap forward when Concorde also made its maiden flight in 1967 which has now become common practice for us all to jump on a jet plane and visit parts of the world we would never have dreamt of back then. Most people experience at least one exotic holiday a year now. But in 1956 when I was born you would have seen this as science fiction, and we are now hearing of people booking flights into space. It makes the mind boggle to think what our grandchildren will be thrilling themselves with in another fifty years in comparison with the changes in our lives. The microchip must be one of the most amazing inventions, which seems limitless in the advancement of technology in our lifetime making everything smaller and cheaper, which makes our lives easier and more comfortable.

Whilst all this development was taking place we were still living in our little shoebox of a home in Lockwood Terrace. However, we were about to start venturing further afield as we started at a newly built school on the Orchard Park Estate, some six miles away on the northern outskirts of Hull, named St John Fisher. This was quite a journey for us at eleven years old as we first had a long walk from Lockwood Street to Beverley Road corner to catch a bus outside the then, Zoological, where the Hull Daily Mail offices are now. Then it was

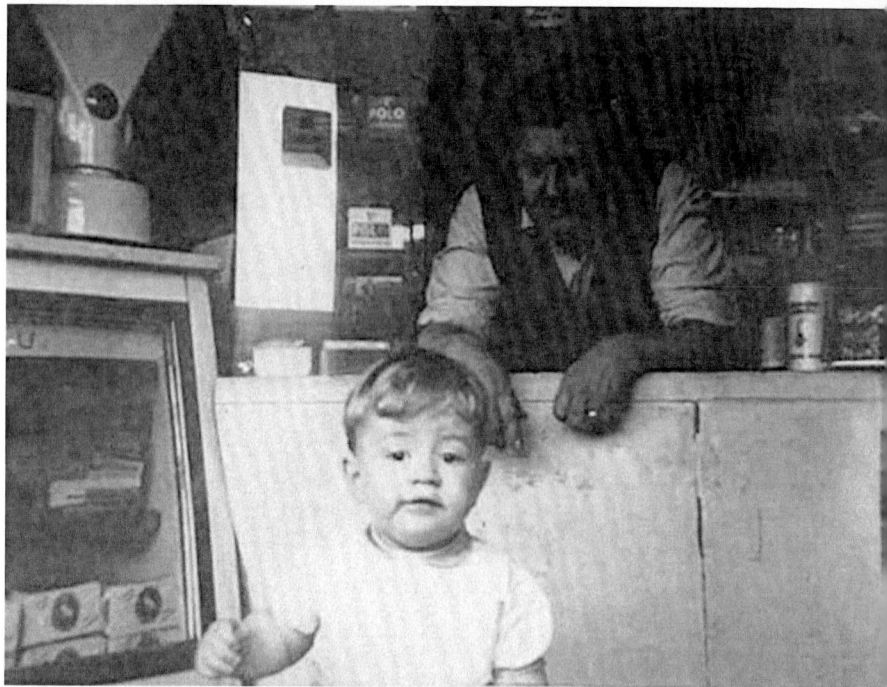

Our John in Eddie Green's shop on the corner of Lockwood Street and Lockwood Terrace

THE POETIC HOOLIGAN

a thirty minute bus ride and another long walk when we got off outside the Orchard Park pub, to walk another fifteen minutes to school as the Hall Road extension had not been built then. We had to walk right through the winter on the muddy roads which ruined our shoes, so my Mam made me wear a bright yellow pair of Tuf boots with animal print soles. I used to feel so embarrassed wearing them and couldn't wait to wear them out but by that time we had moved onto Orchard Park in the December of that year and didn't have far to walk. It infuriates me now when you see lazy women driving their kids a short distance to school.

Before we left Lockwood Terrace we were looked upon as being quite well off as we had a telephone, albeit a Dixon of Dock Green type, the big black Bakelite one with a chrome centre dial. We also had a television with two knobs on, volume and contrast I think. Our other luxury item was a Morris car that my Dad paid £12 and 10 shillings for. All this was thanks to my Mam and Dad who worked hard to give us these things plus a two week holiday every year and rides each weekend into the country or to the seaside to places like Brantingham or Hornsea and Withernsea. Our favourite place to visit was to our family roots of Sunderland where my Mam and Grannie were born.

We would all travel up to Sunderland including my Gran and Grandad and stay at Aunt Ruby and Uncle Alf's, my Grannie's brother who lived at 31 Sea View Road.

They have two sons and a daughter Vic, Dave and Kath. Our Dave, as he is affectionately known to us all down here is still a close relative, even though he is my Mam's cousin I am closer to him than anyone and see him more than my own cousins who live in Hull. Dave now lives in Portugal but we still see him twice a year when he comes over with Michelle.

Aunt Ruby, Grannie, Mam, Gary, Dad and Me on Sunderland Beach.

Grannie, Gary and Mam in tent on Sunderland beach.

THE POETIC HOOLIGAN

Dave's always been a jack the lad and is a natural with cars even though he is not a trained mechanic he had his own garage. When he was eleven or twelve he could be seen driving around Sunderland as he used to pinch his Dad's, specially adapted hand controlled Morris 1000 or Moggy thou' as they were commonly known as Uncle Alf had lost his legs due to gangrene. It was often a comedy of errors when we set off in my Dad's car. He was famous for running out of petrol in the middle of nowhere or something going wrong with it. But to give him credit he took us on some fantastic holidays to places as far as Edinburgh, Blackpool and Sherringham in Norfolk in the days of no motorways or sat navs and yet he always got us there and back safely.

One of my Dad's better cars was his Ford Consul with column change gears and bench leather seats front and back. The six of us plus Gran and Grandad all fitted in comfortably. I remember us all pushing the car on several occasions though, sometimes late at night in the middle of the countryside, with my Gran doing her bit with her little stumpy legs pushing away and panicking that a mouse or other tiny creature would scurry up her leg.

We would visit Sunderland for a couple of days at the weekend or a week during the school holidays. We would all cram in and sleep on the settees and matresses on the floor in every room. All of us kids slept in one room which made us think we were at home when we woke in the middle of the night. But that got me into trouble one night when I woke up, as I got up for a pee and instinctively set off to where our pee bucket would be at home. I proceeded to pull the curtain back and pee up the wall until I realised what I'd done. Needless to say I wasn't my Aunt Ruby's favourite person for the next few days and she never did let me forget it.

I used to love walking around the corner to the shops

Clockwise from top left:
Me and Gary at Butlins, Filey

Me and Gary on top of
Tunstal Hill overlooking
Sunderland.

Dad and Gary at
Marsden Grotto,
north of Sunderland.

for stotty cakes as they call them up there, or bread cakes to us, and then making ham and pease pudding sandwiches.

Sunderland is a beautiful part of the country and not as industrialised as people may imagine. Since the ship building trade died, it has become more developed for tourism. It was the shipbuilding that gave Sunderland its nickname of 'Mackems' due to their accent when they referred to the shipbuilding they would say, 'We Mackem,' instead of make em. Don't make the mistake of calling everyone from the Northeast a Geordie as that term is reserved for the true Geordies who were born within a few miles of Grey's monument in Newcastle town centre. As is the right to be called a Barbery Coaster in Sunderland if you were born on Dock Street or a cockney having to be born within earshot of Bow Bells.

We recently went up to our Dave's son Andrew's wedding to Kelly and it's always nice to visit the places we used to go as kids like Marsden Grotto that is a few miles up the coast from the town centre. The Grotto was a magical place for us as kids, it's a pub/restaurant cut into a rock face looking out to sea. As you drive along the coast road you see what looks like a small building with a lift shaft. As you go down there are different floors with bars and as you come out at the bottom you're inside a bar that's cut into the cliffs. As you walk outside there is a large patio area onto the beach which looks onto a large piece of rock about one hundred feet tall and diameter, as the tide goes out there are caves and tunnels to explore. It is a big bird sanctuary covered in Puffins and other sea birds.

A couple of years ago we stayed in the Roker Hotel which is situated on the sea front and overlooking the old stone pier that pushes out nearly a mile into the North Sea with a large lighthouse on the end. My Mam

Clockwise from top left:
Me Dad with our Gary and
me outside Mrs Tuthill's.
(Sheringham)

Dad with our Gary and me on
the concrete slope where I got
lost (Sheringham)

Dad, David Whitfield and
Norman Collier.

told me of how my Grandad used to fish off the end when he was a young man and if the weather turned bad they would have to go down some steps and walk the full length in a tunnel back to land. It was a surreal experience to walk the same steps my Grandad had all those years before. Just around the other side of the harbour wall is the mouth of the river Wear and the large iron Wear bridge we used to stand on as kids with my Mam and Dad and hundreds of others to see the ships get launched sideways off one bank. We would watch in amazement as it almost keeled over and then sent a huge wave crashing onto the opposing bank.

It's a pity those days of shipbuilding are no longer part of Sunderland's economy after six hundred years, the decline of which started during WW2 when the ships could not be built fast enough and had to be built in America. The last ships to be built in Sunderland were finished in 1989. Whenever we go back up there I get the feeling that you get when you've been away on holiday and you then see the local landmarks again as you get nearer to home…

Top: Karen, Me, Mam and Gary on the Pier.

Grandad Percy Haldenby with Aunt Doris, my Dad's sister.

CHAPTER TWO
MY DAD,
'BIG RALPH'

My Dad took us on holiday every year and one that I remember particularly was to Sheringham in Norfolk. We stayed with an old lady called Mrs Tuthill of Station Road for two weeks. I was about eight at the time and enjoyed the most memorable holiday and remember it like we were there yesterday. It was a beautiful cottage where we stayed with apple and pear trees in the large back garden. We could not believe our luck having never seen gardens with fruit trees before. We gorged ourselves with them and even stock piled them under the mattress which again, got us into bother as we forgot we'd put them there until Mrs Tuthill changed the bedding and found them going mushy between the mattress and the old diamond shaped wire sprung base. I was surprised how far it was even on today's fast flowing roads. When I think how my Dad would just set off on the old winding roads with no breakdown recovery service to back him up in case of emergency. Even though there was the AA and RAC the average working man could not afford them. Everything still looked as I remembered it with a little old fashioned railway station, apart from Mrs Tuthill's not being there which was a shame as I'd have loved a photo of us in front of it. I instantly recognised a concrete slope down to the beach, which helped me lay a ghost to rest as for years I had nightmares of being lost. What had happened was my Mam was playing bingo in an old rickety green wooden building and I wandered off and panicked. The building was next to the slope and I had

Clockwise from top left:

Gary, Me & Karen outside Madame Tussauds.

Mam and David Whitfield, who was the first British artist to have a UK No1 single in his own country and in the USA at the same time with Cara Mia. David was a Hull lad born & bred.

John and Me

walked down to the sea front crying until a policeman found me and took me back to my Mam. When I saw the slope I remembered how it was even though it didn't have the wooden building there just seeing it brought back all the other happy memories. We used to go from there and have cruises on the Norfolk Broads. It was fantastic to see all the beautiful scenery and stop off at riverside pubs for lunch and to see all the swans on the river was something I'll never forget.

As you get older and look back and remember all the things your Mam and Dad did for you and then see them in their twilight years it really makes you appreciate and understand them.

Another memorable holiday we had was in Blackpool in 1963 when we were invited to go and stay with my Mam and Dad's best friends Lucy and Norman Collier. Norman was doing a summer season along with Cliff Richard and the Shadows, David Whitfield and Little and Large.

Lucy and Norman were always known to us as Aunt and Uncle and we called their children 'our' Victor, Janet and Karen. Lucy had lived next door to my Mam from about eight years old and spent a lot of time staying at my Grannies and going on holiday up to Sunderland with them so Lucy was looked upon like a sister to my Mam. As they got older and Lucy met Norman he became a friend of the family and a good mate of my Dad's. When we went to Blackpool with them we shared a great big house just off the sea front. We didn't realise at the time that the friends of Lucy and Norman who came to visit the house were such big stars. We obviously knew who Cliff Richard was but didn't know Little and Large or David Whitfield were also famous. We would sit in the sunshine on one of the promenades and watch them all perform.

Just around the corner from our holiday home was a

The Haldenbys
L-R: Cyril, Dad, George, Ray,
Pete, Doris and Ted.

Grandad Percy with Me,
Mam and Karen.

fishing pond where we used to spend most of our time. It was here we saw our first crane fly whilst fishing, the dragon fly type with its beautiful electric blue colouring and double wings, looking very similar in colour and movement to a kingfisher. Coming from the city it was something we had never seen the like of before which frightened us to death. We had many more family holidays but those few were the ones that stuck in my mind. It's funny how silly little things like the crane fly stick in your mind but other things that my Mam and our Gary remind me about had completely slipped my mind.

Happy days…

It always amazed me how my Dad knew where to go without ever looking at a map. But being a wagon driver for years he had learnt how to navigate as I have without using sat navs. My Dad Ralph had been a long distance lorry driver since coming out of the Royal Horse Guards in the fifties which he later regretted as he could have ended up with a good pension. But back then the money in the horse guards wasn't good and wagon driving was. He became known to the other drivers as 'Big Ralph' a man not to be messed with. My Dad had a tough upbringing, as his Mam Sarah died when he was young and with him being the eldest of six he had the responsibility of helping his Dad to raise the kids. Grandad Percy only had one leg and found work doing whatever he could, including a toilet cleaner at Baker Street toilets that are still in use now. When my Dad got to sixteen he joined the Army, so the kids had to be split up and were sent off to Barnados' children's homes around the country. I know this upset my Dad and according to my Mam made him feel guilty.

Clockwise from top left:

Dad in overalls having repaired an armoured car.

Dad in Jaffa. Egypt.

Dad in Chindits' style uniform.

MY DAD

Big Ralph as he was known back in the day,
When life was tough but the sun shone all day.
1925 down Walker Street
Was where young Ralph first stood on his feet.
To mother Sarah and Percy his dad
He soon developed into a bit of a lad.
A storm like no other did rage that night,
The Norse Gods warned he was here to fight.
He went to war he could do no other,
Too young to care for his sister and brothers.
He met Chrissy Cox, a match made by hell!
And how they would fight a ring a ding dell.
For 65 years they never did part,
They loved one another with all of their hearts.
His proudest days were at Windsor Castle,
As a Royal Horse Guard he would take no hassle.
The rest of his life as a long distance driver,
With a wife and kids he was a better provider.
Three boys and a girl they brought into the world,
A kiss from me Mam would make us a girl.
He'd curl up his lip when he would get mad,
But when all's said and done, he's still our Dad

My Dad had an interesting career in the Army, his proudest days of which were in the Royal Horse guards at Windsor Castle. He spent a few years in Germany and Palestine, where he told me of his time as a motorcycle dispatch rider which was a very dangerous job with lots of the lads getting shot or decapitated by wire ropes that would be stretched across the road at head height.

He was only given a gallon of petrol that would just get him from one camp to another and back again. This was done in case they were captured, there wouldn't be much fuel for the enemy to use. But it also meant that on the return leg he would often run out of juice, so as he got to the top of a hill he would have to freewheel down into the camp.

I recently bought a double DVD called 'The Prize', which was about his time there and is a true story. When he watched it he was telling my Mam step by step what was going to happen next.

One of his other stories was about his time in Southampton on the day of the D-Day landings. He was stationed three miles from the docks repairing the armoured cars that were been brought back damaged from Normandy. He would drive one off the landing craft and up to the lay-by to carry out repairs and then take it back and swap it for another car. On this day however as he drove one onto the landing craft and was walking off to get another that was parked on the quayside he was stopped by a officer who asked him where he was going, he replied that he was going to get another armoured car to repair. The officer said, 'No you're not, you're going over to Normandy,' and was told to stand in line to get a helmet and rifle.

As he stood in line he looked up and saw his own commanding officer up on the quayside who just happened to turn and saw my dad in line and asked 'Corporal Haldenby what are you doing?' When my Dad told him what had happened he said, 'No you're not, get in that car and repair it!' His officer tore a strip off the other and said 'He's worth more to us repairing them than fighting.' If he had gone over I may not be here now. I recently found a small photo of my Dad and posted it on 'Hull, The Good Old Days', which is a local Internet site about days gone by. Someone contacted me and said, 'You must be proud of your Dad being in the Chindits' Special Forces.' I looked up photos of them and it does look like a Chindits' uniform. See the photo with the cap folded up and khaki uniform.

THE POETIC HOOLIGAN

ADOLPH, THE BIGGEST RACIST.

1939 was when it all began,
Over in Germany lurked an evil man.
He ruled his country but wanted more,
So crossed the border into Poland next door.
He sailed the oceans to the far Far East,
He bombed and slaughtered, the evil beast.
He joined with the Japs and their big mistake,
Was to attack the Wild West who they thought they
could take.
By bombing Pearl Harbour they thought they knew best,
But ruffled the Eagle who protected its nest.
Closer to home his target was Britain,
For to break us down he was smitten.
To rule the skies he tried and tried,
But underestimated the British pride.
Our British bulldog and Churchill our leader,
Were much too strong for the super race breeder.

We hardly saw or knew my Dad until we got older, although I was the one who spent the most time with him. I always loved wildlife and enjoyed setting off at the crack of dawn during the summer holidays to see all the rabbits and wood pigeons, which I never saw being a townie, unlike now where they are as common as sparrows in your garden.

Driving a wagon then was one of the hardest jobs going as the cabs had no heaters in them or any suspension as such; the basic suspension they did have was usually knackered and rightly earned their nickname as bone-shakers. We would regularly set off early in the morning and not get back until late at night. You would literally get bounced all over the cab as you hit potholes. I used to love sitting on the big engine cover to keep warm in the winter and be all snuggled up in a sleeping bag. It actually is bringing a tear to my eye

Barmston drain looking from Lockwood Street bridge. Fountain Road bridge in front and monkey bridge in background. Notice the kids swimming near the bridge.

Fishing on Barmston drain, near Toogood Street

now thinking back to those happy days and seeing my Dad now at eighty nine with dementia is hard after a lifetime of looking at him as an 'iron man'.

I remember setting off to Southampton on a three or four day trip with a yacht on the back, we had to deliver it to the docks which were a very memorable trip for different reasons, when we got there the Queen Mary 1 was in dock. I think this would have been around 1964. While we were sat in the wagon waiting to be unloaded a Docker was killed by a swinging hook of a crane. It was a shock to me as it was near us and we could see him laid out with a blanket over him.

When we were unloaded my Dad had to try different companies on the Dock to get a return load which meant we had to stay overnight and find digs. An experience I'll never forget due to the snoring and farting of about ten drivers all in the same room and the awful smell of sweaty socks. I shared a bed with my Dad and remember waking in the morning and seeing all the drivers stood at a hole in the wall - not a cash dispenser - waiting to get their English breakfast and mug of tea, which they ate sat on their beds.

We ended up finding a load of bales of wool to take home. On the way back we met up with a couple more Coastal transport pals of my Dad's in a greasy spoon cafe and all drove in convoy for the rest of the journey home. The drivers were good mates of my Dad's, Pete Young who ended up being a good pal until recently passing away. The other was Slim Palmer who always made us laugh due to him always wearing slippers to drive in. As we neared home we came to the roundabout at Howden which used to be the main road into Hull before the M62. As we all came around the roundabout Slim lost his load of whale meat that was in cardboard boxes that were roped and sheeted, obviously not roped down very well. A lot of the boxes ended up on the grass

Me and Gary on my Dad's
wagon that we went to
Southampton in

On my bike in
Lockwood Terrace.

verge. My Dad and Pete Young stopped to help him reload the boxes. My memories of that day were seeing Slim climb from his cab in his mucky old tartan slippers and seeing all the dogs that came from nowhere to fill their bellies along with cats, crows and seagulls. It was like an African waterhole where all the animals that normally kill each other seem to have an amnesty when drinking. We eventually got Slim reloaded and set off home with no real fuss, par for the course in those days. No trackers watching your every move or mobiles ringing to see where you were and no coppers jumping on your back checking your tachometer to see if you were ten minutes over your time.

I wish my Dad could have had some of the comforts that today's wagon drivers enjoy such as heated cabs and night heaters, air conditioning when it's too hot, air suspension axles and air suspension seats, telephones, sat navs, microwaves, television, DVD players and CD players. Even wipers and washers would have been nice for him.

The times I remember driving along and he'd have to lean out of the window to operate the wipers by hand in the cold and wet. One of his tricks was to tie a piece of string to the wiper and run it along the windscreen and back in through the quarter light window on the passenger side. Then along the inside of the windscreen, out the driver's side quarter light and onto the other side of the wiper, creating a loop and then pull one side of the string then the other, which became my job and I loved doing it to help.

When the front or rear lights stopped working, they'd have to sit in a lay-by and wait for another driver to pull in and have him drive either in front or at the rear to 'cover' your lights. Or they'd tie a front or rear bicycle light to one side or the other if a light had failed. Coppers were more interested in catching criminals then, rather than doing you for having a light out.

An old friend of my Dad's, Keith Simmister, who worked with him at Coastal Transport told me of how he had set off down south early one cold winter's morning with a thick frost. As he got near Grantham he passed a lay-by and saw my Dad's wagon parked up. He pulled in to see if he was okay and found him asleep behind the wheel. He tried to wake him but couldn't. He was like a block of ice and unconscious from the early stages of hypothermia. Keith covered him in blankets and rubbed him all over to warm him up and eventually woke him. He then gave him a hot drink out of his flask before taking him to his own wagon to warm him through as he had a heater.

It turned out that my Dad had set off early doors but he had broken down so waited to flag down a wagon but none came. With no mobile phones, your fate was in the lap of the gods, or in my Dad's case, Keith's.

I recently spoke to another old driver who said that he jumped in his wagon one day to set off on a long haul trip and found that the driver's seat was knackered so complained to the boss. He had the fitter take the seat out and fit an orange box in, then said, 'If you don't like it I'll get someone else to drive the wagon.'

You either liked it or lumped it. No unfair dismissal or tribunal to go to then. Driving was hard enough back then, but the real work started when you got to your destination. Everything was loaded by hand with hardly any forklifts then. Whether it was bricks, tinned fruit or boxes of whale meat it all had to be loaded by hand and then roped and sheeted. That was no mean feat lifting an ice sodden sheet that must have weighed 16-20 stone from the ground to the top of the load and then laying the sheets out and roping them down nice and square with no bits flapping about or loose rope ends. When you rolled into town with my Dad it was like being with John Wayne, everyone seemed to know him as he'd earned himself a reputation as a hard case, a real man's man. My Dad was never technically clever even though he had been a mechanic in the army during the war. He was more the typical heavy-handed driver. However, when you say someone couldn't organise a piss-up in a brewery, well that he could do, much to my Grandad's satisfaction. My Dad used to collect from Tetley's breweries in Leeds and used to take my Grandad for a ride out with him. Whilst my Dad was loading his lorry my Grandad would frequent the visitors' centre and enjoy half a dozen pints of Tetley's best.

There were never any kisses or cuddles because that would make you a puff in my Dad's eyes but everybody liked and respected him…

Mam wearing bonnet with Me and Gary.

Mam proudly showing her nappies.

CHAPTER THREE
MY MAM

Looking back on our adventures and exploits in those days it's only by the grace of God that I survived. Our entertainment and excitement was all self-motivated with no X-boxes or PS2s. We would dare each other to do things such as climbing the bridge of death as we called it at the age of about ten years old. In the days of steam engines the trains would pass under Monkey Bridge near Fountain Road on the Hull and Barnsley line which went under another rail line and went over Wilmington Bridge and the River Hull. Monkey Bridge looked like the ones you see in Newcastle over the River Tyne with a semi-circular top. I would estimate from the top of the bridge to the railway lines was about fifty feet. The two rainbow-shaped arcs were approximately 12" wide with big round rivets on the top. We would wait for a train to pass and then walk over the steel arc in the midst of the thick steam not able to see a foot in front of you, hence the name, bridge of death. One foot wrong and we'd have plummeted to a certain death.

A few hundred yards from the bridge was 'Leccy' as we called it. This was a large electric generating plant that pumped the water from the drain and through the generating plant I imagine to cool it down and then up to the top of a great big cooling tower like the ones you see at power stations. The water was sucked up from a dam alongside the drain with iron grills to stop debris been sucked into the pumps, we used to climb over and into the dam where the water was warm from been pumped through the plant. The water in the drain was also a bit warmer throughout the year which made the fishing better; the fish always seemed to be a bit bigger from there. We used to get threepence off my Mam and tell her we were going to Beverley Road baths and then spend it on goodies. That was till she got a whiff of the stinking water on our trunks and put a stop to that with a clip around the ear. One day my Mam was telling me off for going in the drain when I ran out of the back yard and into the passage slamming the gate behind me. Then, thinking there was a barrier between us I stood putting two fingers up at her and quietly saying, 'F' off,' when the gate suddenly opened and she caught me in the act. I was dragged in and thrown up the stairs to bed, with a warning of those most feared words, 'Wait 'til your Dad gets in.'

It was always bad enough being sent up to your bedroom in the middle of the day, but knowing my Dad would be telling me off put the fear of God into me, unlike now where kids spend all day upstairs and hate being outside. When he did get home we all sat around the table for our tea as families did back then and weren't allowed to leave the table until you were told you could. As we sat eating, or should I say trying to eat, as I was so afraid, my Dad calmly said, "A little birdie told me a young lad down this terrace swore at his Mam today."

There was a pause of deadly silence that seemed to last forever, as we all expected him to explode at me as he normally would. But instead he just said, "If I ever found out that any of you ever swore at your Mam, you wouldn't be able to sit down for a week."

That was good parenting and was as good if not better than a slap on the arse. They had every right to be annoyed and worried about me playing in the drain as a friend of my Mam's had been dragged into the impellers when they were young. A few people were killed in the dam by being sucked through the bars and into the impellers of the pump. We used to wait for the pumps to fire up and then swim against the current. I'd have had a fit if I thought my kids had done a fraction of the things we got up to. The everyday hazards we faced were a danger to our health as Barmy drain was full of rubbish that everyone dumped in. Along with the bloated stinking dead sheep and cows that would end up at our end of the drain as it finished behind our terrace where the lock gates joined the River Hull in front of the Whalebone pub. The poor animals would drown after falling in up at Dunswell or somewhere up stream in the country.

Lockwood Street Bridge crossed the drain here and it was another daredevil game for us. The bridge was about fifteen feet above the water from where we would dive off headfirst into the murky water. It's a wonder we were not killed from all the junk that was thrown from the bridge like bikes, prams and iron framed beds with diamond shaped wire sprung bases and springs all around the edge for suspension. The beds were so noisy that at the slightest movement they squeaked like hell. It must have been awkward for our parents to sneak a quiet bit of nookie when we were all in the next bedroom. I dived off the bridge one day headfirst into the drain but didn't curve my body enough to prevent me hitting the bottom. The result was my head got stuck in the sloppy mud and then as I struggled, my hands were getting stuck as I tried to push myself free. How lucky I was not to have seriously injured myself on one of the sharp objects. When I walked up the drain bank to where all my mates were I had the piss taken out of me mercilessly and was called 'shithead' and words to that effect. I was convinced over the next few years that this was the reason for my hair turning from platinum blonde to mousy brown. Which now I realise is as silly as thinking that my now balding crown is a solar panel for a sex machine.

Once a year Barmy drain used to be dredged out by the old clutch and cable dragline cranes - RB22 types - which was exciting for us to watch and see what came out. The items they pulled out varied from the usual bikes and prams, to more interesting objects like an old cannon of the type you see in American civil war films with the large cart wheels and tow bar with the cannon perched on the top. Another time they dredged directly under Lockwood Street Bridge and pulled out a safe that reportedly had been stolen in a bank raid.

I was just talking to Mike Shipley at his sixtieth birthday party and he asked me if I remember when they pulled out the safe and it was full of pennies. I reminded him the pennies were not in the safe but were buried in the mud at the water's edge opposite Kirby Street. I found them when I was fishing with Mike and Dave Field and I had a psychic moment and started digging deep. When they said "What are you digging for?" and I replied, "I don't know." When I got about a foot deep I came across a massive pile of pennies that was a proper treasure haul for us. There was about five quid's worth. That may not seem a lot today but to eight-year-olds it was a fortune, and especially the sheer volume of approximately twelve hundred coins. For you post decimal people, there were two hundred and forty pence to a pound. That number originates from two hundred and forty silver coins weighed one pound.

We had the biggest 'goody' spending spree we'd ever known on pink 'Anglo' penny bubblies, 'Refreshers', that were a yellow chewy toffee with a sherbet inside. And 'McGowan' toffees, the ones that had the long brown haired bull with long horns on the wrapper. Our Gary and Graham Field enjoyed the feast too.

THE POETIC HOOLIGAN

We also saw an army rifle which my Mam swore was one that my Grandad had dumped, He had smuggled one out of the army when he left and then dumped it in the drain when he found out there were going to be house searches for army weapons that had been stolen.

My Mam said he had one during the war and used to put the fear of God into everyone by lining them up when he'd had a few beers and saying, 'If them bastard square heads (Germans) invade England, they won't get to you lot, I'll put a bullet through you all first.' She said they were more frightened of him than the Germans. Other stuff we would dig out of the piles of mud on the drain side where bullet tips and live bullets that my Grandad said were 303s. And larger ones about six inches long that looked like the ones fired from a plane. Some of these were live as we would throw them at the back wall of Teal & Mackrell paint factory to get the mud and rust off and the copper case would go pink and hot. Luckily the water had got inside them and dampened the cordite. A couple of other items were an old six-shot revolver that Mike Shipley gave to his brother I think, and a bayonet complete in a black bakerlite case, both of which we did not know what they were until we threw them at the wall to get the rust off. Any lump of metal was tested like this and more often than not it was just a lump of metal.

On the other side of the bridge was a row of houses on the drain bank that faced onto Northumberland Avenue, where one of our mates Tony Nightingale lived. We were stood talking to him one day through his fence. He was leant with his arms on top of the steel spikes when just for a laugh and not realising what might happen, one of us tapped him on the top of his arm. To our horror one of the spikes went straight through his upper arm muscle. I watched in shock as we lifted his arm back off and saw all the pink flesh still on the spike.

As I am sat writing my notes now I suddenly thought, bloody hell, my Mam would have had a duck fit reading some of the things we used to get up to behind her back. I told her that I would never misbehave, being the good little catholic boy that I was, and thinking she'll never know, but forgetting that years earlier my Mam had done all the things that we did and was wise to all our little white lies.

Another thing my Mam had done before me, was attend my first school, St Gregory's Primary on Lockwood Street, which was run under the iron glove of the nuns and the headmistress, the much-feared Sister Mary Catherine. Just the mention of her name sends shivers down the spines of generations of children who went there. That brown leather belt of hers lashed the legs and arses of many a kid including my Mam and her siblings. She was like Sir Alex Fergusson of United but instead of using the hair dryer she used the belt. People in their eighties still talk of how hard she was on the children.

My Mam said Sister Mary Catherine disliked my Mam because she was headstrong and wouldn't back down to her. She once handed out a bible to all the class except my Mam and said she did not deserve one, which made her cry. But as they say, all things happen for a reason and a priest called Father Keating, who was also a teacher said she was wrong and gave my Mam a rosary bead necklace. My Mam treasured it to the day she died and it helped her get through her last days, as we put it around her neck when she had her last rights read to her.

Thankfully she pulled through and I'm sure the beads helped her as even though she was unconscious for long periods of time she would feel the beads with her hand. My Mam finally gave up the fight on February 16th

2015 shortly followed by my Dad on July 3rd. When people say about receiving messages from your loved ones, I have had several in the shape of a white feather or a special tune coming on at an appropriate time. A few weeks after my Mam passed I sat in my car outside the nursing home they had both been in and sat looking up at their bedroom window. As I sat there I said to my Mam, 'If you know I'm here let me know.'

Nothing happened for a few minutes, then as I set off driving the song that always reminded me of her, 'Crazy' by Patsy Cline, came on the radio. I absolutely cracked up, as this was the song I requested for my Mam's funeral. A year later, on my sixtieth birthday we were going to the old Lockwood Arms down Lockwood Street for a drink at the exact time I was born on March 4th. I pulled up just before the time I was born and said to my wife, 'Sixty years ago as now I was just entering the world.' As I said it, the song that was at number one the week I was born, 'Memories are made of this,' by Dean Martin came on the radio. As if that wasn't enough, as I looked in my rear view mirror, a white feather floated down.

OUR CARING MOTHER

We love our Mam, our caring mother,
That lovely lady like no other.
Who gave us life and taught us well,
Protected in our family shell.
Dad would shout when we were in trouble,
All made well by her secret cuddle.
Her tender care and little kiss
Among the things I'll always miss.
We're all grown up, their home is bare,
They're both together in heaven somewhere.
We visit often to return the love given,
Now they're looked after up in heaven.

Mam and Dads wedding.
Grannie and Grandad behind my
Mam. Aunt Lilly in front of Gran.
Grandad Percy Haldenby behind my
Dad. Aunt Doris far left.

Mam in white with a Persian cat.

THE POETIC HOOLIGAN

I LOVE YOU MAM

I love you Mam and always will,
The day you left my world stood still.
A light went out within my heart,
My life goes on though were apart.
I try to think of love and joys,
The fun we had when we were boys.
People say do not be sad,
Just think of good times that you had.
Although I try and show a smile,
My heart still aches and will a while.
I know you're near and will be forever,
You let me know with a song or a feather.
I'll live my life as you would wish,
Your tender care and love I miss.

TO SEE A SMILE

To see a smile upon a face
Not knowing what that heart has faced,
It may be sad, it may be glad,
It may have lost a Mam or Dad.
We live our lives with a plastic smile,
And have to go that extra mile.
Our lives will change along the way,
We live to fight another day.
Some lives long and some lives short,
Some of joy and some of fraught.
Be thankful what the good Lord gave,
Enjoy your life and loves to save.

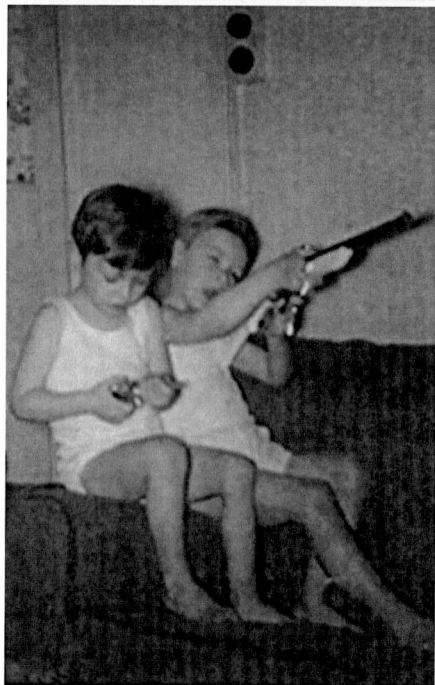

The Splashboat at East Park. My Dad with our Gary & Me. Uncle Ted's wife, Aunt Sylvie Haldenby, and Steve Field 3rd from left.

Me and our Gary playing with our Christmas toys, a pistol and a rifle.

CHAPTER FOUR
CHILDHOOD MEMORIES

We left St Gregory's and went onto St Charles on Prime Street where my Grandad and his brothers went. All these Catholic schools seemed to be heavy on corporal punishment for the slightest thing. Even not going to mass on a Sunday morning was punishable if you didn't have a note from your parents excusing you. We would get demerit marks for silly things and when you accrued so many you got six of the best. This was either from a bamboo cane across your fingertips or the paddle on your arse, and even if we'd been away on holiday but my Mam had forgotten to give us a note.

Sometimes though it was our own doing, as my Mam would dress us up all bonnie and send us off to mass with some money for the collection box. But instead we would meet up with the Fields and Shippo in the Oval after they'd finished Sunday School on Mason Street. I always wanted to go to Sunday school but it was run by Prodyhaddocks (Protestants) and we were Roman Candlesticks (Catholics) so they wouldn't let us in.

We used to go to the 'goodie' shop and stock up with peanut brittle that was our favourite sweet. 'Oval' as the name suggests, was an oval shaped garden for the public, with an iron fence around it containing grassed areas, benches and trees. We used to climb into the trees and get hidden to eat our stash. The same trees are still there fifty years on. It all seemed worth it at the time thinking we could forge a letter or get my Grannie to write one saying my Mam wasn't well. Sometimes it worked, sometimes it never. It wasn't much fun then on a Monday as the sadistic teachers got their thrills from hurting young children. I'll never forget or understand how grown men could bring themselves to apply such force and with such venom. The look on their faces was like they enjoyed it. And that's not just my opinion; I've spoken to many people who say the same. I'm sure that a stern telling off for most of the things like talking in class would have been suffice or maybe one whack on your arse. My own upbringing is a testament to that, as my Dad brought up three lads and never laid a finger on us. Just a growl and the threat of a smacked arse was enough and has been the case for my own three children as they've never been hit either and none of them have ever given us any bother.

Our playgrounds and adventure parks were not Alton Towers or Flamingo Land, mainly due to the fact that there were hardly any theme or leisure parks in those days, and the ones that did exist were beyond the pockets of our parents. I do remember going to Flamingo Land as a ten-year-old on a school trip which was a rare treat. We made our own fun on the local docklands or in empty buildings and warehouses where we would get up to no good borrowing things from the yards of local businesses. We would take five gallon and forty-five gallon drums from 'barrel yard', which was a storage yard for a tank and drum company that backed onto Lockwood Terrace and then go to the other side of Lockwood Street and borrow some lengths of wood from the Arnold Laver timber yard. We would then lash them together to make a raft and simulate a Sunderland ship launch off the drain bank and set sail up Barmy drain on one of our adventures. We would be loaded up with an arsenal of weaponry to shoot rats on the drain bank ranging from our Gat and Diana 177 air pistols which were very inaccurate and could not hurt a fly. I don't ever remember killing one but I remember hitting the odd one, which was more by good luck than good judgement. They would give a little squeal in surprise that you'd hit them and then swim away laughing. We also carried a catapult, either hand made from a Y-shaped tree branch with square section rubber bands and an old leather tongue from a shoe for the slingshot or a steel Milbro Professional. These could kill a rat, as I was a good shot with them using marbles from Glamog factory down Oxford Street.

The other weapon was a bow and arrow made from green bamboo canes that you would bend and tie a string from end to end. The arrow had bird feathers at one end tied on with fishing line as a flight and at the killing end was either a nail fixed between a split in the cane and bound with line, or a piece of wire wound onto the end. Dave Field felt the sharp end of an arrow one day, as we were larking on 'Barmy' drain when their Steve shouted, "You better start running or you'll get this arrow in you."

We started running as Steve fired it into the air. We looked up and saw it coming down towards us so we stopped and tried dodging out the way. We were both dodging about when it hit Dave in the head, leaving a hole. It could have been much worse as a couple of inches the other way and it could have taken his eye out.

The bamboo canes were also used to make kites by binding two canes together with the horizontal one being slightly shorter. We would then cut an old bed sheet or a polythene bag and tie it corner to corner with some fishing line and then tie a string from the top of the cane to the bottom and then adjust it to suit. We then finished it off with a long ribbon to give it balance. The kites flew better than the ones from the shops and gave us more satisfaction having made them ourselves. A lot of our toys were self-made as you just could not afford them. Most kids would play simple games like hopscotch or football with a goal drawn on a wall with chalk. Another popular game was to play marbles or use the marbles to play 'arches'. Arches was a game using a shoe-box with arches cut into the side with numbers above the arches. We took turns to aim at the arches with a set number of shots each and the one with the highest score won.

We also made parachutes from a piece of polythene or an old hanky with four pieces of string tied to each corner then attached to a toy soldier with a weight on it. And played other games such as 'whirlybirds' or 'helicopters' using the seeds from sycamore trees that we would collect from Oval.

October was always an exciting time when we would gather up the horse chestnuts from the trees on Leads Road outside the army barracks, which was the only place to find them in the town. We would then drill a hole through them and leave them to soak in vinegar before putting them in the oven to harden and turn into 'Stoney wallers' before challenging each other at 'conkers'.

Our proper toys that we would get at birthdays and Christmas were very basic and you would only get one unless your aunties and uncles were feeling flush. Then you sometimes got a little extra at Christmas like a selection box to share or a box of toffees. One Christmas I got a cowboy gun in a holster that fired caps along with an apple and tangerine in my stocking. They were all I got but I was still over the moon.

One of the best toys I ever got for my birthday was a Johnny Seven OMA gun. The OMA stood for 'One Man Army'. This was seven weapons in one, which consisted of a grenade launcher, anti-tank rocket launcher, anti-bunker missile, armour piercing shell, ten bullet rifle, slide bolt action machine gun, a detachable cap pistol that fired shells, and a detachable stock and built in bi-pod. The overall length was three feet, what an impressive toy that was for a nine year old boy, even by today's standards that would be good.

Another of my favourite toys was a Thunderbirds' Tracy Island model. There's no wonder the authorities have scaled down the advertising of children's toy guns and advise us not to encourage children to play with weapon style toys the way society is developing with gun and knife crime at an all time high. When I think of all the toys we had they were mainly guns, knives, swords, bow and arrows etc. There's no wonder I was such a little twat and ended up shooting my cousin John and half my mates with my air pistols. We even made a shotgun when I was about fourteen from a piece of steel pipe that I flattened the end with a hammer and bent it over, then drilled a hole a few inches from the bottom using a little hand powered crown and pinion type drill. We secured the tube to an old air rifle stock and poured gunpowder into the barrel from some fireworks with the fuse paper from the fireworks poked into the hole. We then rammed some cotton wool on top to keep it in place then put some small ball bearings in and again packed it with cotton wool. We took turns at firing it at targets like tree trunks or pieces of plywood. It was so powerful that the bearings imbedded into the wood and even went through a round steel traffic sign on the corner of Northmoore Lane. We were so lucky not to have blown our heads off as the metal was only soft malleable steel conduit and got hot after you shot it a few times.

My air pistol got me into bother on several occasions, the first of which was when my cousin John Cox was playing cowboys and Indians. He was dressed as an Indian with a head-dress and bow and arrow, and I thought it would be more realistic if I played a cowboy having just got my new Gat air pistol. He was firing arrows at me with little red suckers on the end so I returned fire and hit him on the arse. He gave out a scream and ran off and told my aunt Kath and Uncle Laurie. As you can imagine Uncle Laurie didn't find it quite as funny as I did and dragged me off to my Mam who clattered me, confiscated my gun and kept me in for a week. Fortunately Uncle Laurie didn't hold it against me and not long after took me on holiday with them to Cayton Bay near Scarborough. However, I think he always looked upon me as a bit of a wild card, as whilst we were there I bought a replica Bowie knife from the novelty shop, which he put in a safe place until we got home but somehow it got lost and I never saw it again.

Another one of my victims was Pat who I went to school with. Pat ended up marrying my brother, to who she had three lovely lads - Perry, Gareth and Adam - who I'm still very close to. We recently went down to London for Gareth's birthday party that was followed by a large family get together meal in a Chinese restaurant the next day. As we sat looking over the Thames Perry said, 'Didn't you ever fancy my Mam Rich, as she's more your age than my Dad's?'

I replied, 'Yes I did, I used to watch her walk past my Mam's and say to my mates look at the tits on her, which everyone found amusing.'

Pat replied, 'I wouldn't have gone out with him, he was horrible. He used to bite pigeon's heads off, was always fighting, and shot me on my backside with an air rifle'. Which I had completely forgot about. I was fifteen at the time and just starting to get into my troublesome teens. Luckily we still get on well although Pat and my brother got divorced.

I was to get into further bother with air rifles that had more power. My first episode was whilst I was building a tree house in the large trees that run at the back of

THE POETIC HOOLIGAN

Schultz's field, Schultz being the name of the school I went to, which has since been demolished but the field is still there and is situated in front of where I live now.

I was about twenty feet up in a tree house I had built with my then girlfriend Maggie who was my mate Howard's sister. A lad off the estate climbed up and into a tree house I had built in the next tree. I told him to get out but he told me to fuck off saying, "You don't own it." But as I had gone through all the bother of dragging the pieces of plywood across the field from the building site and then up the tree, I did see it as mine. I warned him if he didn't get out he'd regret it. Again he told me to fuck off. I wasn't going to be embarrassed in front of my girlfriend so I shot him in his leg. He yelped and lost his footing, falling from the tree and then ran off. I thought no more of it until a little later I heard police sirens and saw the police running across the field towards me. By this time Pete Brown had joined me so we climbed down the tree and told Maggie to go home before 'legging it' across the fields towards Beverley, and hiding the gun in a ditch on the way. When we got to Plaxton Bridge at Dunswell we got into further trouble by a farmer who set his Alsatian on us for running through his crops. Then when we got home I got another clip around the ear off me Mam as the cops had been and left a warning. It was always funny when my Mam hit me as it never hurt and then she'd spoil us rotten with guilt. We would lay it on and say, "You really hurt me with your ring," and she'd spoil and cuddle us even more. If it was nearing a Thursday we were laughing as we always got a treat anyway off my Mam as it was payday. But when she was on a guilt trip we got a bit extra. Thursday was the only night we had a special treat and looked forward to our Bar Six, Double Deckers, a packet of Custard Cream biscuits, McVities' chocolate digestives and my Mam's

Top: Mam aged 16 with workmates at Murleys Bedding. Back L-R: Dot Simpson, Mam, Jean Baker. Front, L-R: Elsie Pullen and Maureen Sulivan.
Below: Lockwood Arms day out

favourite, Fig Rolls. And although she denies saying it now I remember her saying, "You can eat what you want but don't eat all the fig rolls because I've put a black clock in one of them." It not only stopped me eating them, but it put me off them for life. Those treats were the only ones you got all week so if you wanted any more you had to earn some extra pocket money by taking lemonade bottles or jam jars back to corner shop or take bags of washing to the coin-op on Waterloo Street. Coin-op was the coin operated washing and drying place also known as 'Bendix' after the name of the machines.

On the way back from coin-op we always looked in Waterloo Street chemist which sold Cinnamon and liquorice sticks which were small branches off a tree that tasted of liquorice. The shop had rows of jars and drawers and tubs full of interesting and tasty things to spend your bit of extra cash on. Our own little Willy Wonka chocolate factory. The other 'goody' shops we used down there were Hancocks and Walkers. The jam jars and bottles were also used as currency to gain entry into a community centre off Mason Street near the Registry Office. We used to go there on a Saturday morning to watch films, I remember one in particular was Mickey Mouse because I trapped my fingers in the big thick swinging fire doors.

On the corner of Lockwood Street and Green Lane was our local pub, The Lockwood Arms which is a beautiful old building that was built around 1870 and is a unique building in Hull for having a faience tiled front. It became a listed building in 1998 and is still trading today albeit under a new name of 'The Old Bull and Bush', which I believe changed names in the nineties when it became famous for alternative entertainment.

My Grandad would turn in his grave at the thought

of this and the bar staff lining up on the bar singing and dancing.

Up until the late sixties, 'Lockwood', like a lot of other pubs in Hull had its ale delivered by Hull Breweries own horse and cart. These were beautiful big horses like Shire horses, fully dressed with their entire brasserie on the neck harness, they were famous locally and named Lady, Bonnie, Bob and Prince. Hulls own answer to Santa's Rudolph, Dancer, Prancer and Dasher. These beautiful animals used to pull the large cart full of ale and stop on the corner of Lockwood Street where the draymen would lower their wooden barrels down into the cellar through large wooden hatches. Hull Brewery Mild was famous all over the country as one of finest ales with its dark rich texture not too dissimilar to Guinness in its appearance and is still spoken of today with great affection. One of the draymen was a giant of a man called Bill Edwards who owned a Jack Russell terrier as do a lot of men associated with horses, especially farmers to kill off the rats that live among the straw. He could be seen walking out of his home in the morning and his dog would run up his side and sit on his shoulder like a parrot. As beautiful as these horses were I used to hate the bloody things because I was sure they waited for me to come out of the off license in Lockwood Arms on the way home from school in my little white socks and short pants before doing the biggest piss you could imagine. It was like Niagara Falls and my legs used to be soaked.

At the other end of Green Lane was the Whalebone pub, on the junction of Wincolmlee at high flags as we called them, which was a pedestrian footpath raised about three feet up for safety from wagons. Whalebone was and still is one of the oldest pubs in Hull. It's over two hundred years old and has had several names including the Splaw Bone. The Wincolmlee area used to be an old village called Sculcoates, not far from Sculcoates Lane. They say that you could stand on the front of Whalebone and throw a stone in any direction and hit one of the many breweries including Joseph Lockwood brewers, from where Lockwood Street takes its name.

That small, condensed area had more than its fair share of pubs to dispense their ale including Lockwood Arms, Oak Vaults. Hull & Barnsley, Engineers Arms, East Riding, Albion, Grapes, Bay Horse, Red Lion, The Rose and the Central Hotel, all of which were in staggering distance of each other and were used by my Mam and Dad and Grandad. My Grannie bless her never drank.

Even though we had left that area before we were old enough to drink, we still returned to our roots when we could and met up with our old friends.

In contrast to the Hull Brewery horses we would occasionally see the local rag and bone man doing his rounds. Tommy Midgley was a little, scruffy, overweight man with a bright red face, who always seemed to have a long grey coat on, tied around the middle with a piece of rope. His cart would be loaded to the hilt until the tyres were nearly flat and the poor scraggy horse could hardly pull it. I always felt sorry for it and if I saw someone nowadays treating an animal like that I'd take the whip off them and hit them with it. But in them days it was a common sight. The scrap men then used to give you a balloon if you gave them some rag and bone.

At the other end of Lockwood Street was the bridge that linked Lockwood Street to Barmston Street. On the other side of the bridge on the corner of Barmston Street was Gladstone's fruit shop that was known for owning a monkey. This horrible bloody thing had the freedom of the shop and the street. It climbed all over the fruit and vegetables and sat on them with its mucky arse. Environmental health would have closed it down today. It used to run out of the shop and climbed onto the bridge, then run from side to side of the bridge. I always hoped it would fall in the water after it bit me one day as I ran across the bridge. It was on our side of the bridge hidden behind the railed fence of Teal & Mackrel and as I ran by it jumped from behind the fence and wrapped itself around my leg and sunk its fangs into my calf muscle. I had Sandy, my Grannie's dog with me and she attacked it and chased it off. I had nightmares for years after, as I was only about eight or nine years old. I would wake up thinking it was coming out of the cupboard in the bedroom or it was outside on the windowsill trying to get in.

They say pets look like their owners, and old Mr Gladstone certainly looked like his, almost to the point that you could have asked the monkey for a bag of Cox's apples. The monkey, and come to think of it, Mr Gladstone looked like the Barbary apes on Gibraltar. I still hate monkeys now and recently visited Gibraltar on a day trip from Spain. People were looking at me like I was mad as they were feeding them to get closer to them while I was stamping my feet and chasing them off…

CHAPTER FIVE
FRIENDS &
NEIGHBOURS

I was speaking to a lifelong family friend recently who I still keep in touch with through business, John Eddie. His family and mine go back a long way. Mr Edwards worked with my Dad, and Jake Edwards was best mates with my brother. All the Edwards family are characters and natural comedians, and you wouldn't want to upset them neither as they were handy lads. Steve was a very good rugby player and well known for giving you a good 'yuk' in the scrum. The first thing he did in a game was look for the opposition's best player and let him know he was on the field by giving him a crunching tackle or a good slap. John told me of when all the family and friends had been out drinking one Saturday afternoon and went back to their house for a sleep before going back out on the night. Their Mam Doreen, or 'Do Do' as they called her, had done some tea for them before they went out. She woke them all up apart from her son-in-law Tony who was in a deep sleep and they couldn't wake him. As they tried he was talking in his sleep and rocking backwards and forwards and making a revving noise like a motor bike. John gave his Dad a kick as he was laid pissed on the floor and said, 'Dad, wake up, I think our Tony's having a fit.'

His Dad half woke up and looking through one eye at him said, 'Ahh, leave the daft bastard alone, he'll quieten down when he runs out of petrol.'

The Edwards family are a salt of the earth type family who are genuine, hardworking people, just like most of the families down Lockwood Street, including

67

our next door neighbours Gladys and Albert Field and their family who again are from the same mould as the Edwards and Shipleys. The Shipleys lived on the front of Lockwood Street with their backyard looking into ours. Their Mam and Dad were called Hilda and Arthur.

Hilda was like Gladys and Do Do, proper women who had balls, and were never dolled up like today's mothers. These women always had 'pinnies', headscarves and slippers on wherever they were. They had to be strong women as it was them who chastised the kids and balanced the bills, robbing Peter to pay Paul. Notice how I never mentioned my Mam alongside her friends as my Mam was younger and a bit of a glamour puss. She was stunning looking and looked like a film star. However, she was also hard and could hold her own against any woman. She had to be, living with my Dad, they used to fight like cat and dog and she never backed down. The fights they had still have them laughing now. As the neighbours said you would suddenly hear my Dad shout, "Chrissy! Get back here you black haired bastard."

My Mam told us of how one night they were getting ready to go out and she was all made up but only had her knickers and bra on when they started arguing. My Dad grabbed her by the hair and she gave him a slap and ran downstairs. As my Dad followed her into the kitchen my Mam grabbed a red hot pot of tea and threw it in his face and then ran out into the terrace in the thick snow still in her underwear. As always she ran around to my Gran and Grandad's for protection until my Dad calmed down. My gran was the peacekeeper, as my Dad would never upset my Gran. My Dad's hair and eyebrows were bleached after that episode.

The times we would be in bed listening to Mam and Dad arguing and then come down in the morning and see my Dad's tea running down the wall as my Dad had lost his temper and thrown it up the wall. However, their fights were never physical with punches thrown, as my Dad would never hit my Mam. It was more shouting, pushing and shoving.

The Fields lived next door to us and were like family, as our ages were nearly the same. Graham and our Gary were the same age, Dave and Me, Steve and my other brother, and Geoff and our Karen. So from being born we lived in each other's houses, as was the case with the Shipley's as our ages matched theirs too with Mike being just a year older than me.

Graham Field was one of the funniest people I've ever known. He should have been a comedian as his memory for jokes was incredible. He could sit with you in the pub and roll off joke after joke that you'd never heard before and have everyone in tears of laughter. He was also a brilliant singer and did a fantastic Rod Stewart when on holiday. Unfortunately we lost Graham recently. It was a terrible shock to everyone. He was one of the loveliest lads you could ever wish to meet.

One thing I'll never forget about living next door to the Fields was the ginger cat they owned that became part of the recipe for some of Gladys's homemade scones. What happened was Mrs Field had made some scones and put them on a tray in the old Yorkie fireplace oven but didn't close the door. She returned and shut the door a little later when the oven had got hot enough from the fire and then came back again to take them out when the time was up. When Gladys opened the door to take out the scones she screamed out at the sight that greeted her. "I'll never forget the sight of the poor cat covered in cake mix," she said later. "What an awful death the poor thing must have endured."

Some of the scrapes we got into were foolhardy, bordering on suicidal at times. Our thrill-seeking activities would lure us off to places usually in search of squeakers, that being the name given to a baby pigeon, as it squeaks until around the age of eight weeks old.

One of the buildings we would go in was on the corner of Lincoln Street and Cumberland Street corner which is now Smiths Engineering. At the rear and between Swifts Skips is an alleyway with windows all along and up to the roof, with bars on the windows like a prison. The top windows are approximately forty feet from the floor and these were great nesting places for pigeons. To get to them we had to climb the drainpipes, take the squeakers from the nests and either put them down our jumpers or into a hessian sack tied around our necks. Depending whether they were old enough or not, we would finish hand rearing them by opening their beaks and popping maize and beans down their throats. When they were old enough we'd either keep them or sell them to Charles Street pet shop.

One of our more unorthodox ways of catching pigeons was to drill a hole through a piece of maize and tie it on the end of a fishing line. We would then go to Victoria Square in Hull town centre or as we called it, pigeon square. The idea was to throw a piece of maize attached to the fishing line on the floor and let a pigeon eat it. Then let it swallow another twenty or so pieces and then reel it in and catch the bird. We then just pulled the line out, which was harmless to it. However, whilst doing this one day someone shouted to "Let it go!" and unfortunately I panicked and didn't lock the reel, allowing the pigeon to start flying with the line still attached. It started to gain height and flew around Queen Victoria's statue until it ran out of line and ended up dangling off the statue. At that point a copper grabbed me and made me climb up the statue and release it. Then yet again I was thrown into the Doctor Who type police box with a clip around the ear for good measure, before he rang my Mam to tell her what I'd been up to. I saw inside the 'TARDIS' - TIME AND RELATIVE DIMENSION IN SPACE - boxes far more times than I should have.

One of our favourite haunts was the Hull docklands on the River Humber where we had to be careful not to get caught by the transport police. We would climb out and under black jetty to get squeakers. This had to be one of the most dangerous feats we undertook as the jetty went out a few hundred yards into the River Humber on wooden legs similar to the piers you see at Blackpool or Brighton with the pavilions at the end. This one was flat on the top for driving wagons alongside the ships for loading. I nearly said 'and forklifts' but when they were built everything was loaded by hand. You forget how fast things have developed since the late fifties and sixties, which was around the time machines started to replace men. We had to climb under the rafters and shinny our way along to get the youngsters from the nests. One slip from off the rafters and we would have been swept away and down the fast flowing river and out into the North Sea. Another shed we visited was No1 Shed on the corner of Princes Dock Street and Whitefriargate, just as you turn right into Princes Dock Street, which is now a seated area for a café. This used to be what we called 'fruit shed', as ships moored alongside and discharged their load, which always seemed to be fruit. We would hang about there and be given the odd apple, tangerine or banana by the Dockers. Trains used to pull into the end of the shed to load or unload. It's hard to imagine now for anyone who never saw the old docks and to see Princes Quay Shopping Centre stood on stilts and see how clean the water is and that there are even carp swimming in there is amazing. When we swam in Princes Dock, Humber Dock and Railway Dock the

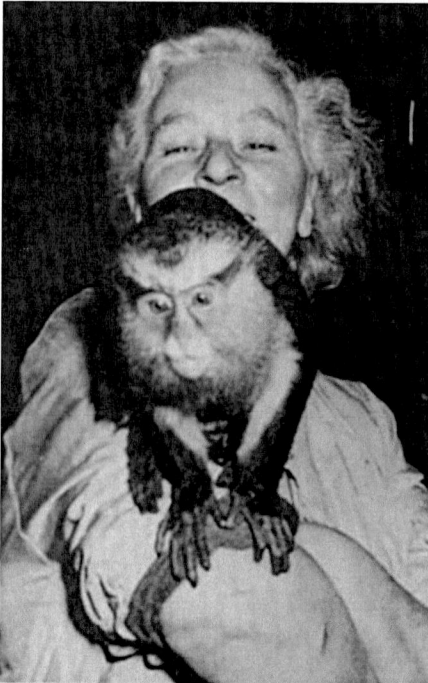

Clockwise from top left:
Dolly Binks, Gladys, Maxine,
Graham, Dave and Albert Field.

TheTardis.

The monkey at Gladstone's
fruit shop

stagnant water was like soup and it was a wonder that we never caught any diseases from it.

Further along the Humber heading east is Alexandra Dock where we would test our nerves and climbing skills at Black tower. Why everything had to be called black I don't know, but we had black hills on Cleveland Street, black jetty and black tower. I suppose it made it sound mystical like Captain Jack Sparrow's Black Pearl. Black tower is still there now and still looks the same. Ironically Graham Field later worked at MMS Ship Repairs on the dry dock where the tower is situated. The upper floors were no longer there due to a fire but there was a bit of the floor left on the edges with about twelve inches of wooden joists sticking out of the brick work. To get onto these bits of floor that were maybe ten feet from the floor we'd lean lengths of wood up the wall and climb up them onto each stage. We would then climb up the brickwork using holes in the wall as hand holds until we got to the pigeon nests on the ledges. The whole floor of the tower was covered in pigeon droppings that had a hard crust on it. When you stood on it where it was thick under the nests your foot would go through into a sloppy cake of pooh! The smell was a rancid ammonia vapour that took your breath away. Fortunately, the tower has recently been refurbished.

The Black Hills that I mentioned were on Cleveland Street where Brooke's Tiles are now on the corner of Foster Street. They were actually piles of ash but seemed like mountains to us. There was a car scrapyard nearby where we borrowed car bonnets from to use like a toboggan and slide down the hills. We would often go hurtling off in the wrong direction and end up clattering into a fence or bramble bushes and ruining our clothes. My Mam would then have to repair our clothes as well as clean up our cuts and grazes.

Lock-keeper's house, Barmston drain, 1976.

One of our less dangerous pastimes was to go to one of the many cinemas that were on our doorstep. We were lucky to have ABC on Ferensway, Tower and Regent, Dorchester where Biarritz bar was next to Manchester Arms and Criterion with its famous white lions on guard at either side of the steps where Comet's offices are now on George Street. The lions take pride of place in a park in Hornsea now. Our favourite was ABC though as we could sneak in to watch whatever we wanted. We used to chip in for one of us to pay and go in and then they would open the side fire escape door to let the rest of us in. We would then spend the rest of the day watching the likes of 'The Guns of Navarone' or Cliff Richard in 'Summer Holiday'. Our favourite film of all was Mary Poppins. Graham Field, our Gary and I watched it seventy-six times. We used to cry with laughter when the old bank owner stumbled down the steps.

Films in them days would take ages to get around to reaching Hull after the premier, not like now where no sooner a film is released than people have seen it on a bootleg or have gone to the pictures and seen it simultaneously all over the country. We would have to wait for months for a film to reach us and hear people saying it will be in Hull next month it's gone from London to Birmingham, Manchester or Leeds. We always seemed to be at the back of the queue.

Just across the road from ABC was Paragon Railway Station, which is still there now but has undergone a complete re-vamp as part of the fantastic developments to the Hull town centre and St Stephen's Shopping Precinct. The station used to be a pokey little hole with a little cafe and shop. In the centre of the station was a telephone box sized recording booth where you could sit inside and close the sound proof door and pay a few pence to record your own floppy disc 45. Our Gary and I recorded our own version of The Beatles' 'I Wanna Hold Your Hand'. The downloading culture of our hi-tech world has taken away the magic and excitement of our then 'try before you buy' vinyl records. When records were newly released we would go into Sydney Scarborough or the music department in Willis Ludlow, and sit in a booth with earphones on to hear the new singles before we bought them. We very rarely bought them but it was the highlight of the weekend to go and meet girls from all over Hull. The other place for getting off with birds was on a Saturday morning at Mecca dance hall that went on to be Lexington Avenue, or LAs as it was commonly known.

I recently visited Withernsea, a small seaside resort on the east coast about half an hour from Hull. When we used to go for a ride there as kids with my Mam and Dad we always looked forward to getting a few miles from Withernsea, usually around Patrington when my Dad would say, "The first one to see the lighthouse gets a tanner." I carried this tradition on to my children and would like to think they will also pass it on to their kids. On Withernsea sea front is a Castle styled building that has some blue glazed interlocking stone sets on the road that leads down to it, these are the same as the ones that used to be down Lockwood Terrace that were the original flooring of the air raid shelters.

Lockwood Street itself used to be a cobbled street, the evidence of which could be seen through the Tarmac. When you relate smells to past memories, the one that always takes me back to my childhood is the smell of tar. It reminds me of when the council workers came to repair the roads with the big tank of liquid tar on the back of the wagon and poured the tar into the cracks of the road. Whenever they came around mothers would bring their bairns that had bad chests like our Gary with his asthma to the wagon to get a deep breath of the tar from the tank, they swore it did them the world of good. Whenever Gary was real bad with his chest my Dad would throw us all in the car and take him to Blackpool for the day as my Dad said the sea air off the west coast was the purest air in the country. That's dedication to your kids.

CHAPTER SIX
DOWN BY
THE RIVER

A few hundred yards from the Hull Marina is the old Hull Corporation Pier or Victoria Pier as it's now called. This is where the old coal fired paddle steamers ferried between the pier and New Holland on the south bank before the opening of the Humber Bridge in June 1981. They were beautiful old steamers that everyone of a certain age remembers.

The Lincoln Castle was known as the Lady of the Humber. She was built in 1940 and was laid up in 1981. She moved home several times after that date and was used as a night club and restaurant before sadly losing her battle for survival and being dismantled and scrapped.

The sister ships that ran opposite to her and as back up were the Wingfield Castle, the Tattershall Castle and the Farringford, which ironically is now berthed in my family town of Sunderland. The Lincoln Castle been the last coal-fired steamer in operation in the UK, I feel fortunate to be old enough to have used them from an early age when we would go across to New Holland on them to go fishing as a child. Years later as an apprentice I used to go over on them in my van to do repairs on forklifts at Immingham docks. They were also handy and very cheap to use for training my pigeons as a teenager. Before the days of all day opening hours the boats were a good excuse for a beer as they served drinks all afternoon and then we came back for an evening sesh around town.

Before the bridge opened the alternative route was

via Goole at a distance of approximately 70 to 80 miles to get to the point at New Holland where the ferry would moor up. You can't talk about pier without giving 'Hoss wash' a mention. It's still there now and a big part of our heritage. There must be hundreds of photos on display all over Hull of the horses getting washed there back in the day.

On the other side of the mouth of the River Hull where the Deep is now used to be a flat piece of land known locally as Sammy's Point. It has been used by many businesses over the years with my last memories of Arnold Laver timber sheds been on there which was another one of our playgrounds. Alan Warfock shipbuilders also operated on there. The name Sammy's Point comes from the land being a small peninsula, which narrowed off to a point as it went out into the Humber. This was occupied in the fifties by another shipbuilder named Martin Samualson, hence the name Sammy's Point.

From the mouth of the Humber and all the way down the River Hull there used to be barges and lighters moored side by side, sometimes blocking the river off completely. They were supposed to leave a fifty-foot through way for other vessels to pass by. All these vessels used to travel down river and under Drypool Bridge and North Bridge to load or unload at the then famous mills, such as JR Rank's at Drypool, Chambers and Fargus on Wincolmlee, Spillers Grain on Chapman Street, CWS-Co-op Flour Mill, and BOCM on Stoneferry.

We used to cross the river by jumping from boat to boat, one slip and we'd have been in the river. One of the docks other little quirky facts from the days of 'If a job's worth doing it's worth doing right,' was to own our own little fire rescue boat named the M.V Clara Stark, which was commissioned in case of fires on boats in the

THE POETIC HOOLIGAN

Hull and Humber. She was moored in the Humber Dock basin and although never brought into action in aid of a ship, she was still well maintained for many years. Luckily she was never called upon in the face of action, which is just as well because she could only leave the dock at high tide due to all the heavy pumps and equipment on board.

Bonfire night was always a time of great excitement for us all, just as it is for kids today. But there seemed to be more danger then for once a year we were allowed to hang around with the older lads and lasses who would tolerate us for a couple of weeks while we did their donkey work on Bommy raids. We were used as slaves to fetch and carry wood on successful raids. We would carry some of the heavier stuff on bogeys that we made from an old door with pram axles nailed underneath. The front axle was pivoted with a rope tied to each end of the axle so it could be steered. These raids would often end up in a big fight if you were caught raiding another gang's booty, or vice -versa. The younger kids would be on watch and sound the alarm if we were under attack for the older lads to come and defend our hoard. They would come running out of passages and hideaways like a swarm of black clocks. One of our other homemade crafts was a raft that we made from barrels in barrel yard, which we lashed together with lengths of wood. However, there weren't many if any fork lift pallets in them days as there weren't many forklifts about then.

These were our first lessons in how to fight, although we had learnt the basics from fighting with my elder brother. He was four years older than me but I never backed down to him. One afternoon while my Mam was at work he tried making me say sorry for something. When I wouldn't he pinned me down for a couple of hours telling me to say sorry. Every time I said "No" he

A raft and two bogeys that we built

would punch me in the face and body, but I still wouldn't until in the end he had to let me go as my Mam was due home from work.

We all turned out to be able to look after ourselves as being a fighter was not an option; you had to be able to fight to survive. I went on to fight for St Charles Boxing Club and St Paul's when they were on Cannon Street. Even though I never carried on professionally I did on the streets and was forever fighting.

Our fires used to be either on Bomby or flats. Bomby was a flat piece of land at the bottom of Lockwood Terrace that had been bombed during the war and then flattened. When I think back to how we used to have these fires it's frightening, as we would pile the wood up on Bomby to about half as high as the houses and only a few feet from the gable end of the house. When the fire was lit on bonfire night the flames were literally inches from the wall. The Aili family in the end house never complained, as it was probably the warmest they'd ever be through the winter. Our other site for a fire was opposite St Gregory's School on a piece of wasteland .

When we built our bonfires they were huge and as we built them we would construct passage ways inside and even had different levels with a den inside. On one occasion I was inside one of the dens, which were like a rabbit warren of passageways lined with doors laid horizontally and then opening up into small rooms, when someone set fire to it. The smoke built up so fast that I could not find my way out. The smoke quickly got thicker and thicker and I could feel the heat and started to panic and cry. My mates heard me and started to pull the wood away and got me out just in time as a gas cylinder exploded and blew the bonfire to pieces, showering us with burning wood.

The bonfires were made up of anything from old

Clockwise from top left:
Larking on bomby with Jeff
and Pete Marshal in 1958

Mike Shipley

Jackie at 20 months old

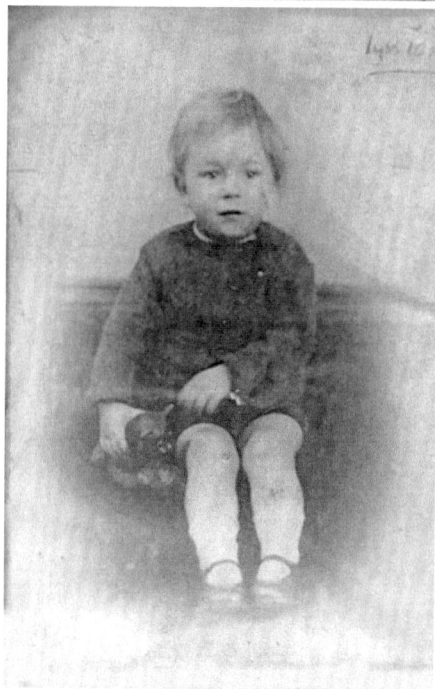

settees and mattresses that were full of fleas. My poor Mam was forever washing our hair in medicated shampoo and dragging a dick comb through our hair. That along with calamine lotion all over our flea bites used to take the shine off bonfire night.

I still have a big scar on my left shin where another bonfire escapade went wrong for me when I was eight or nine years old. We had been playing on Barmy drain and had a small fire going when a gang of older lads decided they wanted to have some fun with us and made us dance around the fire by throwing stones at our legs. One of them threw a piece of glass that hit my shin and cut it wide open. As if that wasn't enough I stepped back and into the fire, which melted my white calf length socks to my leg. I had to go to Hull Royal Infirmary for treatment which lasted for six weeks, each day I had to go and get my dressing changed. I'll never forget those dressings they were about six inches square netting in a flat tin made by Smith & Nephews Elastoplast.

I was to have several more visits to HRI for different accidents including a few days in there when the Queen came to open it in 1967. I had a suspected fractured skull after I had been playing hide and seek at my mate Mike's home which was the Masters Bar pub in Hull town centre. I was hiding in a bedroom with his sister and stood up to get hidden and fell over her and split my head wide open down the middle of my forehead. I had six stitches but never got to meet the Queen.

Steve Field was the only one of the Fields who was cheeky, the rest of them were always well behaved. My Mam said he was always as good as gold with her and loved sitting and talking to my Mam. Gladys however couldn't control him as he led her a right song and dance. He was the only one who swore at his Mam. Steve's Dad Albert was a chief engineer on the trawlers and was a quiet, polite man. He had been home on leave one time and was setting off back to sea and said goodbye to my Mam and Gladys as my Mam was doing her hair. Albert was carrying his kit bag as he walked out of the door and waved at Gladys through the window. At that point the glass shattered on a large round-faced clock that stood on the fireplace.

Gladys panicked and said to my Mam, "Oh Chrissy, I don't like that, it's a bad omen."

She found out months later that Steve had been sat on the stairs that day and fired his peashooter through a gap in the planks on the stairs as soon as his Dad walked out the door.

Another time when he was about seven or eight years old he had come round to our house and had climbed up onto the back passage wall asking my Mam if he could come in. She said to him 'Give me a minute, I'll think about it.'

So again after a minute he asked, 'Chrissy, can I come in?'

This went on for a few minutes. As he was waiting one of our neighbours Minnie Cubby who was a lovely woman came walking down the passage and said to Steve, 'Hello Steven, are you being a good lad?' to which he replied, 'Mind your own fucking business. I don't fucking like you.' Every other kid in the street would have given a polite response but not Steve.

Not many people in those days owned their own houses as I have just had to explain to my twenty-eight-year-old son, Jonathan who was surprised and said, 'You mean to say that someone came to your house every week and collected rent money.'

I recently found my Mam and Dad's rent book when clearing their home out for them to sadly move into a home together after nearly fifty years there. The book showed that on March 5th 1956, the day after I was born our rent was seven shillings, eight and a half pence which equates to approximately 38 pence in today's money. When I got married in 1976 our rent was £2.00 a week, so it's all relative.

Our rent man was a Mr T. A. Hudson who had come around for years and had known him from been born but that mattered not to Steve, Mr Hudson came into our house after been in Gladys's and went on to tell my Mam that when he first walked into the Fields house next door to us that Steven had said to him 'what have you come for?', so Gladys said 'Steven shut up and get under that table out of my sight.' As she walked into the kitchen Mr Hudson sat having a cup of tea waiting for Gladys to get the rent money when Steve popped his head from under the table and said 'I don't know what you've come for, we've got no money so why don't you fuck off!' Gladys walked in and heard him. She waited for Mr Hudson to leave and thought she'd teach him a lesson once and for all and dragged him to the toilet and shoved his head down the pan and flushed it. He pleaded with her to stop and promised that he would be good. As soon as she let go of him he ran up the stairs and got under the bed knowing she couldn't get to him and called her every name under the sun.

Gladys called my Mam in and said, "Listen to this. Have you ever heard out like it?" as he shouted, 'Shut up you big fuck off'. There was no taming him, a complete one off. The rest of the lads were relatively well behaved although they all share one trait, which is their wicked sense of humour.

Another time my Mam was upstairs cleaning the bedrooms with the window open and could hear Steve and my brother talking. She heard Steve say, 'Have you seen that Mandy over there? I'd love to look up her skirt,' to which my brother replied, 'Yeah, so would I.'

My Mam shouted, 'You dirty little buggers, wait till I get down there.' Considering they were only about eight or nine years old they ran out of the terrace and stayed out as long as they could hoping my Mam would forget.

Our bonfire raids took us to different neighbourhoods where we could explore different areas, Oxford Street and York Street were areas we used to go raiding the old warehouses. There was a new factory that was being built on the corner of Oxford Street and Barmston Street that we took some used packaging cases from for the fire. The steelwork had been erected complete with the roof trusses, which stood about 30 to 40 feet from the floor. A large area of the floor was stacked high with packs of insulation like the fibre glass you have in your loft all ready to be clad onto the walls, they must have been piled six to eight feet thick like a giant mattress. We dared each other to climb up onto the steel roof supports and dive off into the padding, which we did. As we dived off we shouted Superman as we were flying down and disappearing into the padding like it was a fireman's safety air bed, and again like when we jumped off Lockwood Street Bridge into the unknown. Anything could have been buried among the padding and seriously injured us but at that age you just don't see the danger. Also down York Street was a works yard we called Glamog factory. Glamogs were what we called some round glass see-through balls that looked like marbles with a green tinge to them. They must have been used for some kind of industrial process but we used them for playing marbles or firing them from my catapult.

On the corner of York Street and Bankside was York Road Service Station that was a small petrol station with a triangular sloping roof over the pumps, it's now McCoy engineering. In front of which was the only patch of grass in the whole of the area, which was smaller than most back gardens today but to us back then it seemed huge. It was certainly big enough for us to play football on without skinning our knees on concrete where we would normally play against a wall with a goal post chalked onto it. On the opposite side of York Street and running down Fountain Road and onto Main Street where Waterloo motor trade is now used to be Cocoa mills which was a huge building for processing cocoa. This was a great place to explore and a good nesting place for pigeons. I climbed into one of the big rooms there one day and took a beautiful bronze chequer squeaker from the nest and dropped it into my hessian sack that I had tied to my belt and set off home with it. On the way an older lad called Eric wanted to know what was in my bag, and when he saw it he stole it from me. As I walked around the corner crying, a copper asked what was wrong. I told him and he arrested Eric. The copper put us both in the TARDIS police box and rang his parents to come and collect him. How the law has changed. Can you imagine someone getting done for that nowadays? He ended up being charged for theft and getting his name in the paper.

Just along Bankside and down Air Street was Sculcoates Lane where Albert Draper's scrapyard used to be. This place was fascinating and still had stuff in there from the war, we used to find English and German helmets and parts of pistols and rifles to play with, pretending to be soldiers among the British and German warplanes that were still there. This place was also the final resting-place of Hull's own steam engine, the Wilderbeast 61010, which had only ever run around Hull on the G.N.E.R line. An old driver complained to the Railways and put forward his case that it would be a travesty to cut up Hulls only surviving steam engine, but as in many cases no one wanted to put up the money to restore this timeless classic. As was the case with the Lincoln Castle steamer and yet another class A1, the

RICHARD HALDENBY

Black five was saved from the chop even though it had spent its time running out of town on the L.M.S line and was refurbished and renamed as the Alderman Albert Draper and is now on show at Loughborough. Ironically the last ever Class A1 named the St Mungo or Kenilwart was scrapped at Draper's yard, however, a brand new class A1 has been built named the Tornado.

CHAPTER SEVEN
MY GRANNIE & GRANDAD

When we started to venture further away from the city centre and out into the countryside we came across 'bandstand' which was on the site, now known as Stoneferry roundabout that joins Stoneferry to Leads Road and Sutton Fields. Bandstand was where the old brass bands used to play on a Sunday morning, the type that you see in Hyde Park. Backing onto Bandstand used to be farmers' fields that we called 'Elephant grass fields,' which were just wheat and barley but seemed so tall to us as grass was rare, this is now Carr lane. We were all larking in the fields one day when Alan Marshal needed a crap. As he delivered his load Pete his big brother pushed him on his forehead and he fell back and sat in it. As if that wasn't bad enough, when he stood up and pulled his denim dungarees up he splattered his pile on his back as he'd shit into the back of his dungarees. You can imagine the job he had cleaning it off with our usual outdoor arse fodder of dock leaves and newspaper. Soft tissue paper was unheard of for us, it was either newspaper, Izal medicated paper that hurt your arse or if you were lucky we'd find soft wrapping paper that was used on tangerines on the dock. Fodder was slang for toilet paper meaning (for d bum).

At the other end of Leads Road where it crosses over Sutton Road just on the left used to be a farm with an orchard that had pigs running wild, and when I say wild they really were. The Fields and Marshals used to dare each other to run across the orchard to pinch some apple, these pigs were like big guard dogs and really fast. A few of us would distract them whilst the others ran and jumped up the trees to raid the apples, but often the pigs would realise what you were doing and chase you. Many a time I've looked down to see snarling teeth snapping at my ankles. It was surprising how far they could jump up the tree; these were what you'd call free range pigs I suppose and were fit as lops.

At the end of Leads Road where it joins Robson Way and Wawne Road, there used to be open fields. One of them had a white gate and a bull inside. We would jump into the field with a red rag and run at the bull and get it to chase us to see who could get the closest to it. On one occasion I let it get a bit too close for comfort and as I leapt over the fence I turned to see its horns missing my arse by only a couple of inches.

Most families in those days had some kind of pets, be it rabbits, pigeons, tortoises or a monkey. The laws had not been brought in then for animal rights however. My sister Karen had a friend called Kathy Tempest who lived on Fountain Road and had two pets, a dog and a parrot that formed a rather unique partnership. When anyone knocked on the front door that looked onto Fountain Road, the parrot would shout, "Come in."

They would walk down the passage and into the living room and find nobody there, but as they would turn to go back out they would be met at the front door by a snarling boxer dog that wouldn't let them out. They would often come home from work and find some poor sod like the gas or electric man stood petrified. One of my best mates Bri also had a parrot called Cluck as it had lived on a farm all its life and was very old when he got it. I think it was fifty years old or so. It could copy any farmyard animal and would cluck like a chicken, he said it had built up such a vocabulary that it could almost have a conversation with you. Cluck had hardly any feathers so could only walk everywhere, when Bri came in from work on a night he would sit in his arm chair and Cluck would walk up his leg and sit on the back of the chair and say, 'I love you Bri.' Then in a morning when he came down stairs Cluck would greet him with, 'Morning Bri.' He told me a tale, which may seem a bit farfetched but Bri is not a romancer and tells you as it is. The story goes back a lot of years when 'Nightmare on Elm Street' was out and they'd got the video to watch on a Saturday night, probably on Betamax. They watched the film to the end and were all thoroughly terrified. I say all because even Cluck was jumpy. Chris and Bri went off to bed and left Cluck perched on the back of the chair as usual. Sometime later Chris woke Bri and said, "Brian, there's someone coming up the stairs."

They could hear a 'thump, thump' as someone came closer and closer to the top of the stairs. Bri jumped out of bed and grabbed his pick axe handle and braced himself for the right moment as the intruder reached the top of the stairs. He then flicked the light on and shouted, "Come on then you bastard!" only to find no one there. As he looked down at the stairs, there stood Cluck. He picked him up and put him on the headboard and Cluck said, "I'm frightened Bri," as if the poor bloody parrot wasn't frightened enough watching the film without being confronted by Bri, standing there in his birthday suit, not a pretty sight. It turned out that what Bri thought were footsteps coming up the stairs was Cluck's beak hooking into the stair carpet as he pulled himself up from step to step. He'd never been up the stairs before and Bri took him back down the next morning and put him on the back of the chair where he sat as normal and never went up again.

When I was ten-years-old I arranged a day out with Terry Longden who was my brother's mate and was a few years older than me. We met at six-o-clock outside our house on a hot summer's Sunday morning and set off to Withernsea on our pushbikes. We had no provisions apart from a few coppers to buy an ice cream when we got there. I had a slight idea of how to get there having been on numerous family days out in my Dad's car, bearing in mind Withernsea is approximately twenty-five miles away so it was no mean feat to complete our journey at such a young age. When we got there we enjoyed the best ice cream and lemonade we'd tasted and had a great day just doing what we wanted instead of been chastised by my Mam and Dad, we played on the beach and larked about in the amusement arcades before setting off home. Obviously we never had a mobile or any cash to ring my Mam to let her know where we were or what time we'd be home, and the day just ran away with us.

On our way back home I got a puncture on my back wheel near Patrington. I remember the exact spot where it happened as many a time I have passed it and laughed at our innovative skills at such a young age and being able to repair a puncture without a repair kit. Another one of my Grandad's invaluable life skills that he had shown me was how to repair a puncture by simply peeling off the tyre from the rim using the palm of your hand. And then when one side of the tyre was over the rim you would pack the tyre with whatever you could find, which on our trip happened to be crisp packets, cardboard and some straw from a field - Bear Grylls eat your heart out! When we finally rolled back into Lockwood Street it was about ten o'clock at night and still light, the kids at the end of the street said, "The Police have been out looking for you."

I turned into Lockwood Terrace and was met by my Mam and Dad who were obviously frantic with worry. I was dragged off my bike and slapped by my Mam all the way to my bed. I couldn't understand it; I thought she'd have been pleased to see me. Never did that again.

Two of the families I mentioned earlier were the Shipleys and the Marshals. Mike Shipley is a year older than me who was and still is one of my best mates, he's a hard little bastard who would fight anybody. It's funny how you never forget some things and my earliest memories of Mike was when we were about four years old playing outside my Grannies and talking to him in his woolly tank top, as our Mams chatted and then going into my Gran and Grandad's to look at my Grandad's New Zealand whites he used to breed in the backyard.

He kept them in an old coal bunker with no door on it and was next to the scullery, the bunker was about three foot wide and seven foot high, the breeding hutches were a few feet off the floor with no fronts on the cages. When I asked him if they were safe from cats he said, "Don't worry, they can more than look after themselves," and said he would often hear a cat squeal and thud against the wall opposite the hutches in the middle of the night as the bucks would turn their backs on the cats as they got in the hutch and then give them an almighty kick with both feet. The buck was huge like a small dog and vicious as hell. We used to see them hung upside down and gutted in the kitchen waiting to go to the butchers.

Like most kids we had a menagerie of pets which were the usual gold fish, mice, rabbits, budgie, cat, dog and pigeons etc, most of which were kept at my Grandad's, either in the attic or the back yard. One of our other pets that we kept at our house was a tortoise what I loved; unlike the bloody horrible cat we had Dusty, it was evil. I was once playing with the tortoise and thought it would look good with a modification and decided to make it look like a tank by innocently sticking a Bic biro pen onto its shell. I was only about eight years old and didn't know that heat would conduct through its shell as I heated the end of the pen on the fire and then stuck it onto its shell just above its head. The poor little bastard set off with its feet spinning on the Lino like the bird on 'Road Runner' and bouncing from wall to wall.

Grannie and Grandad's attic was a magical place, our own Lockwood Street Narnia, where we used to sneak our pets up to. There was a pulpit shaped window with a platform you could stand on and look out over the tiles and down into Lockwood Street and coal yard across the road. My Mam told us of how they used to play up there themselves when they were young and that during the war they would look out and see dog fights going on above them from the same window. They also saw a parachute coming down and said to my Grandad, "Look at that Dad. It's a man on a parachute."

When my Grandad saw it he told them to get down as it was a landmine which was a massive bomb that had devastating effect, these bombs were aimed at Rosedown & Thompsons that was only a couple of hundred yards away from Lockwood Street. It used to be a munitions factory during the war and is still a successful engineering company known as De Smet & Thompson. It would have been a travesty had it been bombed as it was established in 1777.

When the bomb landed it flattened a large area of Waterloo Street I think and nearly killed my Grannie who was looking after someone's kids. The house she was in was badly damaged and when they got to her she was covered in black soot and could only see the white lines down her face where she'd been crying and still had the kids tucked under her arms. My Mam said the worst thing of all was hearing the Doodlebugs going over and hearing their distinctive engines and hoping the engine never stopped and dropped on you. People don't realise that Hull was the second most bombed city in the country.

No matter what we did wrong my Grandad would never tell us off. He would always laugh and say it would be all right, like when I took some maggots up to his attic in a biscuit tin with small air holes in the lid. I left them there for when we went fishing, as my Mam wouldn't let me have them in our house. But I forgot that I'd taken them up there until my Grandad reminded me a few weeks later after he had gone into the loft for something and heard a buzzing which led him to the tin. When he took the lid off hundreds of blue bottles filled the attic and the whole of the upstairs of the house. It must have looked like a scene from an Alfred Hitchcock film. You would expect a bollocking or some kind of punishment for that, but not my Grandad, he just laughed it off. I also used to breed white mice up there in an oblong shaped fish tank and then take them to Charles Street pet shop and sell them for a few pence. My Grandad said I wasn't to let me Grannie know that we had mice in the attic or she would never have slept. Grannie and Grandad were chalk and cheese, my Grannie was an absolute little angel who was beautiful until the day she died in 1984, a week after my Grandad died. A few years ago I went to the cemetery to have a natter with them and said, "Grannie, if you know I'm here, please give me a sign to let me know that you know I'm here." I stood for a minute looking round for a sign and when I looked down I saw a white fluffy feather land between my feet. I was shocked and took the feather home.

At the time I was working for my mate Mike's company, Clearway, as a supervisor and was on 24/7 standby. I had a pen and pad alongside the bed, it got to 1.30am when I woke up with the following poem going through my head, I thought I'd best jot it down before I forgot it, which took only a couple of minutes. The next day I took it to show my Mam who cried her eyes out and said how beautiful it was. This was the first time I'd ever written any poetry but since then I have done many others as you will see...

GRANNIE COX

In times of darkness, in times of fear
I think of you and know you're near.
In times of sadness, in times of doubt
I feel your warmth as I look out.
I sometimes ask to let me know
If you are with me wherever I go
Then hear your song on the radio.
Years have passed with many a baby
As you have seen my silver lady,
I came to see you and read forever
That we will always be together.
As I looked down to give my love
I found your white feather from above.
I know you watch and wish us well,
You are forever our guardian angel.

I think the reason my Grandad was so tolerant with us was due to them losing a son called Jackie or (Jonty) as a baby of about two years old. My Grandad had come in from the pub and left a hot drink on the table edge, Jackie pulled it onto himself and Grandad pulled the baby's top off in panic, which pulled his skin off resulting in pneumonia. Apparently he should have poured cool water on and left his clothes on for a while. Grandad never got over this and always had to have a few beers to help him sleep.

Grannie was born in Sunderland as Lilly Austin and was related to the shipbuilders of Austin & Pickersgill, so she was a true Mackem. Grannie Cox as everyone called her was small and chubby but with the most amazingly beautiful face. At 79 her hair was white not grey and her complexion was perfect, with a lovely glow and not a wrinkle on her face. She was always smiling and singing and forever the peacemaker, never seeing wrong in anyone.

There were never any family fall-outs when Grannie was alive as none of us wanted to upset her. She never smoked, drank alcohol or swore, when Grandad swore it made us laugh, as he never had his teeth in, which made his Fs become Ps, so everything was "Pucking hell". My Grandad was the opposite to my Grannie, he swore like a trooper, smoked baccy like a chimney and went in Lockwood Arms every night for a few pints of Hull Brewery mild.

It was funny when Grandad let rip with a tirade of abuse at my Gran for something that was neither here nor there and usually not her fault. Grannie would laugh at him and say "Eeh you Laurie, there's no need for language like that," which would normally bring a smile to his face as he didn't mean any harm.

Grandad was born in Castle Noch, Southern Ireland and was introduced to my Grannie by her brother Uncle Alf Austin whilst serving in the army with the East Yorkshire regiment.

They had courted by letter for five years without ever meeting and proposed by letter. From being born to getting married in 1976 I saw more of Grannie and Grandad than my own Mam and Dad. We would be woke in a morning for school by my Grannie who would have our breakfasts ready which would usually be eggs on toast or porridge oats with butter and salt in it whilst my Mam was at work. When we came home from school at dinnertime my Mam and Grannie would be there. Then when we came home in the afternoon it

Clockwise from top left:

Grannie and Grandad with Sandy

Karen, Gary, Sandy and Me in
Grannie's scullery (kitchen)

Barmston drain, 1955, looking
from Toogood street

would be just me Grannie again singing away and happy as Larry, starting the tea for my Mam who would get home about six. In-between times I would spend as much time as possible with my Grandad learning all sorts from him, Grandad was a Jack of all trades, and as they say a master of none. He finished his working days as a sprayer at Weeks Trailers down Oxford Street.

His general knowledge was vast and he could talk to anyone about anything and could relate to them. As I got older I realised that all the stories my Grandad told me were not all exactly true, including the one about the stallion that lived up in the attic. He told me this when I found a wire rope coiled up like a cowboy's Lasso in a cupboard alongside the fireplace. He told us that when we went to bed the stallion would come out and play. It could only be seen during the night and would then go back into the attic at daybreak and that's why we never saw it. I'm sure my love of wildlife, nature and sport is from him. When I was about seven or eight he told me that pigeons need to eat maize in the winter to keep their blood warm. As I got older and raced pigeons I studied their diet and found that maize is by far the most important food and gives them energy by building up their glucogen level which in laymen's terms puts 'fuel in your tank' by increasing the sugar level. He also taught me how to pluck and gut a bird, gut and skin a rabbit and gut and fillet a fish. These were all carried out with the use of his gutting knife from his ceremonial Gurkha knife complete in its black leather case with the two matching gutting knives built into the case either side of the blade. The main knife had a blade of about twelve inches long with a slight curve and had an M-shaped notch cut in between the blade and handle for taking aim when throwing.

Grandad had a fantastic array of tools which he handed down to me when I started work, it broke my heart when some low life broke into my van in 1986 and stole my tool box with some of the tools inside it. Fortunately I still have some including a large pair of pliers which always makes me smile when I use them as one day I was just about to walk through our back gate at our home in Clanthorpe when I saw my mate Ian Wilson knocking at our back door. We had moved onto Orchard Park by then and were dead posh. We had an outside loo as well as an inside one. As he stood knocking at the back door I said to Pete Brown, "Watch this!" and I threw a big heavy bomb type dart that belonged to my Mam that stuck in the toilet door next to him. He shit himself and pulled it out of the door and threw it back at me, thinking it would stick in the fence. However, it didn't go to plan and the dart came through an inch gap in the fence and stuck in my skull. There was no pain, but as you can imagine I was panicking trying to pull it out but to no avail. I tried pulling it out myself but couldn't budge it so I got Brownie and Ian to have a go, but they couldn't either. The more they tried the more they laughed. It ended up with me laid flat on my back with Brownie's feet on top of my head as he pulled, all the time they were both singing Robin Hood. The pair of bastards! We ended up walking over to my Grandad's, which was only a few hundred yards away and had him pull it out with the large pliers, which I still have in my collection today. I always love using my Grandad's tools as I get a warm feeling knowing his hands held them. I spent as much time in my Gran and Grandad's if not more than our own home and every time I walked in I would be greeted by our Sandy, a golden retriever cross. I would often go in and be led by her to the corner of the carpet where Grandad's chair was in front of the fire. She would scrat at the corner of the carpet for me to pull it back and find my pocket money, which consisted of the old pennies and threepenny bits that Grandad had left there and taught her to show me. We all absolutely loved her like she was our own. If ever we got a graze on our knees or elbows my Grandad would say, "Come here and let Sandy lick it and make it better, dogs have healing powers that are better than anything you'll get from the chemist."

I would never doubt a word he said. But as lovely as we thought she was, I remember the police coming to my Gran and Grandad's one day and giving them a warning. Sandy and another dog had swam across Barmy drain onto an allotment opposite and had got among the chickens that were kept on the drain bank and killed a few. The poor bloody chickens were everywhere down Lockwood Street and swimming down the drain.

When we had to leave Lockwood Street in December 1967 due to a compulsory purchase order we moved onto Orchard Park. We took Sandy and my Mam's bloody cat Dusty with us. My Dad had brought Dusty home from work as a kitten from a nest of feral cats and it never was tame, however, it loved my Mam and followed her everywhere. It would follow her the mile across town to work and then walk home when she got to work and knew instinctively what time she was leaving work and walk back and wait for her outside. The same happened on Orchard Park. My Mam would go for the bus at 6am and he would walk her to the bus stop in all weathers. Then at dinnertime, he would go back and wait for her at the bus stop. Although we had moved the six miles across town Sandy and Dusty would both often walk back to Lockwood Street for quite a few weeks after we had left and sit outside our old houses until they were demolished.

Grandad in East Yorks uniform, approx 1920

My Great Granma.
My Grandad's mother Christina, holding the above photo of her son, that my Grandad had sent her from China.

CHAPTER EIGHT
'HALT!
WHO GOES THERE?'

Some of my Grandad Cox's other stories were not so exaggerated, like the ones about his years in the army just after WW1 in China, Egypt and India. We have a photo album that he built up depicting his times there and show a spectacular insight to his exploits that only a photo can. The album is approximately 12 x 8" and has a hand-written description of each photo in white paint. The photos are all of his East Yorkshire Regiment pals in the mid 1920s. I was told that some were of the region where the Boxer Rebellion took place, as depicted in the film '55 Days At Peking' and starring Charlton Heston, Ava Gardner and David Niven.

When Ronald Reagan visited China in the late eighties he was supposed to be the first white man to see inside the Forbidden City, and yet we have photographs taken by my Grandad inside the walls. He told us of the death of a thousand cuts that was not to be seen by the outside world and was carried out on criminals where the thousandth cut killed them, he said he had sneaked in and witnessed this.

We were told many a story of when they were based in India. One of them was when they had to do a guard duty during the night and had to stand in the sentry box with their rifle loaded and a light above their head as a deterrent to anyone. He said not only was it annoying with all the flying insects, but you became a perfect target for anyone wanting to take a pot shot at you. His answer was to either take the bulb out and risk a rollicking from his superior if caught, or to prop his hat and coat up to look like he was stood in the box when he was actually stood near it.

One night while he was doing this he heard a noise coming from some bushes nearby and shouted, "Halt! Who goes there, friend or foe?"

You were supposed to shout this three times, but he didn't want to give them a chance to shoot first so after the second shout he got no reply and so he fired into the bushes. The response was a groaning noise. All the camp lights came on as other guards had heard the shot, other soldiers came to his assistance and asked what had happened so he told them he shouted three times and feared for his own life so fired to where the noise was coming from. When a search party went to the bushes they burst out laughing and said, "Coxy, come and see what you shot."

When he got there he saw he had shot the Doby's donkey. The Doby was the Indian laundry man who wasn't too pleased with him and he never lived it down. One night, many years later, he was stood in Lockwood Arms when he heard someone shout, "Coxy! Who shot the Doby's donkey?" It was one of his friends who'd been in the army with him.

Another one of his night patrols ended in similar circumstances. Whilst he was stood alongside his box, he heard an unfamiliar noise and looked out across the sand dunes and saw in the bright moonlight what looked like someone crawling on their stomach. He could see their head, shoulders and bum moving up and down as they crawled towards him.

Again he shouted, "Halt! Who goes there? Friend or foe?" and again after the second shout he fired.

All the camp lit up again and soldiers came to see what had happened. When they went and investigated they found three large Bull frogs that had been following each other and saw he'd shot all three of them.

THE POETIC HOOLIGAN

Another one of his stories was about him catching a golden eagle in India. A tall story you may think, however, I saw the photo of him holding it from wing joint to wing joint with his arms at full stretch and it still drooped down to the floor. Apparently there had been a big storm and it had been battered to the ground by the strong winds. He could see the crow's dive bombing something and making a racket as they tried to kill it. He picked it up and put it in a small wooden shed on the campsite and fed it scraps of food and whatever he could trap like rats etc. The cook gave him all the fatty meat that had been left and after a few weeks the eagle was raring to go. He had just fed it one day when his CO asked him what he'd been doing and went to have a look in the shed. As he opened the door it came flying out and knocked him flat on his arse. Forever the joker. When we emptied my Mam and Dad's house for them to move into a home, I searched through all the photos for that picture but to no avail.

He also told me of the Vultures and 'Shitehawks' as he called them. I never did find out what they really were. He said that if you needed to carry your bacon and eggs across the camp from the cook house to your billet you would look up in the sky first to see if there were any about and then ran with your hand over it. But if a new recruit started they wouldn't tell them and watch as they swooped down and snatched their grub.

Another gruesome story he told me was how they had to take someone with them to stand around the back of the wooden toilet block when they wanted a crap. The toilet had a long wooden plank with holes cut out for you to sit and shite through that went through each cubicle. What would happen if you went by yourself was that the rebels they were fighting, the loose wallahs, would sneak behind the toilet block and prize the boards off. So that when you sat down your meat and veg was dangling down and they would slice them off with a knife. Ouch!

We have a boxful of medals that my Grandad won for marksman competitions and different tours and achievements. He was a chip off the old block and would have gone far in WW1 had he not missed it by a few years. His Dad Capt. George Cox was promoted to Kings Corporal for his heroics in the Boar War 1900, or the South African War as it was also known. He and a few other soldiers held a rift to cover the retirement of 20 soldiers, he noticed a wounded officer at the front and returned to rescue him on horseback whilst under severe fire and rescued Lieutenant B. A.W.C Moeller of the 2nd Battalion Middlesex. My Great Grandad Cox was promoted to Kings Corporal for gallantry in the field, and was known in the regiment as Kings Corporal Cox, an honour that was only given in the Boar War, the tradition in the army was that he should only reduce in rank by the King himself.

He retired from the army after the Boar War and came to live in Hull at 75 Alica Street. He tried to re-join the army for the 1914/18 war but was deemed too old at 44 so he falsified his age and reapplied and joined the East York's regiment at York. However, he was recognised and marched in front of his CO who promptly told him to put back on his two stripes that he won in the Boar War. They sailed to Gallipoli in Turkey to fight in the Battle of Gallipoli, otherwise known as the Battle of Canakkale, on August 7th 1915 and landed at Sulva Bay and dug in at Lala Baba. It was a military disaster and technically doomed. They should never have landed on these beaches as they faced near vertical cliffs that they had to climb and were picked off easily by the Turks. It was known as the Dardinals campaign, which was supposed to capture Ottoman with the eventual aim of capturing the Ottoman capital of Constantinople (modern day Istanbul) and secure a sea route through to Russia. However, due to delays on a full attack the Turks were able to gather troops and successfully defend their homeland. He was killed around midnight by a sniper on August 9th 1915. He was married to Christina Cox of 3 Valance Terrace and is commemorated on the Hellas memorial. God bless him. The Battle of Gallipoli is remembered worldwide as Anzacs Day on April 25th which is a bank holiday for them due to the large number of Australian, New Zealand and Canadian troops that were killed there along with British and French soldiers.

This disaster laid heavy on Sir Winston Churchill's conscience for a lot of years as he gave the order to attack but the men in charge of the ships delayed resulting in the massacre. Some military men of power labelled him as gung-ho. However, this made him more resolute and developed him into the greatest leader of our country that we've ever known. A leader who stood alone against Hitler when the rest of the country were ready to sign a peace treaty.

Throughout my life Grannie and Grandad were always there for me and were always a source of inspiration to me. If ever I had a problem I would go and see them and come away feeling better. When I was first married at 20 years of age I often had money problems and could not get through the week. They would always bail me out and lend me something until I got paid. Then on April 3rd 1984 at the age of 78 my Grandad died suddenly of a heart attack. This knocked me and the rest of the family for six, especially my Grannie. Grandad had been there for me every day of my life and then suddenly he was gone. It broke my heart and I cried continuously that week. Up until then my Grannie had always struggled to walk the few hundred yards to our house but always managed it without complaint. We had moved to Orchard Park by then and our houses were not as close as down Lockwood Street, yet she never failed to come over whether it was rain, snow or shine. We've seen her come over even when it's been thick snow and told her not to come. But still she would trudge over in a little pair of black ankle boots with a pair of socks over them to stop her slipping with snow up to her bloomers. What a laugh it was when she dried her long-legged bloomers. However, the day Grandad died she completely lost her will to live and could not walk anymore. And exactly a week later my Grannie passed away to be with Grandad. The doctor said she had died of a broken heart, when my Grannie died I could hardly cry like I did with Grandad and felt guilty. I could not understand how I could not let go in the same way for someone I loved more than some people love their own parents. Then three months later I was talking to Mrs Penna of Penna's ice cream in her shop full of people when she mentioned something about my Grannie and I broke down in front of everyone. After that I felt better having got rid of the pain I'd been carrying for months. But even after thirty-odd years I still get upset just writing about them.

One of my fondest memories of my Gran was watching her answer the telephone; she never liked 'these new fandangled things'. They were probably the same to her as computers are to me, much to my son's annoyance. When my Gran answered the phone you'd hear her saying, "Hello, Hello, I cannie hear you. You'll have to speak up."

By then we'd be crying with laughter and telling her to turn the receiver around as she'd be speaking into the ear piece with the flexi cord wrapped around her neck.

Bless her, no cordless phones then.

When we lived next door to the Fields down Lockwood Terrace we used to make our own phones by having two tin cans with holes punched in the bottom. We then run a length of string through the middle with a knot tied at the end and threw one across to Dave or Graham and pulled it tight. We would then put the can to our ear or mouth and speak or listen. The cans used to be left dangling inside the bedroom window so that we could use them to speak to each other whenever we wanted.

Top: Grindells pet shop.
Below: Holding the trophy with Kev Green.

CHAPTER NINE
THE YOUNG
PIGEON FANCIER

Most of the lads round 'our end', as it was affectionately known had pigeons. My first attraction to them was whilst I was at St Charles School on Prime Street in the early sixties. I would stand outside school and gaze up at the roof opposite and watch the pure white and jet-black pigeons that a lad called Paul and his brothers kept up in the attic like my Gran and Grandad had. I was fascinated watching them flying in and out of the attic window.

My first pigeons were from Charles Street pet shop and were a blue racing hen and a red grizzle tippler cock that we paid a shilling each for. Many of Hull's present day fanciers originally got birds from there. It used to be a good little earner for some of them as people would buy them and try breaking them off, meaning to get them to return to your home, only to return to them and be up for sale the week after.

Our first home for that pair was in my Gran and Grandad's backyard that was bigger than our tiny backyard, their home was an old wooden tea chest that was 24" square which we lovingly painted white inside and out, the inch wide lats on the front red and white and a 6" landing board with a bob wire on the entrance that let them in, but not out. This tiny little home for them was comparable to our own little two up, two down home when we moved up to Orchard Park, our new home seemed massive. As was the case with our new pigeon loft we built which was only 6 foot square, we literally went from tea chest to not much bigger when compared to other fanciers lofts that were 20 footers.

When we'd finished our little tea chest we climbed onto my Grannie's scullery and painted our own personalised homing mark on the tiles. It was a red, white and blue cross inside a circle, and like every other backyard fancier we believed that this mark would let the birds know exactly where they lived. I would like to have seen all these rooftops from an aeroplane, as they would probably have looked like a modern art display.

A couple of weeks after getting our pair of birds we saw our first pair of eggs. Every lunch and afternoon we would run home from school to see if they'd hatched out, and then after seventeen days we saw them chipping out of the shell. It was the most exciting thing I'd ever seen to see two little squeakers pop out of their shells. Unfortunately though they did not live very long as the next day I developed my first hatred for cats. We progressed from my Grandad's backyard to the local barrel yard, where we secretly kept our birds in one of the large wooden packing cases, which were about ten feet square. We had a secret passage way through all the drums and tanks and up into the case. To let them in and out we had a small hole cut in the side with a landing board and bob wire as before. We managed to keep them there for a while until we moved up to Orchard Park.

In December 1967, we built our first proper loft, which was six-foot square with strict instructions from my Mam that we could only keep twelve pigeons in the winter and eighteen in the summer for young bird racing. This meant that only the best survived, as I had to cull six in the winter when racing had finished. This became a valuable lesson when I became an established fancier as when I was at my peak racing and became top prize winner in several clubs it proved that its quality over quantity that counts as on many occasion I would send an average of six birds and win the top prize and all the money against fanciers sending fifty-plus.

Mam hadn't realised that by making me cut down for winter I would have to cull some of my birds, until one night she came in from work and said, "Mmm, that smells nice son, what are you cooking?" When I proudly lifted the lid to show her some pigeons bobbing about she went mad and called me an evil little bastard and all the names under the sun.

In my first season racing as a fifteen-year-old schoolboy racing in one of the strongest clubs in the town 'The Hull Newland Pigeon Club' racing from the Rising Sun pub on Beverley High Road, I won the most prestigious young bird race of the year, 1st prize from Perth 212 miles and taking 5th federation.

This earned me the headlines in the Hull Sports Mail, "Young Richard shows way to old hands."

I still have the newspaper cutting now which is my pride and joy. I went on to win many accolades in my later years including the Yorkshire Middle Route federation channel averages and top prize winner in several clubs. A question I often get asked is how pigeons get home? I can tell you now, it's nothing to do with psychedelic paintings on scullery roofs. When I've had pigeons win races for me and they have flown more than 500 miles, they couldn't see the little paint mark on the roof of our back garden.

In those days there were no pigeon transporters, or if there were, they were few and far between. Our birds used to be sent around the country on trains. When we were teenagers we would go to Cottingham Railway Station to see the baskets all lined up on the platform and then watch the pigeons being released to fly back to their lofts in whichever town they came from. To see a bird come darting out of the sky and straight into its nest box after flying 12 to 14 hours on the wing is a fantastic feeling. But knowing that you watched it hatch out of an egg and you trained it to come home, it's an even better feeling.

They become as much a part of the family as any cat or dog. My birds were so tame they would come up to the house and into the kitchen looking for me and then fight each other to sit on my head and shoulders.

The secret to a pigeon's homing ability and every other living creature is down to a magnetic field, which is situated in the skull between the eyes. I saw a science programme years ago that carried out an experiment with a nest pair of pigeons that were trained every day together from the same place and always arrived together taking approximately the same time.

Then one day one of the birds was placed in a box at the liberation site that had an electronic field running through it that could reverse polarity and switched it on so the North and South poles were reversed in the bird's skull. When they were released, the one that had been reversed went in the opposite direction and never came home and the other went straight home. They took a pigeon's skull and tested it with a small electronic charge and found there was a north and South Pole, they x-rayed it and found small metal particles of iron that had built up. These magnetic particles are basically the pigeons built in sat-nav, this is what they use when released a long way from home or closer to home in poor visibility. The magnetic field is said to pick up on the earth's magnetic core and position of the sun, the moon also has an effect, as we all know that the moon affects the tides. Pigeons are said to be better if bred on a full moon. They will revert back to local landmarks when nearing home by using rivers and motorways, I've driven alongside pigeons on the motorway heading into Hull and when they've got near the Humber Bridge they've branched off and headed north. When I've been fishing at Spurn Point on the mouth of the Humber, I've seen a flock of pigeons coming down from the north and a flock coming from the South. When they got to the Humber they circled round together then some went down the river that were heading into Hull and the others have carried on north and south.

If not by using the sun and moon to navigate, how can I explain how two youngsters I gave away at three weeks old to Arthur who lived a few hundred yards away? I gave Nicky Sawyers a squeaker straight out the nest at three weeks old and soon as it could fly at six weeks it took up into the air from his loft on the next block and came flying back into the nest box it was bred in. That Schailie Janssen cock became known as 'Wobbly Gob' due to a slightly deformed beak. He won a few prizes for Nicky until he finished with pigeons and gave him back to me as a two-year-old. The following year he twice topped the fed from Abbeville in France, one of which was disallowed due to the clock setter not putting enough tape in my clock.

The other young bird I gave away to Arthur came back to me when it was a few months old. I came in from work one night and found a blue flighty walking around the garden and thought how strange that I had locked one out in the morning after they had exercised. I opened the loft and saw the one I thought it was sat looking at me. I picked it up and checked its ring number and realised it was a brother I had given Arthur as a baby. It turned out that he had took it on its first training toss that day and its instincts brought it back to me although it had never seen outside my loft when bred here.

One of the strangest experiences I ever had with pigeons was when I lost a young bird on a training toss and then a few days later I received a phone call from a

Newspaper cutting: Young Richard shows way to old hands

friend who lived near Goole, which is approximately twenty five miles.

He said, "I have two pigeons in my loft with your name and telephone number stamped on its flights, the other belongs to your brother."

Unbelievably we had both lost them around the same time and somehow ended up in the same loft, our homes were a few miles apart and the birds had never been in each other's loft. When you consider there are hundreds of lofts within this area it's incredible how they landed there.

I've always had a close affinity with pigeons and won their trust much in the same way as the dog or horse whisperer. My pigeons would often come looking for me, up to or even into the house if the door was open, much to the annoyance of my wife. Even on a race day when I've been waiting for them to come back from a race they would fly up the garden and land on my shoulder or hand, then let me take the race rubber off their leg and clock them in, saving me valuable seconds. I've mastered a pigeon's coo to perfection and used this to either pair up to a young hen, or wind up a cock bird when he's protecting his nest box. This has often been a source of amusement to my friends like Harry Dooley who would request a rendition over the phone when he was having a bad day by ringing and saying, "Do me a pigeon the Hald! I'm having a bad day!" and then he'd cry with laughing asking for me to do it again.

I've had pigeons come to me in the most bizarre circumstances like a few years ago when Harry was organising a show jumping event with his wife and family at Dunswell just outside of Hull. We were stood near the commentary box that he was announcing from, when I heard Jackie shout, "Look out Rich, it's going to land on you." I looked around expecting to see a horse out of control when I felt a thud on my shoulder and saw

a young racing pigeon complete with its race rubber on its leg. It had dropped out the race exhausted and of the hundreds of people that were there that day it decided to pick me to land on. I went to see Harry for a box to put it in and told him what happened and his reply was "Why doesn't that surprise me?"

I took the phone number of the owner stamped on its wing and let him know where it was so he could send for it by Amtrak, this type of thing has happened to me countless times. Even recently when camping up in Runswick Bay, we were in the pub one night when some women started screaming that there was a pigeon in the pub. How it got in I don't know, as there was a double set of doors. Our friends laughed and said it must have known you were in here to help it find its way home.

My greatest achievement was having the King of Dubai order a young bird from two of my champions at stock with my mate Eddie Wright of Fountainhead lofts. Eddie rang me one night all excited and said in his unique country accent "Rich! You'll never guess who has just ordered one out of Lionheart and Norsea?" which were two champion long distance racers I had bred, I raced Lionheart and a friend at the time Mike raced Norsea.

Just off the top of my head I said, "Oh I don't know! The King of Dubai?"

He went quiet and then said, "Who told you?"

It transpired that the King's loft manager had rang Eddie under instruction from the King and specifically asked for "One out of Richard Haldenby's Lionheart and Norsea."

Lockwood Terrace party.
L-R: Me bottom left, Mickey Bowers, Pattie Forth, Irene
Edwards, June Appleby, Lorraine Shanks, my cousin Diane
Jackson, our Karen, Pat Ling, Peggy Bowers, Linda Appleby,
Anne Folan, Mary Shanks and Steve Field

CHAPTER TEN
RE-HOUSED

We were sadly re-housed from Lockwood Street under a compulsory purchase order, which was a bittersweet experience as we were separated from our lifelong friends like the Fields, Shipleys and Marshals.

We all had the choice as to where we wanted to live among the many new council estates that were being built all around the outskirts of Hull in the late sixties. The only problem we had in choosing somewhere was that we wanted my Gran and Grandad to be near us. The first house they offered us was on Spring Cottage Estate, which was a beautiful house and a nice area, however they could not offer us somewhere for Gran and Grandad. We eventually accepted one on Orchard Park with a promise of a house nearby for them. We moved in on December 1st 1967 and it was a month later before we got them near us after constant protests from my Mam. Everyone had moved out apart from my Gran and Grandad. Every day my Mam would go to Guildhall and complain as all the houses were knocked down around them. She went to see them one day and they were blathered in soot and dust from surrounding fires. Enough was enough. She shot around to Sam Allon's office and demanded to see Sam.

When he showed his face she screamed "Have you got a mother and father?" and he nervously replied, "Yes, why?"

She took him to their house and said, "Is this how you'd like your parents to be treated?" So he apologised and stopped all work until they got a house near us.

RICHARD HALDENBY

When we moved into 16 Clanthorpe, we couldn't believe our eyes. It was like we'd won the football pools. To have hot running water and an upstairs and downstairs toilet, an upstairs bathroom and our own bedroom was such a wonderful feeling.

The first time we walked into the house we were overawed by the amount of space and light. The kitchen was large with a big window overlooking the garden and two doors leading off into the dining room and hallway, which both adjoined the living room. We ran through each of the doors in a circle diving and sliding on the shiny tiled floors. The living room had two large windows, which allowed the light to stream in and enabled us to look out over the open fields towards Beverley. The living room also had a large tiled open fireplace with a back boiler to give us hot water as well as an immersion heater. We had four bedrooms, which meant Gary and I shared a room but as we were nine and eleven it wasn't a problem considering four of us used to share a bed down Lockwood Terrace. To go from cramped, squalid conditions with ice on the inside of our windows in mid-winter and contending with blackclocks in the middle of the night to a beautiful, clean, spacious and warm room was a dream come true. What a pleasure it was to have a bath in the privacy of your own bathroom and not have to worry about being caught having a strip-down wash in the kitchen sink by Mrs Field or one of our other neighbours. Moving there was nearly comparable to the life our children were born into, except we didn't have double-glazing, central heating and the Internet. We felt like we'd been transported through time from the Edwardian days to the modern life we live now.

We were lucky to have moved when we did as shortly after we had the worst snowstorm we'd ever seen. I still haven't seen one as bad. The snow was so high in front of the house that when you opened the front door it was just a wall of snow that reached up to the bedroom windows. Even though we never had full central heating the coal fire gave off heat throughout the house and gave us hot water. We did however get a storage heater in the hallway, which took the chill off the bedrooms. The storage heater used to come on at night when the electric was on 'Economy Seven' which was a tariff that Yorkshire Electricity offered for off peak electric. The special furnace bricks within the heater would get hot during the night and then give off heat all day long.

The house seemed so big that we played hide and seek. If ever we were grounded and sent to our bedroom we would wait until after tea knowing my Mam would have the soaps of the day on such as Crossroads, Emmerdale or Corrie. We then put our record player on and climbed out of the bedroom window onto the front door porch and shimmied down the support pipes and sneaked away to play, and then came back a couple of hours later just before Corrie finished.

When we moved onto the estate we lost some of our old friends who I've never seen to this day, but others such as Mike Shipley and the Fields are still good friends more than fifty years later. The Fields ended up living down Blythorpe, a few doors away from my Gran and Grandad and only a few hundred yards away from us. Other families from round the old end came up near us such as the Sellers family, Christine and Julie Savage, Mrs Plumb, Minnie and Paddie Forth, The Freers, Joan and Dennis Routh and Gwyneth Taylor now Witham. It was an exciting time for us all moving onto a massive estate which gave us a whole new circle of friends with whom I'm still good friends with today.

I suppose the upheaval of moving at such an early age was comparable to adults emigrating. We left the safety of a close-knit community and the comfort zone of knowing everyone, to the insecurity of a large estate where we were all dropped into the middle of other small clans from different parts of Hull.

It was not a safe place in those early days as every time you went out the door to walk to or from school that was at the other end of the estate you had to pass through areas with small gangs who wanted to challenge you. We had plenty of fights through which we made good friends as we asserted our positions into rank and file. As with most estates that were built in the late sixties or early seventies there was no thought into any social activities to occupy the large groups of testosterone filled teenage lads who wandered around on a night in large gangs. And with girls hanging around with them who they had to impress, as one group crossed paths with another you would inevitably have gang fights.

On Orchard Park there were only a few places you could go on a cold dark winter's night - pre-legal drinking age - one of which was Schultz's youth club that was based at Sir Leo Schultz High School where I eventually ended up. The school did a lot to keep the kids off the streets with a number of activities. We could go and play table tennis, listen to music or watch films like Easy Rider, Bonnie & Clyde or 2001 A Space Oddity. It had a TV room that was nice and dark to snuggle up with your girlfriend, and also had its own indoor swimming pool where we would often go.

The highlight of the week for us all on the estate was Sunday night at St Michael's Church that hosted a disco called The Voodoo Club, named after Jimmy Hendrix's 1970 number one hit single Voodoo Chile. This was a fantastic place for us all, as kids from the age of twelve to eighteen would mix and listen to the music of the day that seemed to be dominated by heavy rock bands such as Led Zeppelin, Cream, Black Sabbath and Free. There was also a lot of Motown, which was big at the time, but to us it was puff music, whereas now it's my favourite. We would play our imaginary air guitars and 'freak out', as was the term used for dancing to such tracks as 'All Right Now', which was said to have been written after doing a gig in Hull at the university in front of around twenty people. Their career was at a low ebb at the time and as they walked backstage completely pissed off, Paul Rogers said that they needed something else. Then as they sat strumming their guitars they came up with the bass chords for 'All Right Now' and between Rogers and Kossof they laid down the first lyrics and chords.

As I write, I've just been over to St Michaels and All Angels and spoken to the vicar Dave about organising a reunion. I've posted it on face book and everyone's excited about the idea.

We used to build up our Dutch courage to dance at the age of fourteen or fifteen by going to Holmes's shops for some booze and putting our cash together to buy a bottle of wine on the wood, whatever that was and a bottle of Woodpecker cider. We'd send in one of the older looking lads such as Ian Lamping, who was a big lad and looked older than the rest of us.

I'm still friends with Ian now and he's just as bad an influence on me as he was back then. He recently picked me up on a nice, hot summer's day from my caravan and took me to his local pub where he showed me the proper way to drink Newcastle Brown from a half pint glass to keep the beer lively. The only problem with that was by keeping the beer lively, eight hours later I wasn't as lively and the usual twenty minutes' walk home took me one and a half hours of one step forward and two back. I hadn't drunk that stuff since being a teenager and now I know why.

One of the other rising stars of that era was David Bowie. A claim to fame story regarding Bowie was told to me by one of the fitters at West Plant Hire, Rick Mumby, who became a good friend. As you may know, Mick Ronson who was in Bowie's band The Spiders From Mars was from Hull and was brought up with Rick. He told me that Mick rang him one day and asked if Rick could do him a favour by standing in for one of the band members who was sick but because Rick could not play any kind of instrument he naturally said no. But Mick explained that due to the band being contracted to have a certain number in the band they needed someone to stand in. He said that all Rick had to do was stand and pretend to play a guitar, which would not be plugged in and that they would cover him, to which Rick agreed. He stood on the stage in Sheffield and although he froze in front of thousands of fans he managed to pull it off, or so he thought. As the adrenalin dropped off he noticed that he was suffering a little pain and was feeling wet and warm down his leg. He looked down to see a big patch of blood. It transpired that as he was hurried onto the stage and set up with his guitar they had forgotten to give him a plectrum and he had worn his thumb down to the bone.

The nearest I got to see Bowie was in early 1973 at Bridlington Spa with my first love, Julie Boynton. We had queued for hours to see him on a cold winter's night and got right to the front of the queue when Julie said, "My Mam and Dad have a caravan at Flamborough," which was only a few miles away from Bridlington. So with no further ado, we ditched the idea of seeing Bowie and jumped on the bus to Flamborough and never did get to see him. Big mistake!

In 1974 Bowie transformed The Spiders From Mars into Aladdin Sane with that unforgettable 'lightning' flash across his face, around the same time as Mark Bolan was creating Electric Warrior. Jackie had heard me talking of both these albums and wanted to buy me a birthday present, a simple task you would think! But Jackie being Jackie tried buying 'two in one' and went to every record shop in Hull asking for an album called 'Painted Warrior' that no one had ever heard of.

It wasn't until a shop assistant clicked what Jackie meant when she asked her to describe the album cover. She realised that Jackie had muddled up Bowie with his painted flash and Bolan holding his guitar in a threatening manner on the cover of Electric Warrior and come up with her own album - Painted Warrior. Jackie has come out with some crackers in her time but none more so than when I got in her little orange Skoda 120 on a cold winter's day and found all the screen defrosters were off. This was the case every time I got into it and I had to turn the heaters on.

I asked her why she turned the heater off when she left the car and she answered a bit sheepishly, "Well, when I'm driving with you or Sarah and Lisa I have the heating on but when I'm by myself I turn the heating off."

I asked her why she did that and to my amazement she answered that she didn't like wasting fuel. When I delved further the plot thickened. I found out that she thought that the heater matrix in the car ran on petrol like a paraffin heater and she did not want to waste fuel. Priceless!

Before we got married we had been to see her sister and husband Neil down Cadogan Street and got the bus home. When we got off the bus we walked down York Road and you could not see a hand in front of you for the thick fog. A proper old 'pea-souper' as we used to call them in 1974, the kind you never see now due to the lack of coal fires. As we walked along we were

Me and Acko in 1975.

suddenly faced with a double barrel shotgun shoved in my face and a man in a clown's mask who said, "I'm going to blow your heads off."

When you see something like that on telly you say I'd do this or do that but in reality you freeze. These were the days of the IRA and the troubles were at a high. I froze in my shoes not knowing what to do until he laughed and said, "You're okay, I'm only joking," and walked away into the fog laughing. Neither of us said a word for a moment and then carried on walking home, not saying anything until we got to her house when I said, "What the hell was that?"

In 1974 Jackie's Mam and Dad banned me from their home feeling that I was not the type they wanted for their daughter. I did not disagree with this as I would not want my girls to settle down with the likes of me as I was in those days. I was basically honest but was always fighting and flirting.

After nearly two years of me being banned from their home and Jackie and me standing outside their gate 'saying good night' in all weathers, they decided to give me another chance. They invited me to go and see them on the last day of their week's holiday at Robin Hood's Bay, where they had rented a cottage.

The whole family were there including my brother in law and good friend Neil. I went up there with my good mate Steve Akril (Acko) in his Wolsey 1500 and nearly killed ourselves on the way, as I was driving and got a speed wobble at Lisset and nearly 'lost it'. We were due to stay at our friend Ken Faichney's place on the Saturday night in the artist's studio. Ken has been a lifelong friend of the family and is like a brother to us having gone out with our Karen and lived with us down Lockwood Street and on Orchard Park. We arrived there at lunchtime and wasted no time in having a few drinks in the Bay Hotel. We spent the whole afternoon there knocking back double rum and blacks. We met up with Jackie on the Saturday night and carried on boozing and by closing time we were steaming. Jackie and I set off to find where I was staying at Ken's but could not find it down all the little alleyways.

We set off up a steep hill that must have been a 3 in 1 and got half way up with her pushing me up, when she said, "Can we stop? I need a rest."

We both had our platform-soled shoes on which didn't make it any easier. As we stopped to rest she let go of me and I fell straight back and landed flat on the back of my head, knocking myself out. Luckily a copper came to my assistance and lifted me up onto my feet. He helped Jackie take me back to their cottage where I stayed for the night. It must have been a nice surprise for Jackie's Mam and Dad when they got up in the morning to find me snoring and farting on the settee.

RICHARD HALDENBY

When I finally awoke I could smell the English breakfast being cooked. I started to feel ill and ran into the kitchen, where they were all getting breakfast ready, looking for the toilet. I didn't have time for niceties and to greet them with, 'Good morning, how are you all?' I just blurted out, "Quick open the door!"

Unfortunately it was locked and no one could find the key. By the time they eventually opened it there was sick pouring through my fingers. I ran straight outside and emptied the full contents of my stomach into the fishpond. The water turned purple from all the rum and blacks I'd had the day before. The fish enjoyed it as they went into a frenzy. John and Brenda eventually agreed to accept me into the family and I can't have turned out that bad as Jackie and I stayed together for forty-odd years.

When we first got married we lived at 154 Division Road that backed onto Hull FC's ground, The Boulevard. We paid £2.00 a week rent for the old four-bedroom house, which shared the yard with my brother in law Les's business. At the back of his workshop was a trapdoor fitted onto the wall around three feet square, which led into the gents' toilets of the rugby ground. When you lifted the door you were looking directly down into the men's urinals of the 'threpny' stand (three pence stand) that's how much it used to cost to get into the ground, which in today's money is nothing. Twelve old pence equated to five new pence so three-pence would be about one new penny.

My other brother in law Neil and me used to laugh as we opened the trapdoor on match days knowing the shock on the faces of blokes stood with cock in hand as we'd say, 'Excuse me mate,' as we jumped through the door. Every one of them made the same comment - "For fuck's sake, you nearly gave me a heart attack you daft bastards!" as they jumped back pissing down their legs.

CHAPTER ELEVEN
A NEW
SCHOOL

Being raised as a Roman Catholic I was expected to go to Marist College after finishing St John Fisher on the estate at the age of thirteen. But I had other ideas. Marist was a bus ride of two or three miles, which I'd had enough of travelling from Lockwood Street to St John Fisher School, so I decided I wanted to go to Sir Leo Schultz High School, which was a multi religion school. The only problem to this was that the authorities would not let me go. I couldn't see the sense in this as most of my new mates off the estate went there and it was only a couple of minutes' walk as it was directly in front of our house. We looked onto a large school playing field full of football pitches that were shared between Schultz and Sir Henry Cooper High School that was another large school at the opposite end of the field. When the first day of term came I walked in with my new-found mates who I knocked about with on the estate. We sat in the classroom and the teacher read out the register to which everyone answered.

When he finished I put my hand up and said, "What about me Sir?"

He looked bemused and said they must have made a mistake and wrote my name on the register. This happened with each class we went to as with this large modern school pupils went from class to class where you had a different teacher for each subject in different house blocks with different lessons such as Cousins house was for maths, metal work shop and cookery block. This was unlike my previous schools where you had the same teacher all day or they'd come to your classroom.

After a week or so the teachers got to know me and everything was tickety-boo. But that only lasted for six weeks until the board man came knocking. I came in from school and he was sat with my Mam and Dad.

He said, 'Richard, why haven't you been going to school?' to which my Mam replied, 'He has.' I said, 'I have been going to school but not the one you want me to go to.'

My Mam and Dad looked surprised as they thought I was going to Marist and said 'You've got to go to Marist,' and for the first time in my life I answered my Dad back and said, 'I don't want to go there Dad,' and then explained to him why.

Much to my surprise he shrugged his shoulders and said I agree. The board man tried frightening me and said if you don't go you will have to go to boarding school, which I said, 'Okay then, do what you want, I still aren't going.'

Luckily he backed down and allowed me to stay at Schultz and I went there from 1969 to September 1971.

Schultz was a fantastic school and far-advanced for the early 1970s. People still can't believe it was closed down in favour of its neighbour, Sir Henry Cooper. Schultz boasted an indoor swimming pool, tennis courts, a specially designed science block that was admired by everyone and stood out on the skyline with its unique triangular shaped glass pinnacle, along with the youth club and it's own TV studios that was used for presenting local news on TV.

The football team was always one of the top teams in the Sunday Leagues and produced some top players such as Pete Skipper and Dave Towers who both went on to play for Hull City. Fred Ramsden was our football coach and had a good relationship with City, Paddy

THE POETIC HOOLIGAN

Doran was one of our PE teachers who I believe was a top national runner along with Paul Newton. Terry Glenville was our swimming teacher who also competed at national level and was said to have come close to been selected for the Olympics. One of our tennis coaches was the beautiful Miss Gosling who always had our undivided attention during her lessons. At the end of each term there was always a tennis match between the teachers on the courts at the back of the school. And all the lads could be found watching the matches, laid on our sides propped up on one elbow, trying to catch a glimpse of her frilly knickers

My first year at Schultz went well, however my second year went downhill as I lost interest in schooling and was more interested in knocking about with girls. I started playing twag and spent most of my days going into school for my mark in France house, which was our base. If I remember rightly the other four houses were Schultz, Cousins, Lumsden & Digby. I'd get my mark in the morning and after lunch and then spend the rest of the day with a couple of girls called Glynis and Helen at one of their houses. This went on for the full year. Mr Hunt, the headmaster, would occasionally catch me and ask where I was going? I'd tell him to the doctors or dentist and he would ask for my note from my Mam to excuse me. When I couldn't produce it he'd laugh and say, 'Get to your lesson!'

When I did go into some of the lessons some of the new teachers had never seen me before and would ask who I was?

Considering the fact I hardly did any schooling in my last year we all attended our very last mass assembly where all the classes got together to see all the swats receive their diplomas. All the 'Jack the Lads' like me, Lamping, Morley, Rumble, Amo, Norm and (Porky) Pete etc., would sit at the back taking the piss.

RICHARD HALDENBY

Mr Hunt got the final laugh over me as he knew I was basically a good lad as he'd often had me in his office for fighting and given me the cane and always said if you stopped messing around you could make something of yourself. When he finished handing out all the certificates he looked at the teachers sat in a row behind him on stage and started smiling and said, "Last but not least is Richard Haldenby who receives a certificate for good attendance."

I've never felt so embarrassed in my life as I walked up onto the stage with the whole assembly laughing and jeering. As he handed me it he laughed and said, "Well done Richard, on paper you did have the best attendance."

It was the same throughout my working life. I've rarely had a day off sick and I'm always punctual, which I get from my Mam and Dad who were always hard workers. I still have the certificate to this day. As I said earlier we had found a new set of friends and soon found out where the meeting areas were. One of the main spots was a row of shops known as Holmes' shops, situated between North Hull Estate and Orchard Park. They comprised of an off licence, a newsagents, a Co-op, a Chinese takeaway and a chip shop, which is still a chippy today and run by a very nice Chinese family.

This was the main area for meeting up with your mates and all the girls in our early teens, a tradition that was going on before we moved up there and still goes on today. You would often see a group of around thirty or forty lads and lasses laid on the grass or playing football on the other side of little Ellerburn Avenue, in front of the small bank especially throughout the seventies and eighties. As we got a bit older and into our mid to late teens some of the lads who could not find work or in some cases did not want to work would make a living out of cadging as they called it. This was basically begging for ten pence to everyone who walked into the shops. They were known as 'The Vulture Squadron'. When they had enough money they would buy a bottle of cider or a bottle of the sickly cheap wine, known as 'wine on the wood'. You would take your own bottle in and have it filled from a cask. The master of his trade was Tony Dolan who was a few years older than us and who we all looked up to as he was a nice lad who everyone liked. Unfortunately he died too young due to his lifestyle.

No matter what we were going to do, whether it be a cricket or tennis match on Queen Elizabeth Park, a night at the Voodoo Club or a game of football on Schultz's field you could always guarantee a good number of girls in the mix. This would inflate the lads bravado resulting in a lot of chest beating and the odd scrap, usually over a girl. I was once showing off in front of my first proper girlfriend, Joy Brown, around 1970 when I was fourteen years old. I was acting like Mr Cool doing 'stoppies' on my push-bike, meaning you ride fast and then pull your front brake on to make your back wheel lift off the floor as high as you can without going over the handle bars. That was going well until I set off to go home and pulled a wheelie, lifting my front wheel off the floor only to see it go rolling away in front of me, leaving me flat on the floor and looking a right prat. This was much to the amusement of Joy who nearly peed herself laughing. I quickly slotted the wheel back in the forks and rode off gingerly.

On the opposite corner of Ellerburn Avenue lived my mate Steve Akril, who I still see a lot of. He owned one of the most powerful Lambrettas ever and even today it would give the TS1 lads a run for their money. It was a GT 200 bored to a 236 with a Delorto downdraught carb, a racing gearbox and a ten-spring clutch and padded crank. You had to pull the clutch lever in with both hands due to the double springs so that when you let the clutch out you had to lean over the headset to hold the front end down.

It beat every scooter on the road and most motorbikes. I used to borrow it to go to work and college whenever mine broke down. It was purple and yellow and well known by everyone. I remember racing Graham Thomas up Orchard Park Road on his Honda 250 super dream and beating him.

One of the funniest confrontations we had was when Acko and me pulled out of Warley Cross Cafe on the way to Bridlington with me riding it and Acko as passenger. Before we could get up to speed a few greabos passed us and started taking the piss by gesturing the wanker sign and trying to kick us off our bike. I accelerated and overtook them leaving them in our wake. Doing 95 two up was unheard of. The average scooter in our day would do 50-60mph. When we got to Brid we were parked looking over the harbour when the bikers came up to us and said, "What the fuck have you got under them cans? We've never seen a scooter move as fast as that."

CHAPTER TWELVE
JACKIE

After school and at weekends we would spend a lot of time out on the large school playing fields in front of our house playing football. These games would go on for hours on end. On a weekend we would be out there at seven or eight o'clock on a Saturday morning and still be playing at ten or eleven at night on the long hot summer nights. The teams could consist of eleven or twelve-a-side and would be constantly changing as we all went for our dinners and tea at different times. The games always took place on Schultz's field which was a field full of pitches with goal posts situated between Sir Leo Schultz High School and Sir Henry Cooper High. I went to Schultz which was handy for me as I could look out of my bedroom window and see who was larking soccer.

We had some fantastic players among this lot who went on to be professionals. And others, such as Graham Thomas, could have become top players but turned down the opportunity to sign for Wolves as he didn't want to live away from home.

Schultz's field was a centre point for all sorts of activities and was never more entertaining than the end of school term battle between the Schultz mob and Sir Henry Cooper School lot. We would line up against each other about two hundred a side and then run at each other with fists and boots flying.

The battle would traditionally take place either on the field or on the green hill, which was another gathering point on the estate. This was a man-made hill in the centre of the estate that was formed from excess building rubble when the estate was built and then topped off with soil. One year we lined up there for our battle and we're all lined up ready to go in but no one seemed to want to go first so I said to Terry Morley and Ian Lamping, "If I go in first are you going to back me?"

They said they would so I ran into their biggest lad and whacked him. A few of his mates joined him to give me a good kicking before my mates came to my assistance which may have been only a few seconds but was long enough for me to receive a right good kicking. Green Hill as I said always seemed to have something happening especially in winter when it was covered in snow. Dozens of kids would turn up with all sorts of sledges that were either man-made ones of wood or dustbin lids, car bonnets or even just polythene or plastic sheets that were faster than anything but not very comfortable.

When the Arctic Ranger pub was built in September 1973 the hill used to be a great place for all the teenagers to lay out in the summer. They would leave the pub at kicking-out time, 3 o'clock, and lay in the sun flirting with the girls or playing football until the pub opened again at 5:30. It was on the opening night of Arctic when I started going out with Jackie, having previously met her whilst going out with her sister a couple of years earlier when I was at school.

All of us back then were crazy for fighting but we have all turned out to be decent, respectable and hardworking men with good family values. Most of us still keep in touch and get together every couple of months and whenever United have a big game.

We always say how good it is to get together without any trouble. At least that was the case until the FA Cup Final against Crystal Palace in 2016. Thirty or forty of us were having the craic when I was talking to one of the lads I went to school with and saying how there was never any bother. With that Palace scored and a handful of Arsenal fans got in our faces taking the piss. Tony and Bri went over to tell them to cut it out and I could see it was getting a bit heated so I went over to pull them away when one of them stood up and said to Bri, "How do you fancy a fucking glass in your face?" Before he'd finished gobbing off I saw red and battered him half a dozen good shots and sat him back down in his seat. I pulled the lads away and went back to talk to Steve, who asked "What were you just saying about never fighting?"

It was a one off as for the last twenty-odd years I have walked away from trouble even though I have been boiling inside. It's nice to know you've still got what it takes to defend yourself when needed even at sixty years old as I keep myself fit.

Tony and Harry still go to most home games on the Hull & District Supporters Branch bus. They take two buses to every home game, one from Howden. We formed the club in 1973 with Demo as secretary. Whenever we get together we often raise a glass to two of the lads I mentioned earlier, Dobbo and Ewan. Dobbo passed away in 1996 at the age of forty-one and was one of the most popular lads you could wish to meet. Lots of people still speak about him. His popularity was evident by the number of people that attended his funeral. He was sent off in good style with a big United badge made of flowers in the back of his hearse that had been put together by the OPE lads and United scarves on his coffin.

One of my greatest memories of Dobbo was when I went away with Brownie to Blackpool for a long weekend and Dobbo said he would join us as he was working and couldn't set off with us. We set off early on the Friday morning with just a sleeping bag and a bit of

On Ewan's 750 Triumph Trident

cash each. We didn't even have the money for the train and jumped on it as it set off from Hull Paragon Station and then avoided the ticket collector all the way there by popping into the toilet as we saw him coming down the train.

We said to Alan, "We'll be sleeping in the sand dunes towards Lytham St Annes," not realising how big they were until the next morning, as we got to them in the dark and having only seeing them as a kid and thinking they were quite small. We had a great day in the sun and scored for a couple of birds from Wolverhampton and got our leg over. We made our way to the dunes and bedded down for the night, we saw a few shadowy figures moving about in the moonlight and were shitting ourselves as we were only sixteen or seventeen years old. We were shouting out threats pretending we had knives saying, "If any bastard comes near me they're going to get stabbed," when we heard a voice say, "Don't be stabbing me you pair of bastards," in that familiar north Hull accent.

We all bedded down again with me sharing my sleeping bag with Alan. When we woke in the morning I said, "I had the strangest dream last night. I was sleeping on an airfield and a plane nearly landed on me."

They both laughed and said, "It nearly did, look there."

We were literally yards away from the perimeter fence of Blackpool runway. We'd had a good drink before we went to sleep and a plane had come in to land, just clearing the fence and nearly blowing us out of our sleeping bags. I had woken up and seen the undercarriage of the plane just feet above us, then fallen straight back to sleep. When we looked at the vast area the dunes covered we couldn't believe how Alan had found us.

Happy days Dobbo. RIP.

Ewan was a hyper personality and always the centre of anything that was going on, a proper joker and very mad. I remember seeing him at a United away game with his mate Lee on a red hot summer's day. They both had full all in one flying suits and leather head caps like the ones astronauts wear. Everyone who passed them was laughing and pointing which just made them act more crazy.

Whenever I think of Ewan I see him stood on the bar or on a table in Hull Cheese playing his air saxophone to the Specials on a Saturday afternoon, he was the double of Terry Hall.

One Saturday afternoon he got us all kicked out of one of the fast food burger bars by starting a chip fight. The waiters had come over to ask us to calm it down and Ewan squirted them with tomato sauce. Not a good

Top: OPE Reds - 1986. L/R: Harry, Bert, Our Gary, Me, Acko, Bri, Fred,
(Rat) John Hindley and (Dobbo) Alan Dobson.
Below: OPE Reds - 2016. Rat's return. Harry, Shaun Tordoff, Me,
(Rat) John Hindley, Gary Gibson, Caz, John Carol and Bri.

idea!

Always the extrovert he had to do things a bit different to us all. We all rode Lambrettas but not Ewan, he had to have a 750 Triumph Trident motorbike.

We've had some great get-togethers and dos, a memorable one was Rat's Australia emigration party in 1986 at Marist Rugby Club.

Rat was always a well-respected member of the OPE reds and a born comedian. He was one of the first, if not *the* first to spray his Doc Marten boots gold, which became a craze all over the country in the height of Glam rock. He also sprayed 'The Doc' on the back of his black three-quarter leather coat in tribute to the then United manager Tommy Docherty.

You can imagine how shocked and bewildered we all were when one night we all met up as usual outside the Rampant Horse pub for a kick-around when someone said, "Have you heard about Rat? He's joined the army."

"What!" We never heard anything from him until years later. In between times someone asked Brownie and me, "Have you ever heard out from Rat?" With just a spare of the moment quip and no malice meant we replied, "Haven't you heard, he's been found dead upside down in a dustbin in Ireland?" not thinking for a minute that it would be taken seriously. Then months later someone else approached Brownie and me again who had received the same story but with bits added on and said, "Have you heard about Rat, he's been killed in Ireland? We were both shocked until he said he was found dead upside down in a dustbin.

We realised the story had gone full circle and fell about laughing. The lad walked away in disgust saying, "You two are fucking sick, he's supposed to be your mate."

The Glam rock days were an innovation and brought us out of the dark and into the light with bright colours and a sense of fun, much to the dismay of my dad and others of the men's men brigade. The likes of T. Rex's Marc Bolan with his cork screw hair were all puffs to my dad.

He would not allow us to watch The Glitter Band with their silver suits and platform soles on 'Top of the Pops'. And I used to pray that he would be away on a Thursday night so I could watch the best band ever, Slade with Noddy Holder's unique voice. Slade were originally a typical sixties band going nowhere until Chas Chandler said, "Hey lads, I want you to shave your heads and wear braces, turned up jeans and bovver boots."

This was the new way forward - to be a skinhead band. They released, 'Get Down And Get With It' and never looked back. Slade were responsible for the abbreviated text we first used on mobile phones with titles to the songs of 'Coz I Luv U' and 'Gudbuy T' Jane.' My dad hated all these bands and nearly kicked me out the house when I wore some beads saying, "Get them off your wrist. Are you a puff?"

Although these bands did look gay and most of them probably were, the music they left behind will be remembered by our generation for decades. But even though our parents thought our music was unbearable, just as we think a lot of our kids' music is not music but boom boom crap, there will always be classics that will be remembered like Slade's 'Merry Xmas Everybody' and Free's 'Alright Now'.

CHAPTER THIRTEEN
MY FIRST WAGE

I started my apprenticeship in September 1971 at West Plant Hire, Southcoates Lane, Hull as a forklift and plant maintenance engineer, cars & commercials. Thanks to my uncle Ken Jackson who was a Massey Fergie 50B driver for Malcolm West. Unfortunately my uncle Ken recently died.

My wages were £6-00 per week of which I took home £5-47, then £2-00 board to my Mam, which left me with £3-47 to pay bus fares and dinners. Unbelievably I still had enough for a couple of nights out in Orchard Park pub where I could buy ten pints of bitter or nine pints of lager for a quid - 10p for bitter and 11p for lager. People can't believe you could buy a pint in the seventies for ten pence! My duties as an apprentice in the early days were mainly cleaning. I think that's where I've got my nickname now as Squeaky because I'm always squeaky clean. I've become a bit OCD with my work cleanliness a bit like someone in the Army who has it drilled into them. The workshop had to be blitzed every day before I could touch a spanner, starting with the work benches that had galvanised tops. I had to work along the bench between vices that separated each fitter's area, each area had to have every part moved and replaced in the exact order whilst I cleaned the bench. I was often the scapegoat as some of the not so bright fitter's would blame me for nut's & bolt's going missing when they had lost them. It was like a surgeon's operating table when I'd finished. In between those duties I would have to go around all the fitters at 9-30 and take the sandwich order, then run down to the shops and return at five to ten to get back in time for the tea break. If I was half a penny short for the likes of Barry the crane driver there was hell on. The next job was to pull up the wooden, latted duck boards from in front of the benches that the fitters would stand on to keep their feet warm in winter. We would then sweep under the benches making sure nothing had fallen on the floor. That could be a small but expensive and important part for an engine that could bring a job to a standstill for weeks, as parts weren't readily available as they are now with overnight delivery.

All the rubbish had to be swept into the middle of the workshop from both sides, shovelled into a wheelbarrow and then emptied outside into a big skip. Then out into the yard and start moving forklifts or plant from the perimeter and again sweep everything into the yard and bin it, that was if none of the fitters had kicked my pile all over the yard for a laugh. The canteen was next, sweep the floor and wash the tables.

The job I hated the most was steam cleaning whatever forklifts or plant were on the wash area, not so bad in summer, but winter you couldn't dry yourself out. Last of all were the toilets. Then, usually about mid afternoon, I was allowed to get my little metallic blue cantilever toolbox out and do some repairs.

At fifteen I was a quiet shy lad who addressed all the fitters by their title, Mr. I thought it was rude to call them by their first names. However, that didn't last long. By the time I was sixteen or seventeen I'd got a bit streetwise and was regarded as a rum lad by the men I worked with. Middy (Alan Middleton) found this out one day when he clipped me around the ear for doing something wrong. I turned on him in a fit of temper and warned him and all the rest of them that if they ever laid a hand on me again I would hit them back. And if they still hit me I'd whack 'em on the back of the head with a lump of 4x2" when they least expected it. This was shortly after they had all cornered me to grease my balls as a birthday present and I picked up my hammer and said, "The first one get's it."

They never bothered me again after that, knowing all the stories about me fighting after work and that I was getting to be a bit of a handful and would do it. Malcolm Wilkinson was my manager, known to everyone in the town as Wilky. Although he's a good friend now, I used to be shit scared of him. He was a hard taskmaster and was always ripping a strip off the lads. He used to look like the actor John Thaw, in his 'Sweeney' days. Considering I was so afraid of him I once plucked up the courage to play a prank on him with Kevin, one of the fitters, who was a few years older than me. I had noticed that whenever Wilky was in the workshop and the phone rang in the office which was across the yard, someone from the office would pop their head through the workshop door and shout "Wilky, telephone!" He would spin on his heels and sprint to the office, mid conversation or not. Why they never had a phone extension in the workshop I don't know.

Anyway, this one day I said to Kevin, "I need to get Wilky near the four poster ramp and for you to get him looking at something on a fork truck on the ramp whilst I pretend to be working on a truck next to it."

Our cunning plan couldn't have gone any better, in fact it went a little too well actually. As they were both looking at the truck I sneaked up behind Wilky and slipped a hook into his back pocket that I had made from an electric welding rod. Next, I tied the other end onto a fork truck, bearing in mind his back pocket was always bulging with his wallet and delivery notes etc. I then sneaked to the workshop door and shouted "Wilky!

Telephone!"

As planned he shot off, but instead of just pulling his back pocket off it also took half of his arse out of his favourite brown cord pants, that he usually wore with a tweed suit jacket complete with patches on the elbows which was then fashionable.

There were papers all over the floor, which he tried putting back in his pocket but all that was left was his undies showing. He glared at me with a face like thunder and screamed, "I'll have you, you little bastard!" And he did for the next few weeks by making my life a misery. I spoke to him recently and he said, "Aye you owe me a pair."

Monday mornings are never good but on the occasions when I'd missed college on a Friday or not turned in on a Saturday morning as I never got paid, as they said I wasn't entitled as an apprentice. So if I'd stopped over at my then girlfriend's Julie Boynton's the last thing I wanted to do was pedal seven miles on a push-bike in the snow or rain. Once I got my provisional licence at seventeen it was not so bad as I bought my first Lambretta, a GP 150, Reg SRH 849G from Kingston Scooters on Spring Bank in 1973. The same company is still there now. Being a Lambretta though I still had to pedal or get a bus on many occasions due to it always breaking down.

I recently went to see Malcolm West to pass on my condolences having just lost his wife Brenda and thanked him for standing by me in my wild boy days and not letting me leave my apprenticeship with six months to go to join the Navy. He made me finish my time saying, "If you wait six months and then join in case you don't like it, then you've got your paperwork behind you."

Whether it was a good move or not I'll never know, as if I'd have done twenty-five years in the Navy and would probably have retired early with a good pension. At least I have my City &Guilds and indentures that state I am a time served forklift, plant, car & commercial engineer, which has helped me get some good jobs over the years.

I take pride in describing myself as an engineer and not a fitter, as when I was taught by the likes of Middy, John Axle or Ray Wallace you were taught the right way how to strip something down and find why it had broken. And not to just fit a new part as is often the case in today's 'throw-away' society, created by cheap imported parts where it's not worth stripping something down to find the fault. However, this does not help you when you're stuck for a part on a Friday night in the middle of a site and everywhere is closed. This is where you need the knowledge to strip and repair a part to get you out of the mire.

John taught me always to present myself clean and tidy, and always have a clean rag in my side pocket to keep myself and the machines clean.

He'd say, "There's nothing worse for a machine man who looks after his machine than to climb into his cab and get blathered in oil and grease. You will only turn them against you and make life hard for yourself. Also, if you look like a grease monkey you will be treated like a chimp. When dealing with customers, if you're clean and respectable you'll be treated with respect."

Back in those days if you had to reline a set of brake shoes or clutch plate you couldn't just go buy one off the shelf or have it delivered out the back of a van in half an hour as you do now. We had to drill out the rivets, fit new linings and re-rivet them, the same with the clutch plate. Pressure plate fingers were compressed on a handmade press and renew the fingers and springs and even skim the pressure plate face if required and reset the fingers. Brake master cylinder and slave cylinders were stripped, honed out and new seal kits fitted. Even cylinder head gaskets were hand-made by thin sheets of copper and asbestos by laying the old gasket onto the new sheets and cutting them out and punching the holes out. The asbestos was sandwiched between the two sheets of copper. Starter motors and alternators were also stripped and overhauled. Dynamos and rectifiers were still in use then, a bit like changing from old money to decimal.

There were about ten or twelve fitters when I was an apprentice, some good, some not so. The ones who made an impression on me were Middy, Ray and John Axle, the others were good men but I learnt a lot from the latter. Ray Wallace once saved my bacon when I was fifteen-years-old and did my first big job. I had been told to service a 26/48 Henley which was a big truck in those days that lifted thirteen tons. He showed me what to do and let me get on with it.

When he came back he asked, "All done Rich?" to which I replied, "Yes Mr Wallace" with a big grin on my face.

As I started the engine, he said "Have you tightened the sump plug and topped the oil up?" I froze and yelled, "Oh no!"

I'd forgotten to put the oil in it and quickly stopped the engine. We filled it with oil and tested it and luckily it was okay. A great lesson was learnt and from that day on I always check the sump plug and oil level two or three times after I've finished a service as I'm doing other jobs.

CHAPTER FOURTEEN
SURROUNDED BY GUARDIAN ANGELS

In 1971 there were only three forklift companies in Hull, West Plant Hire, Croslands, who were then based on Hedon Road where Trinity Hotel and KCFM are now situated, and Liptons Fork Lifts down Marvel Street that is now Barek lift trucks owned by Mike Leak.

My good friends Tony Trigg and Mike Asquith were manager and foreman of Liptons.

Westies in their day were a huge company, founded by Malcolm who was only about twenty-one and was helped by his dad Fred of FK West builders. He was also a self-made man, who earned his money just after the war by cycling to Bridlington and the surrounding area, a distance of approximately thirty miles from Hull, with a bag full of tools in his front basket and repairing bombed buildings.

West Plant had a large variation of machines including Hyster, Henley and Coventry Climax, they were the main forklifts of the day with the odd makes trying to get on the scene like Hudswell total which had the first hydrostatic drive motors we'd ever seen. Then Stihl introduced the first diesel/electro drive forklift, which was where the modern Hybrid cars originate. They had an engine driving an electric motor that in turn charged the batteries basically. Side loaders were mainly Boss and Shawloader.

The plant consisted of cement mixers, Wickham beam pumps, Thwaites dumpers, up to the bigger stuff like Cat, Fiat Allis, and International drotts and Coles

Clockwise from top left:
Kevin Edwards,
Paul Clarke and Albert Priestman

cranes and several MF50B diggers. These were driven by the likes of Ken Jacko, Brian Woolace, Ken Wallace, Dave Brown, George Harris, Bob Grundy, Peter Johnson, Peter Wray, Ray Galloway and Barry Buckton. The Bri mech tipper body driver was Rod Guernel and low loader driver was Tommy Masters. Jimmy Irwin was the diesel bowser driver and old deafy, Herbert Lonsborough, the Green Griffin ten-ton road roller driver. Deafy lost his hearing during his days as a petrol tanker driver when he turned over a tanker that blew up. He was also known for having one bollock that would swell to the size of a coconut if he lifted anything heavy. It was his party trick and would often whip it out for a laugh. The old twat caught me out by sneaking up behind me and shouting, "Richard!" Then, as I turned around I got a big bollock in my face, much to the amusement of all the lads who were stood waiting to see. All the men were good to work with including the aforementioned and Martin Tate of South cave, Albert Priestman, Fred Rhodes, Roy Watts, Rick Mumby and John Hardy, who is still a good friend now. Paul Clarke was the apprentice after me and was the brother of my life long friend Tony. Unfortunately Paul, bless him, has recently passed away.

I have good memories of all the men. Fred was an old slogger who had worked on barges all his life and was the oldest of the fitters. I used to have some fun with him. Once, we were all stood around the coffee machine in a morning having a drink before we started, I had found a piece of sponge packing from a parcel the night before that looked like a house brick. As we stood I waited with the sponge behind my back until Fred was lifting the cup and then threw the lookalike brick at him. He tried dodging out the way and poured the coffee into his ear and then chased me up the workshop throwing everything he could get his hands on. Another time I

George Harrison

Fred Rhodes

caught him out was when I again found some yellow polystyrene packing that looked like Quavers. So I bought a packet of the real things and ate them and then filled the empty packet with the fake ones. I offered him some, which he scoffed down before he realised anything was wrong and they nearly choked him.

The best one though was when I got a piece of bike inner tube and cut a piece off about six inches long and fixed it over the end of his exhaust pipe. I secured it with a jubilee clip and told everyone to watch him leave at five o'clock. He duly jumped into his Mk 1 Cortina and revved the engine, which made the loudest farting noise as the gasses blew out. He got out and walked around the car but whilst it was ticking over it didn't make the noise. Everyone was hidden behind cars and even the office staff were looking out the window. He got back in and set off through the gates with his car

154

farting all the way up Southcoates Lane and people on the bus pointing and laughing until the exhaust got hot and melted the rubber tube.

Another night as he was leaving I jacked up the back wheel of his car and put a brick under the axle which held one wheel off the floor slightly. When he put the car into gear the wheel just spun around making him think his clutch had gone.

Bless him if he's no longer with us - or if you're reading this, my sincere apologies Fred.

John Hardy and Kevin were about four years older than me so we had a lot in common and got on very well, before I passed my test I used to love going out on site to breakdowns with them. When Haworth Park Estate on Beverley Road was being built we spent a lot of time there. Kevin and I were called out to a cement mixer that was broken down there one day. When we got to it we asked this huge Irish man what was wrong with it? He said it had an oil leak and he could not turn the engine over with the starting handle. I asked if he'd checked the oil level and he said, "Yes I've filled it right to the top."

He literally had, right to the top of the rocker cover causing it to lock up. He didn't know where the dipstick was - we did, he was stood in front of us.

On another occasion we were working there inside a huge coffer dam that they were building. It was about sixty-feet deep by about thirty foot across. It had to have wooden stagings made out of large wooden beams, which spanned from one side to the other about every ten-foot down, so that the Wickham beam water pumps could pump up into a 45 gallon drum on each staging, and then be sucked out of that drum by another pump, and so on to the top.

There were ladders lashed from beam to beam, the times you would be working on a pump when a low flying jet would scream above you. The first you would know about it was when the sonic boom exploded into the hole, bouncing from wall to wall and nearly knocking you off the beam with shock.

No such thing as health & safety then.

Harnesses hadn't been introduced in the building trade, the lack of which nearly cost the life of a man while we were working there one day, as he fell off one of the beams and landed vertically onto a piece of a bar that was stood vertically to the ground.

It entered his backside and came out through his neck, miraculously bypassing every major organ in his body. The Emergency Services cut off the bar and took him to hospital, where he was X-rayed and found to be okay. They pulled the bar out and stitched him up. A few years later I saw the photos in a construction plant magazine in a site office.

A less serious but very painful accident happened to my apprentice Paul Clarke. He was unloading a trailer from the land rover with old Bob Dunn, father of Industrial Tyres' Bob Dunn. As he lifted the trailer off the ball hitch it dropped on his hand, his initial reaction was to pull his hand out, which pulled all the flesh from one of his fingers like a finger of a glove, including his nail. His finger bone was bare and split. I rushed him to hospital to be treated. This happened on a Friday afternoon. On the Saturday morning, I looked under the trailer and found the sleeve of flesh. And when I later took the sandwich order I asked Kevin if he wanted it in his sarnie, which nearly made him sick, much to his horror and my amusement.

I was lucky to escape a couple of near fatal accidents as an apprentice. The first was helping Middy strip down a hydraulic lift cylinder that he had locked in the vice. It was about six feet long with a rod diameter of about three inches. The gland nut had been removed from the cylinder which holds the seals and stops the oil coming out of the cylinder and centralises the rod. The rod was jammed in the cylinder so Middy decided to blow it out with compressed air. If I'd have been doing it now I'd have left the gland nut in for safety, but he must have forgotten. As he pumped air into the cylinder with an air line I was bent down looking at the end of the cylinder to see if it was being held central by one of the lads. As I stood up the chrome rod shot out like a torpedo clearing everything in its path, which would have included my head if I hadn't moved. It imbedded itself into the breeze block wall of the stores and protruded through the other side by about six inches. Another time I was servicing Dave Brown's Fiat Allis drott just before lunch. I was laid across the tracks fitting a fuel filter to the engine when I heard oil gushing back into the hydraulic tank. I pushed myself off the track with a fraction of a second to spare as the main hydraulic rams that lift the big steel bucket at the front came crashing down onto the tracks and brushing the back of my head. If I hadn't moved I'd have been cut in half.

It transpired that Dave had come back to get his pack up bag from behind the seat and leant across the levers thus lowering the bucket. Another valuable lesson in growing up was learnt as I should have had a safety support in place whilst I worked on the engine. My guardian angels must have been on duty that day just as my daughter Lisa said after going to a psychic in Bridlington and being told, "Your dad is completely surrounded by guardian angels."

I think I must have been after some of the near misses I've had…

During the early days of my apprenticeship a lot of the forklift and plant companies used to have regular darts competitions at different pubs around the City including 'Kingston', 'Blacksmiths Arms' off Williamson Street and 'Dixons Arms' at Woodmansey, now 'Warton Arms'.

They usually ended up being lively affairs with a strong smell of diesel from all the talk of work that some of them could not leave at the gates. And there was often a punch-up with a couple of opposing teammates rolling about on the car park.

Unlike nowadays, drinking and driving was common back then so there was always a lot of the lads who would drive to the pubs, which resulted in a few pranks by some of them sneaking out to the car park and messing about with someone's car.

They stuck a roast tatty up the exhaust pipe, removed a HT lead or jacked up a wheel and 'blocked' it so that it was off the floor. They once went as far as to remove a starter motor one night. I seem to remember it being Maurice Coward's who was one of the office staff at Westies.

The pubs that hosted these nights always put food on, such as pie and peas or fish and chips. Some of this food was also used for pranks on the cars. One of these was to put fish skin on the radiator or engine block so that as the engine got hot it would bake onto the block and give off the most awful smell as it worked its way through the air vents into the car. No matter how you tried to clean it off the smell lingered for ages...

CHAPTER FIFTEEN
THE BEST NIGHTCLUB EVER

When I got my provisional driving licence in1973 I was allowed to drive the fitters in one of the old vans, which were a Ford Transit Mk 1 Bedford, with a narrow wheelbase that made you rock from side to side like a roller coaster, and Middy's Mk 1 Escort. After driving them things about and jumping into a little Austin A40 to take my lessons, it was a doddle to pass my test and luckily I passed first time and was allowed out into the big wide world. I was sent to sites to do small jobs like fuel blockages or 'out of fuel'.

As I gained more experience I was allowed to do jobs like head gaskets on Thwiate or Winget dumpers that had single cylinder Lister or Petter engines. Fuel blockages were regular breakdowns as the lads on site would pick any old drum up and give it a quick swill out and then fill it with diesel to top up a machine. The old Perkins 3152, 4108 & 4203 and Ford 2700 series would run on contaminated fuel then flush it through with fresh diesel and bleed it. Then after a bit of coughing and farting it would usually run well. Unlike the new high-pressure engines that only have to get a thimble full of shit in the fuel system and it ends up costing you thousands of pounds.

One of the first places I ever went to out of town by myself was Howdendyke near Howden. This seemed a long way away back then yet it was only about twenty miles. We had a few Hysters on hire to a company there called East Coast River Services. I went there with Ray Wallace in 1973 to do some servicing. We serviced a few trucks during the course of the day and got down to the last truck, a little S40 c Hyster, which was a two-ton with solid band tyres for use in a warehouse.

RICHARD HALDENBY

We'd finished the service and just had to give it a blast off with the steam cleaner and lube the lift chains by way of climbing onto the overhead load guard and pour oil onto the top of the chains which Ray said he would do whilst I loaded the van up and brought it out of the shed. He had done the chains and put the gallon jug on top of the load guard and climbed down, he must have got busy doing something else and forgot about the jug of oil on the load guard and climbed onto the truck to drive it back in the shed just as I was driving out of the shed. I was about fifty feet away and could see the jug bouncing about on top of the load guard directly above his head and could see what was going to happen.

I tried warning him by blowing my horn and pointing above him, but he thought I was messing about and started waving back. Then as if in slow motion the jug lifted and landed on a side emptying the lot which run through the slots in the flat steel roof and down onto his head. He froze as the oil ran down his head, over his glasses and down his neck. The look on his face was priceless but for that split second that seems to last forever, I didn't know what to do as I was dying to laugh but didn't dare. He eventually did and then we both burst into laughter. He ended up stood in the toilets stripped down to his polyester Y fronts washing himself and his clothes in the old green Swarfega that looked like gorilla snot.

Another memorable day I had working there was when John Axle had just serviced the transit van and was ready for me to take it to Howdendyke to do some repairs. As I drove out the yard the van was not driving well and was misfiring, so I drove it back in and had John check the points and timing. He said it was okay and sent me on my way. It was better but not right. I got there okay and did a few jobs, but as I drove from shed to shed looking for another truck I was looking back over my shoulder and through the windows in the back doors for another truck when I heard a strange roaring noise. As I turned and looked forward there were flames shooting out of the windscreen and heater vents and down at my feet. With it having the old carburettor system what had happened was that it had backfired and set fire to the petrol in the carburettor then the heater fan was sucking the flames through the vents and straight into the cab. I ran and left the van before realising I'd left my little cantilever tool box inside, which I ran back and rescued. As I ran away the full van exploded. The van had to be recovered by Rod with his wagon.

I had another explosive experience as an apprentice when we were all sat having our lunch in the canteen at Southcoates Lane when there was an almighty bang. We all ran into the workshop to see the oxyacetylene bottles on fire and blowing a jet of flame about twenty-foot down the workshop. Nobody knew what to do so I calmly walked up to it and turned the acetylene off with the bottle key hung on the carrier as all the lads shouted to keep away. If it happened now you wouldn't get me anywhere near them, but at seventeen you don't see the danger.

I have always been keen on photography and was never far from my camera in my teenage years, much to the annoyance of my mates who were always telling me to, "Fuck off with that camera!" However, when they see my vast collection of photos from the early seventies now, of us either at Manchester United games or on our Lambrettas they all say how fantastic they are and wish they'd taken some.

One photo I wish I had taken is of all the lads from Westies who turned up at my wedding on November 27th 1976 outside Hull Register Office. They blocked the street off in the crane, a low loader and vans. Although I do have a photo of them all on the day in their overalls I wish I'd thought on and took one of the vehicles blocking the road off.

On November 26th, the day before my wedding, I went on my stag do to Bier Keller on High Street that was the best nightclub ever in Hull. It was an old

Wedding photo with the Westies lads. L-R. John Hardy, Rod Gurnel, Kevin Edwards, Me, Alan Middleton (Middy) and Ken Wallace.

Me and Bri at Hoffbrau

warehouse with three floors and had many nooks and crannies and even had balconies on the outside of the building where people would go and stand for a cig. I started going there at nineteen years old with John Hardy who I worked with at West Plant Hire and was a few years older than me as were most of the people there. It was a proper eye opener as you would walk up the stairs that were dark and dinghy with small rooms only big enough to get a settee in but big enough for couples to be groping away and even shagging I had been told. On this particular night of my stag do we bumped into an old school mate called Steve or Kojak to everyone who knew him due to his bald head, the result of Alopecia. When we were at school he used to have bald patches and was the subject of a lot of piss taking from some of the lads, so he started to wear a wig, which made it worse. He eventually gained confidence and started to remove it and had his head shaved completely. But during this transition he would wear his wig for a laugh and go on the dance floor and dance with some unsuspecting girl. Then he would suddenly take hold of his wig and throw it into a corner of the dance floor ordering it to "SIT!" which would have the poor girl running off screaming. This became a regular occurrence, which never failed to have everyone in fits of laughter.

There was another bar on George Street that was nicknamed 'Beer Keller' but was actually named the Hoffbrau or the 'Oompah' bar as it was known due to the German brass band that played there. It was a traditional German bar that served Steins of beer in 1 litre jugs, and very much stronger than the average beer on sale at the time. When the band played everyone would get up onto the bench seats and link arms swaying from side to side. We'd never experienced anything like it in Hull and for quite a few years after it was the most popular bar in the town, with Scamps Nightclub next door that we would fall into after leaving Hoffbrau.

One night we were in there when a crowd of Royal Navy lads came in. They were soon up on the dance floor with all the girls. One of them grabbed hold of a girl around the waist and lifted her off the floor. He was dancing with her and swinging her about, which resulted in a similar shock and awe experience for both of them. As he spun her around with her feet off the floor and her head leaning backwards her wig parted company with her head and shot across the dance floor, leaving her own hair pinned up and looking a mess as she ran screaming to the ladies.

I don't know who was the most shocked him or her, as the loud confident sailor suddenly went quiet and walked off the dance floor, a bit like the 'Kojak' experience at the other Bier Keller.

I stayed at Westies until 1977 when Malcolm West sold out to Harvey lift trucks and restarted as Malcolm West Lift Trucks on Clough Road next to R.S.P.C.A. I stayed with him another two years until I got a job for Aaronite fire proofing who specialised in fireproofing the legs of oil rigs based up in Middlesborough where the modules were built. I only did a couple of trips and was offered the position of foreman fitter at Stoneledge Plant and Transport in Cottingham.

Stoneledge wasn't the best job I ever had as I had to work long hours in terrible conditions. The workshop let in as much snow and rain as there was outside, and the floor was just hard standing compressed mud with a pit that was always full of water and rats crawling about everywhere. When I started working for Graham Greenwood in 1979 he had only been in business a few years having started in a war time nissen hut in the bottom of a chalk quarry on Eppleworth Road on the outskirts of Cottingham. The workshop backed onto the quarry wall of chalk, hence the name Stoneledge. When I started he had ten of everything which included Leyland boxer tippers, J.C.B 3Cs, two-ton dumpers, cement mixers and various other plant like an old

Michigan dump truck that was huge. Half of all these machines were broken down and cannibalised, yet within six months I had every piece of kit up and running and out on hire, having worked from seven in a morning until sometimes twelve at night. There were times when I was just about to go home at six when a JCB would come in with a blown head gasket or clutch burnt out and have Graham pleading with me to have it ready for the following morning. I could usually do one in around six or seven hours and a head gasket in four. Despite all the praise I got from Graham for putting every machine on hire with a minimum of cash being spent and saying he'd never had every machine out before, he then put me on forty hours as they were all running so well.

I left at the end of the year, having previously taken on a fitter I had worked with at Westies who I won't say I worked under as he never taught me anything but how to bodge. He stabbed me in the back and stayed after telling me he was going to leave and then took my job. I did however return to Stoneledge some thirty years later to work for Graham's son Philip. A few of the lads were still there including John Kerman, Pete Cassanelli and Bruce Kendal who is one of the most intelligent men I'd ever worked with considering he was a Cat bulldozer driver. He would spend all day in between loads reading and could give you an educated conversation on most topics. He was also a fantastic artist and a well-established oil painter in the Hull area. I will return to my second stay at Stoneledge later.

I went from Stoneledge in 1979 to Croslands Forklifts, which turned out to be one of the best fun jobs I ever had with a great set of lads who made everyday a pleasure to go to work. They were made up of mainly young men in their early twenties, with a few older ones like Col Brookes, Bob Walton the sprayer (Cat Weasel) and kinky John who were only maybe in their early thirties. Every day was one big wind up from morning til night. How we ever got any work done I don't know as every time you laid under a truck or bent over one, someone would be shoving a brush handle up your arse or slapping a handful of grease on your back. I started there in the December a few weeks before Christmas, we had been given a few cases of beer which is customary in the motor trade by our suppliers, not so much nowadays.

Come Christmas Eve we started drinking at 8am ready for the traditional dinnertime finish and then straight into the pub. We sat in the canteen drinking cans of Skol or whatever was popular at the time, getting more and more boisterous which resulted in Bob the paint sprayer getting de-bagged and having his knob painted by kinky John while we held Bob down. John always had a sexually explicit story that you never knew what to believe and had you wondering if you were safe, especially when we played five a side football and he would go round the showers offering to wash your bollocks for you. As it got closer to dinnertime we were well on our way to being pissed when Keith, one of the outside engineers came in. I got a handful of barrier cream and rubbed it in his face then ran out of the canteen laughing. The joke was on me though as the door had half shut and I ran straight into it breaking my nose. As this was the third or fourth time I'd broken it I decided to straighten it and got a hold of either side and pulled it, and then put a plaster across it. I have photos of me through my teens and early twenties with my nose on different sides of my face. The first time playing rugby at school, the second time fighting, then the last by the door. When we finished work we went across to the Oriental pub that was situated on Hedon Road backing onto Alexandra Dock. This was a 'proper' pub, used by all the dockers and local factory workers, with a good atmosphere and a good mix of sailors and working girls. While we were in there I bumped into an old school mate, Ian Lamping who I still see regularly now. He had a white carrier bag with him and when I looked inside it, there were two skinned rabbits complete with head and eyes. I took one out and slapped it around Tony's chops, which covered his white shirt with blood, completely spoiling his original 'medallion man' image as his shirt was always open wide with a gold chain on. We ended up staying out all day and ending up at Bier Keller and completely ruining Christmas Day. I was twenty-three at the time and looking back now I can't apologise to Jackie enough.

I enjoyed my time at Croslands and I met some good mates like Mike Puckering. We still reminisce of the times when you needed a crap but you dared not go to the toilet in fear that someone had seen you go in. And you ran the risk of a welly full of water coming over the top of the door or a hosepipe shoved under it. So we would sneak out of the yard and have a crap either on the dock behind a bush or go into Victoria Coffee Club or the Oriental if it was between twelve and three. The money was not good and I had to move on.

Top: United fans on Kop
Below: United fans on the pitch at the final whistle

CHAPTER 16
WHY BE
A UNITED FAN?

As I look back now I realise how foolish I was in my teens and twenties and also how lucky I was to have survived some of the kickings I had. Some of the injuries I received were life threatening. A few times I had my head kicked from side to side when taking on gangs by myself resulting in a broken nose and my front teeth going through my top lip. Each time my face was unrecognisable. I must have a skull like steel.

I was brought up never to go running and grass but to always sort it myself. At the time I thought I had something to prove being the son of Ralph Haldenby who had a reputation for being one of the hardest lorry drivers in Hull. Being brought up on the Orchard Park Estate, which was a new estate in the late sixties and had a bad name for being a rough council estate, we soon learnt how to fight and earned our rank and file among all the other lads who were thrown together from other compulsory purchase areas of Hull. Having lived the life I did and realising how stupid I was, I have brought my son, Jonathan up to be the opposite to how I was and teach him to respect people and only fight if you have to. We're so proud to have done so and have just been informed of him achieving first class honours in Bachelors Engineering Management and winning the Hull Association of Engineers Cup as nominated by Hull University.

People always ask why I'm a Manchester United supporter when I live in Hull, but as with most kids you select your first love of a team around the age of ten with the team who is the top at the time. In my case and that of the lads on our estate it was United having been the first English team to win the European Cup with the Holy Trinity of Best, Law and Charlton in 1968, the year after we moved onto Orchard Park. George Best went on to become the best player the world has ever seen and the first playboy superstar footballer, known as the fifth Beatle.

In the early 1970s after we had started our first jobs, we had a bit of money to enable us to go see United live. My first game was at Old Trafford in 1973 against Q.P.R. with a young George Graham playing for them who later became the manager of boring, boring Arsenal.

After going to United for a few years we developed a reputation as the O.P.E. Reds and were always in the thick of it at either Old Trafford or at away games. There were about twenty of us who were best mates and would never let each other down with a pact that no matter how many of the opposing fans we faced we never ran and left anyone.

We would often go to watch Hull City if United were away at a crappie ground, even then we never mixed well with the City lads even though we would fight the opposing fans with them. City were always an underachieving team considering the size of the old Boothferry Park and the large crowds they could get. It was said that the people who owned them did not want promotion into the old first division as they were getting first division crowds and paying second division wages. Unlike now with the recent ownership of the Allam family who have done a great job of developing the club regardless to what some of the fans think of them wanting to change the name of the club with a brand name of Hull Tigers. Their club, their money, their ball.

THE POETIC HOOLIGAN

Then employing Steve Bruce, an ex-United legend, they became a good footballing club with good ambitions. I still however support United although I wish City well. Unfortunately as I write this they have dropped down into Division 1, albeit four points clear at the top,

To start supporting City again just because they got into the Premiership would be like divorcing your wife and then wanting her back because she won the lottery. I saw blokes at work suddenly start wearing City shirts who had never mentioned football in all the years I'd known them. Then when they were relegated they stopped wearing their shirts. That's the difference between true supporters and glory seeking fans. We supported United in the years of decline of the early seventies and would go when there were only 20,000 there. During the 74/75 season I went to every home and away game in the old second division, sometimes hitchhiking down to London on a Friday night to see them against the likes of Leyton Orient.

Today, at sixty-four years old, I haven't been to United for a couple of seasons but I go when I can with the same lads who I've knocked about with for over fifty years. The only difference now is when we get together we just laugh and joke all day instead of fighting. The craic is brilliant. Whenever there's a big game on away and the lads who go to every home game don't go away, we often all get together in the Haworth Arms to watch it, which is like being at Old Trafford with the singing and piss-taking.

By the time I was in my late teens and twenties I was fighting every night to a point that if I missed a night's fighting I would feel rusty. I remember thinking how slow I felt after a night off scrapping.

We had some great weekends away with United when we were relegated into the old second division courtesy of that ill fated goal by our once King Dennis

Top: L-R, John Hope, Dave Towers, Gary Gibson, Me, Hoss, Tony Clarke
Below: Dave Towers with the United fans

THE POETIC HOOLIGAN

Law in 1974 when he'd been transferred to Man City. The '74/75 season saw me go to every home and away game that season as in those days there were no mid-week games.

Around 1975 Martin Holiday and I went to a night game at Man City's Maine Road to see a Man City all time greats for I think what was Mike Summerbee's testimonial against Manchester United's 1968 European cup winners. This was one of the most frightening experiences of my hooligan days. As we walked through the side streets next to Maine Road in Moss Side we were punched and kicked by black women and kids who were poking us with knifes while the men stood laughing and telling us to get out of their street, which we did without a word back. When we got to the ground we were walking through the crowd and brushed shoulders with Lou Macari and Stuart Pearson, Stuart of course was an ex Hull City lad and lived not far from us. When I realised who it was I said to Martin, "Hey look, it's Stuart Pearson." Stuart spun round and smiled, I think he recognised the accent. It wasn't much of a game due to them all coming out of retirement but it was worth the journey just to see Best, Law and Charlton who still showed flashes of brilliance.

United v Derby County in the FA Cup at Sheffield Wednesday's ground on April 3rd 1976 was a great day. The weather was hot, there was lots of beer, and lots of AGGRO. All the OPE Reds were out in force. United took over the ground. We won 2-0 and Gordon Hill scored both. The good thing about being in that division was that the team was already a great team, so we had some good high-scoring results most weeks.

One of the most memorable weekends was Blackpool away, we went for the full weekend with Jackie and her sister and Neil, my then brother-in-law. We got the train there and stopped in a B&B called

Holmelea. United had a good result by winning 0-4 and the fifteen thousand United fans were in jubilant mood as we descended onto the beach with thousands of us up to our knees in the sea singing "I do like to be beside the seaside". A bit later on, around tea-time, Neil and I were walking along the sea front when we saw United's team bus down a side street.

I said to Neil, "Come on let's try and get some autographs." We went to the front of the coach and sat right at the front was Tommy Doc and his assistant manager, Tommy Cavanagh, an ex Hull City man. I asked the Doc if we could have a autograph and he said, "Come with me son". He took me down the coach and had every player sign my programme. What a prize to have the likes of Stuart Pearson, ex Hull City, Lou Macari, Gordon Hill, Stevie Coppell, Sammy McIlroy, Martin Buchan, Brian Greenhoff, Gerry Daly, 'Six foot two, eyes of blue, Jimmy Holton's after you,' and Alex Stepney, all on one programme.

Leyton Orient away saw Neil and I hitchhike down to 'that there big London'. We set off on the Friday night from Fiveways roundabout and got a lift in a wagon as far as Pockley on the A1. We could not get a lift from there after a couple of hours of thumbing it so decided to try and bed down for the night. We tried sleeping in a dried out ditch bottom and covered ourselves with newspaper and hay until Neil whinged that he couldn't sleep due to spiders and insects crawling over him. We then walked into the village by the side of the A1 and came across a car sales garage. We tried all the doors until we found one that was open and got a good night's sleep there, then set off back to the A1 and got a lift into Doncaster.

We got some breakfast there and then saw a fifty-two seater coach full of United fans, they were Donny Reds, our guardian angels looked after us that day as we were taken straight to the ground. Bearing in mind we only took a fiver each with us, I don't know what we'd have done if we hadn't seen them. The whole weekend was good fun and what you may call character building, even got into a bit of aggro to finish the weekend off nicely. A mate, Shaun Tordoff, recently posted some photos of the trouble that day between United supporters and Orient, there was someone who looked the double of me, but not sure.

Our weekends to London were something to look forward to, the build up and excitement among the lads was electric. The bigger the game - against West Ham, Chelsea or Arsenal for example - the better. They were the ones you wanted even though we had some lively affairs against Tottenham who once put all our windows in on the coach as we passed down White Hart Lane. We laid on the floor to avoid house bricks hitting us but they still fell on us, very frightening. I'd rather face a hundred lads than have bricks thrown at you.

We had the same at Elland Road against Leeds. I think it's the most cowardly thing you can do to throw bricks, you don't know who might get hurt. It was the mid-seventies and Leeds were having some building work done. As we were walking away from the ground there were hundreds of Leeds fans on the building site throwing bricks that were hitting people of all ages including women and kids. You could hear the sickening thud as a brick hit someone on the head and gashed it wide open. I saw a woman get hit and I don't mind admitting I was scared shitless. You can do nothing but look for something to cover your head or put your hands over your head.

Arsenal in 1973 was one of our best-ever away games. We went down by train on the Friday night without Dobbo, Bri, Bert and a few others. We slept in Euston station on the floor which had underground heating and just laid on newspapers, we still had a good crowd of about twenty OPE reds including Harry, Tony, Caz, Ewan, Brownie, Budgie, Gibbo and Hopey, all good lads that would never run. We were up and about by early doors when a gang of Chelsea lads came in and ran at us. There must have been two hundred of them all in full war paint. In those days it was fashionable to have stripes across your cheeks in the colour of your team like Indians. In this case they were blue with Chelsea scarves around their heads and wrists. As they ran at us they must have expected us to run but we never and instead we ran back at them and started fighting.

Most of them ran as we chased them out the station just in time to see our reinforcements of Bri, Dobbo, Bert, Rosey and a few others getting off the bus who jumped in to help us clear them. A crew of the Cockney reds joined us throughout the morning as they knew we were coming down, the rest of the morning carried on like that as other cockneys were coming in to get their away trains. We had a good face off with Tottenham who were going away and was just like the opening scene to Green Street, when the Hammers' lads were facing up to Tottenham and calling each other out and then go battling in. If ever you want to see what it was really like in those days watch that film, that's just what it was like.

We left Euston and went for a walk to find something to eat when an open-backed bus passed by with a bus conductor stood holding onto the pole. He had a turban on so was Asian of some kind, we had rarely seen anyone like that before coming from Hull where up until recently you hardly saw black people. As the bus passed someone thought it would be funny to throw a gammy tomato at him along with a lot of other rotting fruit that was piled on a dustbin outside a fruit shop. The poor sod was covered from head to toe and jumped off the bus and ran at us. We were all laughing as he attacked the first lad who was one of the Manchester lads and he went down followed by Budgie who ran in and then shied away holding his shoulder. As he came running towards me I went to hit him then realised he had a big curved knife in his hand as he slashed across my stomach. I jumped back but could go no further as my back was against the railings on the roadside. Luckily I had a black suede jacket on that prevented my guts falling into my hands but left a permanent scratch across my jacket. As he slashed me I whacked him on the back of the head and gave him a few good punches until he ran and got back on the bus.

I read about the exact same thing that happened that day by one of United's notorious supporters Tony O'Neil in a book called 'Red Army General' that I bought whilst on the way to Tenerife about ten years ago. He must have been with us that day.

When we regrouped and saw what had happened to the Manchester lad and Budgie I realised how lucky I was as the Manchester lad lifted his shirt up he had a hole of three or four inches in his stomach with guts popping out. Budgie had a hole of about an inch or so in the muscle below his neck and above his shoulder.

When we used to travel we always had a change of clothes ready in Paragon train station in a locker that we kept paying for week after week. We would get changed in the toilets so that if we were photographed and the police were waiting for us on our return, they wouldn't recognise us. This paid dividends that day as when we got to Arsenal's ground, Highbury, half a dozen of the Hull reds ran across the pitch and stormed their end. We dived into the middle of their Kop and started scrapping. I was punching an Arsenal lad when a copper got hold of me and gave me a few good clips and kicked me out as in those days coppers were allowed to. I think it's a practice they should never have stopped as the little arseholes like I was then deserved it and it didn't use up police time and resources. We lost 3-0 that day.

When we got home late that night I went straight to bed and was rudely awakened by my Mam slapping me and calling me all the names under the sun whilst wafting a Sunday paper in my face. On the front page was a clear-cut picture of me holding the Arsenal fan by the throat with my left hand and with my right fist raised in the air.

I pleaded my innocence to which she replied, "I know my own son."

When I pointed out the black suede jacket and denim jeans the lad in the picture had on and then showed her the Slade styled, multi-checked bomber jacket lying on the bedroom floor with my white jeans, I got lots of kisses and cuddles and apologies. I never did tell her the truth as it would have upset her. On the other hand me dad would have been secretly chuffed I'd been scrapping.

Our return trips from Manchester were often eventful when we stopped at Leeds and clashed with the Leeds fans. Again we were always outnumbered but that was never a problem. We would either clash on the platform and have an all out battle or pull alongside other carriages from all over the country and hurl abuse at each other.

One time in particular we were alongside another train waiting to depart and were winding some other fans up as they were threatening us. Bri was being as sarcastic as ever saying, "Oh don't! You're frightening me", then he dropped his trousers and shoved his bare arse against the window saying, "Kiss that you wankers".

They were going berserk while we fell about laughing. Bri often dropped his kegs for the fun of it.

THE POETIC HOOLIGAN

One of his favourite tricks was to disappear in the toilet and come running out and around the pub with his kegs round his ankles and a yard of burning toilet roll hanging out of his arse cheeks, much to the amusement of his mates but bewilderment of strangers. He called this the dance of the flaming arseholes.

During the week on OPE we were still faced with the other gangs of lads who had been uprooted and planted into the jungle away from their own safe havens.

All of these gangs had their own hierarchy who would challenge and test the cock of the other gangs until you eventually found your rank and file. Some broke off to be a quiet, peaceful group who were not a threat to anyone. Our gang, which totalled about thirty, and the top five or six were fighters who were all respected by each other and never really took each other on. They knew from watching each other fight against other gangs that they would have a struggle on and never needed to fight each other.

The only two who ever got into a fight were Ewan and Caz. This fight was not a pleasure for any of us to watch as it was two of our best friends knocking lumps out of each other. It took place on Chanterlands Avenue outside the chippy and seemed to go on forever. At the time it was fashionable to wear leather soled Brogues, the same as the ones I wear now.

The ones then though had steel segs in the heels and toes that we fitted so they were just overhanging the sole at the front, so that when you kicked someone the steel cut into them. Caz and Ewan both wore these and made a right mess of each other until we parted them.

We all knew our capabilities having watched each other fight, as was the case one night when we were at a party at my girlfriend, Julie Boynton's house.

Suddenly her next door neighbour came banging on

the door and making threats to the lads. He was a thickset bloke, about forty years old and we were in our late teens. He started punching a few of the lads, which made me see red. I laced into him and knocked seven shades of shit out of him.

As he staggered away he said, "I'll have you," which he threatened a few times whenever I saw him but he never took me up on a repeat performance.

I had never dared do anything like that until then, as my Dad always warned me to respect my elders. But when I told him what had happened he was chuffed as he loved me fighting and being able to defend myself.

The only other time any of us got into a fight with each other was when Bri and me had a bit of a tussle in the Chinese takeaway on the corner of Dundee Street where Julie lived. We were skylarking about when it started to get a bit serious. Neither of us were giving it our best but all the same we were getting nasty. It got to a point where Bri had me in a headlock and I didn't want to hit him in the face but lost it a little and bit his head.

As I sunk my teeth into the top of his scalp he gave out such a scream. And at the same time pelted the cash he had in his hand at the Chinaman behind the counter who was screaming at us in Chinese, which made us laugh and diffused the situation.

Bri was always an irritating bastard but the type of lad you could not help but like, always winding someone up just for the craic.

CHAPTER 17
'WHO'S RICH HALDENBY?'

Some of our other run-ins with the Leeds fans happened when we went to Bridlington or Scarborough for the weekend on our Lambrettas, fully flagged up in our United scarves.

The weekend always started off by meeting outside our house on a Saturday or Sunday morning and set off in convoy of about twenty of us, when we got there we would come across the 'Wessies' (West Yorkshire lads). They all had Vespas and Leeds scarves, which was as bad as having motorbikes and leather jackets, these being the days of Mods and Rockers. We always ended up scrapping with either the Leeds lot or the greabos.

If we were there for the weekend we used to take our sleeping bags and doss out in Bridlington in the 'glasshouses' as we called them. They were basically a round structure like a conservatory with sliding doors and wooden seats in them for the old people. We would settle down in them for the night with our Lambies booked inside after we'd been on the pull and the piss, often being woken in the middle of the night by a copper telling us to move on.

We went one bank holiday weekend with no money to see how we could fare on a survival weekend of three days. I remember Brownie was there with Bri, Harry, Clarkie and Lawrie. We set off walking from Bridlington North Bay early on the Saturday morning and along the beach through Dane's Dyke and to Flamborough. When we got to Flamborough we walked up onto the main road and nicked a crate of milk along

Top: L-R, Paddy Brown, Graham Soare (Joe) Me. (Olly) Graham Oliver,
Bruce McDonald, Steve Waller.
Below: L-R, Pete Brown, Paddy Brown, Me, Graham Oliver

with spuds and cabbage. We lit a fire and roasted the spuds but ate the cabbage raw. We went onto the beach at Thornwick Bay and found an injured seagull. We put it out of its misery and I plucked and gutted it as my Grandad had taught me and then spit roast it over a fire. When we tried eating it you could not swallow one mouthful as it was like chewing leather and tasted like a block of salt. Next on the menu was a crow I killed with a stone. When I said I'd kill one, they all laughed but I was a crack shot with a stone. We had another fire with spuds on and cooked the crow and ate it. Again it was leathery and the dark meat was not very nice but it made a small meal.

As I mentioned earlier our two main hates were Leeds and Greabos. Greabos or Greasers was the name given to them because of the greasy hair gel they used to keep their hair in style to form their quiff at the front and the DA at the back - ducks arse.

Although we loved fighting none of us ever carried knives, unlike today with all the deaths and injuries we keep hearing about. We had hundreds of fights all over the country supporting United and Hull City. We even went on our Lambrettas to different estates to fight. These were the Skinhead days of the early seventies which were a follow on from the Mods and Rockers of the late sixties. There were still a lot of Rockers about including a chapter of Hells Angels in Hull that had become quite well known. I remember seeing a photo of a couple of them who had got married using steel washers as wedding rings and received publicity all over the National papers. This pissed us off that they had been recognised and we hadn't. We decided to give them a visit on our Lambies and considering that they were grown men in their mid-twenties and we were 17 and 18 years old we gave a good account of ourselves. A later confrontation with another gang of greabos saw

Top: L-R, Olly, Me, Paddy Brown and Pete Brown
Below: L-R, Paddy Brown, Graham Oliver, Pete Brown and Me

THE POETIC HOOLIGAN

a few of the lads 'going down' after they had clashed at Hull Fair. Our fair is said to be the largest travelling fair in Europe, even larger than Nottingham Goose Fair and has been going as far back as 700AD on Walton Street apparently. There were some serious injuries on that night and some of our lads had been named and shamed with photographs published in the Hull Daily Mail. For years we would often clash on the waltzers as this is where all the birds used to gather. I was fortunate that night as I'd just started seeing Jackie and was with her, otherwise I'd have been one of the lads arrested.

All these fights were either football related or local territorial fights, which stemmed from us all being thrown together on large council estates. We were all trying to out-do each other and get ourselves a reputation. The more fearless and crazy you were the more respect you received from your mates, or so we thought.

One of the best and funniest nights we ever had fighting was in 1975 when I was 19 and a crowd of around ten of us went to see the band, Thin Lizzy at Hull College in Queens Gardens. As usual, once the word was out that the OPE reds were in town there would usually be a fight, normally against the Albermarle lot who were a gang that hung around the Albermarle Club in the town centre, also known as the Station Gang or the Monte Carlo Boys, all Hull City fans. On this occasion though it was a gang of Holderness Road lads who picked on us. There was about forty of them so we were outnumbered by four to one. It all started as we were watching the gig and one of them kicked one of our lads up the arse, we had a bit of a scuffle with them and thought no more of it until we got outside after the gig and found ourselves lined up against them. As per usual we never hesitated and just ploughed straight into them which made most of them

Top: L-R, Gillian Busby (Buzz) Kim Ponsonby (Mock) Mike Moses, Graham Oliv
Below: L-R, Pete Brown. Graham Oliver. Paddy Brown.

run and left not many more than us. I was bang on form that night, nineteen years old and fit as a butcher's dog. We were on the corner of George Street, opposite the old Queens Pub, which later became the Pozition nightclub. They were coming at us thick and fast. I was hitting one after the other and dropped a few of them as we were starting to get the better of them. With that, a taxi pulled up and one of them shouted, "We're alright now, Froggies here."

A big lad stepped out of the taxi wearing a sheepskin coat and shouted, "Come on then! Who's the hard man?" Before he could take two steps out the car I ran at him and punched him square on the side of the jaw and sent him flying back into the still open taxi door, banging the back of his head on the roof of the car and knocking him out sparkers. That finished the brawl as one of our lads, Hopey shouted, "Rich croaked Froggie!" which made everyone laugh as we all dispersed.

The Albermarle lot were our biggest hate along with the Greabos, Leeds and Man City fans and the Mickey Mousers (scousers). We had to pass through their backyard to get into Hull Paragon station to go to United. We would often battle with them, sometimes winning or sometimes them giving us a kicking. One night we arranged to have a showdown with them behind the LA's nightclub on a car park. We all lined up against them with roughly the same amount of lads on each side of around twenty apiece. We stood in line squaring up to each other when one of their lads stepped forward and said, "Who's Rich Haldenby?" Without hesitation I stepped up to him and said, "I am," and whacked him and knocked him backwards onto a car bonnet. My fight with him must have looked like a scene from a comedy film, as I had him held by the throat with my left hand whilst trying to punch his face

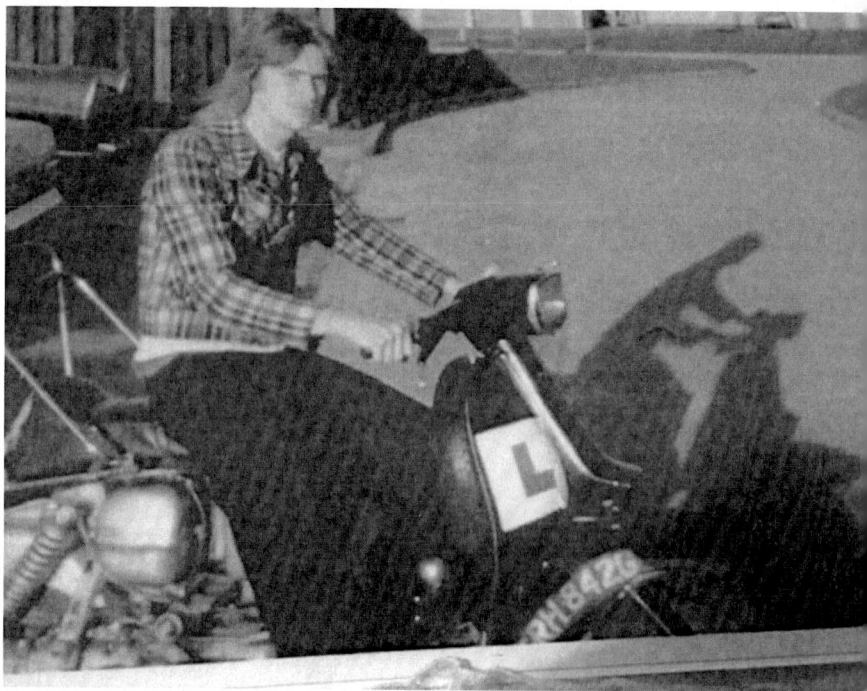

Top: On my GP 150, in 1973 - Photo courtesy of my good friend Lawrie Lee.
Below: A recent photo on my SX 200

in with my right. He kept bobbing his head from side to side as I was hitting the bonnet. I won the fight with him but can't remember how it ended between the two gangs. I think we got the better of them but I would say that wouldn't I? As much as we hated each other back then we have met up recently and got on with them as we've all mellowed over the years.

Opposite Paragon Station in Hull town centre was the Hammonds store, which had a restaurant on the top floor called Pickadish, where all the teenagers from all over Hull would meet on a Saturday morning to eye each other up and compare the clothes and records they'd bought.

There used to be a great scam with a lot of the lads who would queue to get food on the right of the restaurant as you walked in with all the food on display behind glass sliding windows where you would select your food and put it on your plate, to the left was a barrier which separated the eating area. The lads used to sit next to the barrier and a couple of others would fill plates with food and pass it over the barrier to the lads sat down. Then just two of them would pay for their food and get squared up by the recipients.

The restaurant looked out over Ferensway to Paragon Station so that on match days they would sit up there and watch out for opposing fans getting off the trains and then run down and attack them. It was said by visiting fans that they were always bemused that they would walk out of the station and see no one and then out of nowhere they'd be faced with a gang of City lads.

Another incident that I will never forget happened when City played at home against West Ham during the 1974-75 season. The Hammers brought a good crew with them and kicked off as soon as they got into station. The OPE lads were there in full strength but got broke up with all the fighting. I ended up with Harry outside Cenotaph and was arguing with a West Ham fan who was a bit older than us and a right smooth bastard, well dressed and sporting a silk Hammers' neckerchief.

He asked, "Can you tell me where your town centre is lads?"

I replied, "You're in it."

He laughed and said, "You're fucking joking aren't you? What a shit hole!"

I ran at him but was stopped in my tracks when he pulled a knife and put it to my throat. The next few seconds seemed like an eternity,

Harry said, "Shiv him Rich", meaning stab him.

I looked at him and said, "I don't have a knife."

Harry winked and said "You have, I gave you one earlier."

It was like a sketch from a comedy film as I pretended to go into my pocket for a knife. Luckily the Hammers fan lost his bottle and ran off. We gave chase and saw some of our lads with some City fans who were outnumbered by West Ham, we joined in and some of the OPE broke off car aerials, the old chrome telescopic type that were like whips. They were used to slash them across their faces, which made them run. We went onto Boothferry Park and fought with them all the way up Anlaby Road and into the ground. We were on the Kempton where most of them were but a few had got over the fence onto Bunkers Hill. One of them thought he was Bruce Lee and was doing all the moves, a few of the City boys went at him but backed off. Brownie went in next and had a bit of a go and then came back. I jumped over and ran at him, again he was doing all the fancy moves and noises. I waited for him to stop prancing about then simply gave him a good old fashioned kick in the balls which dropped him like a sack of spuds. Kung Fu my arse! Much to the amusement of all the City Kop who cheered me on.

CHAPTER 18
A-G, A-G-R, A-G-R-O, AGRO!

Most nights in the seventies you'd get into a fight if that is what you wanted. Most of the lads such as our Gary weren't fighters and would go out with never any bother. However, trouble always seemed to follow me even though most of the time I wasn't looking for any. Like the night I'd been in the Orchard Park pub for a quiet drink with Jackie and stopped off at Holmes's chip shop for supper.

As we walked into the chippie there was a gang of greabos who I'd never seen before and they were taking the piss out of a mate called Tony who was disabled with leg irons. He was also a bit of a biker fan too and had his leather jacket on. A big lad grabbed hold of him by the throat and was roughing him up a bit. He obviously wasn't a fighter due to his disability and was too nice a lad anyway. There were five or six of them and this big clever bastard was showing off so I said to him, "Leave him alone and have a go at me if you want to fight."

He said something back so I just flew at him and knocked seven shades of shite out of him. But what I hadn't bargained for was Jackie jumping on my back trying to stop me fighting, just as I'd nearly finished him off. He got back on his feet whilst she was still trying to pull me back and he kicked me square in the balls, which pushed them that far into my stomach that I thought I had mumps. It was then his turn to give me a good kicking with the help of his mates.

There have been a few times I've been in a fight and

been glad it's come to an end when you've both been going hell for leather and are both knackered and thinking, Shite! Isn't this bastard ever going to give up?

Then one of you would say, "Have you had enough?"

Then cracking on that you were not bothered you'd say, "It's up to you, what do you want to do?"

Then you'd either shake hands and go for a beer or if you really hated the bastard you'd wait till he was halfway up and try and get your last good shot in to put him down. That sometimes didn't work and you'd end up even more knackered until someone stopped it or you both agreed to call it a day.

Twice I've been beaten so much that my face has been unrecognisable when taking on more than one person. The first time was when I'd got off the bus on the corner of Dundee Street where Julie Boynton, my first proper girlfriend, lived. I was togged up to the nines with my new beige suit sporting the then fashionable, exterior black hit and miss stitching along the lapels and four-button, high waistband from Arthur Mason's. And burgundy loafers from Ravels, complete with steel segs overhanging the leather sole toe by a quarter of an inch for fighting. If you got a kick in the shin from them you knew about it.

I wasn't smart for long though as I saw two of the Bricknell Avenue lads who'd I'd been fighting with a few weeks before. We had been at a club when the OPE reds started fighting with the Bricknell lads. We beat them and I beat the cock of their gang only to find out later that he said he'd beaten me.

When I saw him I said, "Do you fancy another go?" and started fighting with him. Unfortunately for me though his mate joined in and proceeded to give me the kicking of my life. They got a hand each and spread-eagled me with the street corner in the middle of my back as they both kicked hell out of my balls and legs until I dropped on my knees where they carried on kicking me in the head until I was unconscious. I made it to Julie's where she cleaned me up. I ended up with cracked ribs, broken nose, teeth cut into my lips, both eyes closed with just little slits to see through and the whole front of my body black and blue. I went home that night and when I came down stairs the next morning my Mam screamed and cried. I was one mass of lumps and bruises and could not eat for weeks or open my eyes. For weeks I went looking for them on Bricknell Avenue and Chanterlands Avenue hoping to see either of them and put the word out that I would make a worse mess of them when I caught them. Fortunately I never did see them again as I would have done time for them.

The next time I got a good kicking was in 1987. I was 31 years old and on my way home from the pigeon club with a lad called Tony. We'd had a good skin-full of ale, about ten pints when we stopped off at the local takeaway for supper.

As we walked towards the doors a gang of lads shouted, "Hey, what the fucks that you've got in your hand, a bomb?" referring to our pigeon clocks.

I said to Tony, "Don't say out, we've had too much to drink and these clocks are too valuable to damage."

But he didn't listen and shouted back, "No it's not. Why, what the fuck's that you've got on your shoulders, a bag of shit?"

We got our suppers and as we were walking out I said, "Keep your head down, mouth shut and keep walking." But as soon as we walked out one of them smashed a cider bottle and said, "You're dead."

As he came towards me, I put my clock down behind me and swung an uppercut on his chin and lifted him completely off his feet and flat on his back, sparkers! Only problem was that I had a brand new pair of Ben

Sherman leather soled loafer shoes on with slippery soles. So as I hit him the momentum carried me on and made me slip on the greasy concrete pavers and fall flat on my back banging the back of my head on the floor. The next thing I remember was waking up with one of them knelt on my chest punching my face in. I reached up and grabbed him by his Mohican hair and pulled him down while I nutted and bit his face. He screamed like a pig telling his mates to get him free.

I was kicked in the side of the head and again by another from the other side as two of them kicked me unconscious. I woke to see them running off as I pulled myself up on a metal pole and shouted, "Come on you bastards! Let's have another go," as they ran off shouting, "Fuck off you old bastard or we'll do you again!"

The bastards. Quite funny though - they reminded me of us lot at that age.

When I said to Tony "What the fuck happened to you?" he showed me a cut on his hand and said one of them held him at bay with a knife. I went back around there with a baseball bat for months after, at different times to try and catch them but never did.

When I woke the next morning and walked down stairs Jackie screamed and cried as my Mam had done all those years before. When she calmed down she did laugh at me because of my chin, it was massive and swollen like Desperate Dan and called it my Desperate Dan chin as it was like a big polythene bag swilling from one ear to the other, all black and blue with a perfect shape of a heel on my cheek bone. My teeth had cut the inside of my lips again, my nose was broken, my eyes were closed and I had lumps all over my head and neck. I'm sure I must have had a cracked or broken jaw too, as I couldn't eat solid food for a couple of months.

When you've had a kicking like that it certainly

makes a good lad of you and makes you wiser not to be so gobby as you often see with some lads who shout their mouth off and have obviously never had a good hiding. Like they say, "Don't worry about the one at the front of a gang doing all the shouting, watch the quiet one at the back."

I recently got myself out of a scrape one Saturday morning at eight o'clock when you would never expect it. I had gone to collect some parts from a supplier when I walked around the back of my van and two lads in their twenties bumped into me. I never said anything but gave that icy look to stand my ground and carried on staring at them as I walked to the front of my van to get in. I then bumped into about six of their mates who walked around the corner and never saw what happened, but sensed something was wrong. They all had beer cans in their hands and sandwiches so had obviously been to an all night club. I quickly diffused the situation by using my streetwise experience and started laughing and said, "Fucking hell lads, you must have had a good night. Have you got a can for me?" as I quickly jumped in my van and shot off. As I looked in my mirror I saw them telling each other what had happened and shaking their fists at me as I drove off.

I had a similar confrontation with a gang of trouble causers that I didn't want to walk away from when my daughter Sarah was young. We had gone to visit Jackie's parents on Orchard Park and as usual there was about twenty lads in their late teens making a nuisance of themselves, swearing and kicking a ball against the gable wall. And as her parents lived at the end of the block it echoed through the house.

I was in my early twenties and had often told them to clear off and just got a lot of abuse and threats from them. That was until the time our Sarah came running in crying and said that the lads had swore at her whilst playing on her bike, and one of them had nearly knocked her off the bike with a motorbike and told her to get out the fucking way. Jackie's brother had seen it happen but didn't want them to see it was him who'd told me so pointed him out through the fence. I walked up to them as they were all gathered at the end of the block with the one who'd sworn at her sat on the seat of his motorbike sideways on and leant against the pebbledash wall.

I asked which one of them had sworn at my daughter and he said, "Fuck off before you get filled in."

I saw red and nutted him repeatedly bouncing the back of his head off the wall and not only busting his face but also cutting the back of his head on the sharp pebbled wall. I proceeded to hit his mates as well who all backed off saying it was nothing to do with them. I went back inside and waited for the police to come as they quickly did. The officer was about to arrest me when he asked why I'd done it. I told him and he said that the lad's parents wanted to prosecute me but bearing in mind this lad was one of the biggest trouble causers on the estate and the police were well aware of him he said, "Oh did he? Leave it with me."

When he came back he said he'd told them that if they wanted to prosecute me he would charge them with attempted assault of a minor. All charges were dropped and we never got any more bother from them again. And every time I drove down the street they all shot off and kept out of the way.

However, I am not proud to say that I have been involved in affrays even though I didn't actually do anything, I would not have dared to cause trouble unless it was with like minded people who wanted to fight due to the fact that my dad had always warned us never to do so. On this one occasion it was funny more than troublesome as we were down Hardane on OPE in the mid-seventies when a new ice cream man came round, we went to the van only to find he was Italian, you wouldn't think twice about that in today's multicultural Britain but back then it was rare to see a black person on OPE or hear a foreign voice so you can imagine the reaction when he opened his mouth, we were all about 17 or 18 at the time. I remember there was Brownie, Rat, Bri and H of OPE. One of them started to take the piss out of the way he spoke and warned him that if he didn't give us a free ice cream we would tip his van over. He must have had a rough upbringing as he refused and started shouting at us to fuck off in a typical irate Italian manner that just made us laugh even more.

They started to rock his van chanting, A-G, A-G-R, A-G-R-O, AGRO!

He picked a wheel brace up from under the counter and jumped out of his van through the serving hatch screaming, "You talk to me about aggression! I'll give you agro you bastards!" as he chased us around his van whilst we pissed ourselves laughing. There was no harm done, just another day on a rough council estate.

One of the last fights I had was when I was in my forties. I was in town one summer's evening with my pal Mike Leak. We were walking past the old Institute Pub opposite Prospect Centre and two blokes were walking a few yards in front of us. A lady came walking from the opposite direction, and as she passed us, one of them pushed her flat on her arse and then picked her stiletto up and threw it in her face as she laid on the floor. I warned him to leave her alone to which he replied, "Mind your own business or you'll get the same."

I told him not to try or he'd come off worse. I looked across the road to a riot van full of Police that was parked up and gestured for them to do something but to my surprise they just turned away. My dad had always advised me never to get involved in a domestic argument as you never know what's gone on between them, but seeing this in front of you, it was hard to ignore. As they were walking away he was shouting at her so again I warned him to leave her alone to which he replied, "I'll leave her alone if you keep your nose out."

I said to Mike, "Let's follow them for a bit to make sure she's okay."

We walked well behind them not wanting to irritate the bloke more than I already had and just when I thought they had sorted themselves out and were going to kiss and make up, he kissed her alright, but with a OPE kiss! He butted her in the face as they turned the corner into a side street where he thought no one could see him. I ran up and saw the poor woman lying on the floor and shouted at him, "What did I tell you?"

As he turned and squared up to me, I was still running and hit him square in the nose and mouth. Then, as his head went back I kneed him in the balls, which brought his head forward again where I hit him again in the mouth which sent him flying on his back and spitting several teeth out. I turned to his mate in a fit of temper wanting to take him on as well but he didn't want to know.

It was then I realised I should have taken my Dad's advice as his wife or girlfriend jumped on my back screaming to leave him alone, scratching my face and pulling my hair. I threw her off and told her they deserved each other.

I know you shouldn't fight in your forties and always walk away when you can but that fight gave me a great feeling of satisfaction of not only teaching him a lesson but also knowing I could still look after myself when I needed to.

THE POETIC HOOLIGAN

I got a taxi home that night and was dropped off at the end of our road, then, feeling like Rocky, I decided to run the few hundred yards to our house. But as I jumped off one kerb as I crossed a side street, I tripped and landed face first, head-butting the kerb on the opposite side. That left me with a gash along my eyebrow, which closed my eye for the week with a big shiner that everyone thought I'd got whilst fighting.

In 1986 Jackie and I went to a fancy dress party down Silverdale Road opposite the Cross Keys pub. We all arranged to meet in there before the party, bearing in mind it was mid-winter and freezing cold, I maybe should not have gone in the attire I chose that had been lent to me by my cousin that was a baby outfit consisting of a woolly bonnet, giant dummy, large safety pin about twelve inches long, a bath towel as a nappy and some woolly booties.

I was advised by my cousin not to wear any undies as "The birds will be wanting to check and see if your nappies full."

As we were due to set off Jackie asked, "Have you any undies on?" and then made me put some on. It was just as well as I was checked all night by different women. Jackie matched my outfit with a romper suit and pigtails.

When we walked in the pub and up to the bar the looks on the people's faces were a picture as everyone was crying with laughter.

The landlord said, "That's a brilliant outfit and takes some balls to wear, especially in this weather."

He then added, "And all the time you're in here tonight it won't cost you a penny for a drink."

As I said about Bri being a wind up merchant, he's probably the one person you would not want to meet whilst dressed like that so you can imagine my horror

Me in baby fancy dress

when I heard a voice shout across the pub, "Haldenby, you fucking wanker! What's that you've got on?"

I immediately bobbed down and tried scurrying away but again he shouted, "Never mind trying to hide you fucking wanker!" whilst laughing his head off and threatening me with, "Wait till I see the lads." Nightmare!

A few years after that, Bri had a fancy dress party himself, the invite to which read: "You have to come as a vegetable."

Jackie made her own green outfit from cardboard and crepe paper with a row of green balloons down the front with a pointy hat and went as a pea pod. I thought it would be fitting for me to wear the same baby outfit as twenty years earlier but dyed purple. When we got to the party Bri laughed and asked, "What vegetable are you supposed to be?"

"A baby beetroot," I replied.

I recently went to a United game with Harry and Tony, and never laughed as much for years. Harry was bang on form and never stopped from picking him up to dropping him off on the night, he had the full coach laughing. I was pleading with him to stop as my cheeks and ribs were hurting through laughing so much. He's always been the same from first meeting him at eleven years old. I remember walking down Beverley Road at the corner of Spring Bank where the Zoological pub used to be when we were about twelve or thirteen and bumping into my Mam and her friend. My Mam loved him as he was such a cheeky little bugger. Harry had a piece of rope in his hand with a noose at the end, my Mam asked him, "What's the rope for Harry?"

He turned and looked at the rope and said, "Fucking hell Chris, me dog's got away, we were just taking it to the P.D.S.A." which we weren't as he didn't even own a dog. I nearly died with embarrassment for him swearing in front of my Mam and calling her 'Chris' when we all would say, 'Mrs' to our mates' Mams, they both just laughed as he is one of those people who can get away with anything. Harry always had a answer to everything like the day we were at City and a copper looked down at his Doc Marten boots and said, "Hey son, do your feet go to the end of those boots?"

His cheeky answer even made the copper laugh as he looked up at him and said, "Yes, Why, does your head go to the top of that fucking helmet?"

I was with Harry at City another time when he unbelievably tried stopping a fight instead of causing one for a change when a copper was about to arrest him, when I stepped in to plead his innocence and got myself arrested. Harry was let go and I was dragged through Boothferry Park to the cells in a headlock. I was getting punched in the head by him and then he opened every door with my head and then slammed it on the counter. I was locked up with one of City's hard men, a big black lad called Johnnie Reggae who helped me fight the coppers that were giving me a good hiding in the cells. However, I have no complaints against the Police as they did release me with no charge. Each time I have been arrested it's always been my own fault but as a mate of mine who was a copper said to me, my arrests were for 'clean' crimes such as poaching and fighting.

The last time I was arrested was for fighting outside a nightclub at Hull's Romeo & Juliet's in 1975. I'd been on my way out of the club with Jackie when we found ourselves with four big blokes in the lift. I kept my head down avoiding eye contact when I heard one of them saying something to his mate about Jackie. I asked him what he'd said and he threatened me. I kept quiet until the lift doors were opening and then launched myself off the back wall and nutted him square on the nose. I then grabbed him by his Elvis style sideboards, as was the fashion back then and run him at the swinging doors. When I got him outside I held his head down with one hand and pummelled him with the other, kneeing him in the face until he was screaming to get off him. Someone jumped on my back so I elbowed him in the nose splitting it. Someone else jumped me so I turned and nutted him. Unfortunately it was two coppers. I was locked in the cells for the night and went to court. I was stood in the dock looking at my Mam and Jackie, the judge read out my previous convictions and then deliberated over my actions that seemed to take ages. He said, "Considering your previous convictions I sentence you to two years in prison," and then paused. I froze and I couldn't breathe. It seemed like time was standing still as I looked at my Mam in tears. I then looked back at the judge and could see his mouth moving but I was not taking in what he was saying. The court usher put his hand on my shoulder to lead me away and I looked down into the cells and saw the white tiles. But then as I started to go down the steps the usher said, "Where are you going, didn't you hear what the judge said? Two years suspended. But if you come to court again, even in twenty years time, you'll serve it."

Needless to say, I've been a good lad since. Romeo's was a great club but there were so many brilliant pubs and clubs open seven nights a week, every night in the early seventies was like a Saturday night. Jackie and I would often go out mid week and then onto Romeo's leaving there at 1.30am and then onto Bun in the Oven for a burger and chips from Sam Frattie bless him, another nice lad who is no longer with us. We would walk the six miles home eating our supper, Jackie wearing her six-inch high heels and soles and me in my Slade style platform soles. We'd get home between three and four o'clock, then be up for work at five. No wonder I was always falling asleep at work or on the bus going home.

Our local watering holes on OPE were the Orchard Park Inn and the Arctic Ranger. In those days they were also full, seven nights a week. It's funny to think of the opening hours back then were twelve till three and five-thirty until ten-thirty and out by eleven.

On a Saturday afternoon we would often get a taxi at three o'clock to Beverley that had all day opening due to the livestock market and go in 'Angel' and then back to 'Haworth' or 'Gardeners' for a change where we would see a bit of fresh talent.

CHAPTER 19
1980
GOING UNDERGROUND

The start of 1980 was a good chapter in my life when I started work for Stepney Contractors of Beverley and met one of my best present day friends Mark (Harry) Dooley who was a sixteen year-old apprentice. We have always been close since then, as when he finished his apprenticeship he was made redundant and I took him on at Malcolm West's and showed him the ropes. We had some good times there and gained a lot of experience on heavy plant. The majority of the men were of agricultural descent and were proper characters. Stepneys were a massive company that was divided up into different departments including contractors, mini tunnels, cast stone, plumbing etc. They had contracts all over the country and would lay new roads for housing or industrial estates and civil engineering contracts. The plant varied from Stihl saws up to RB 38 cranes. Some of the cranes were actually from the war, which were the old Jones KL33 and 66s and the RB22 and 38s. The 38 was a beautiful machine that was like working on a ship's engine as it had walkways all the way around the engine compartment, which housed a Paxman four cylinder with pistons like dustbins. Learning how to set up the clutch and cables and brake bands from some of the old fitters like Mick Drew, Eric and Bill (Trunky) Grummit was something to be grateful of as they were ex-drivers. There are not many fitters today who know how to set these up as we did with Wylie gear on which would ring to let you know you were overloading or lifting with the stick too far out. The works manager was Paul Fearn who was a good man to work for and knew what he was talking about. Others were Bill the Grummit, the foreman, Jack Redmore and his son Mally, who was a mate of mine from school and went to the top in the police force. Arthur Burns was a fitter who looked like Amos Brierly off Emmerdale with his big sideburns and was the proud owner of a Honda Goldwing that he always talked of. Mally Mewit (Mad Mal) was a wagon driver and had everybody in stitches, especially on a Saturday morning when his pigeons were racing and he spent half his time on the phone seeing if they'd been released. Then you would hear a loud shout of "They're up, they're up!" meaning the birds had been released. No matter how busy he was he'd be off and hobble out of the workshop. Other memorable mates were Phil Depner, Keith Masters and my good friend Harold Corner of Bempton near Flamborough.

I eventually left Stepney Contractors at the end of 1982 and returned to Westies where I ended up working for five times and haven't ruled out a sixth yet as I'm still good friends with them, as I write now I'm on my sixth term.

I returned to work for Stepneys in 1984 but this time for Mini tunnels. Stepney tunnels specialised in underground sewage replacement or pipes for electric cables, telephone wires etc. which needed to go under somewhere that could not be open cut like under a motorway or railway line. This was similar to the job I worked on from early 2015 to late 2016 in London - The Crossrail Project, the £17.5 billion pound railway project - but on a much smaller scale.

THE POETIC HOOLIGAN

HOLBORN

To work away I told myself and live a better life,
For twelve long months in London town and leave behind my wife.
Rewards were good they had to be to compensate the pain,
Of seeing a tear run down her cheek as I left her on the train.
To Holborn town old Holborn town and way beneath the ground,
To build a cross rail tunnel for £15 billion pound.
Whilst busy lives do rush above not knowing we're below,
We work so hard to earn our pay to please the ones we love.
I count away the days till I'm in her arms and lain,
But sooner than I think I'm back down here again.
It will not be forever as to work at home I miss,
To go to work each morning and come home to a kiss.

PARAGON STATION

Busy people with different lives,
Leaving husbands leaving wives.
Some to work and some to play,
A different station every day.
Boyfriends, girlfriends, and some same same,
Kiss goodbye, then board the train.
Leaving London, all concrete,
Then out through the fields where the birds tweet, tweet.
Brothers, Sisters and their friends too,
Sit and nod to the choo, choo choo.
Aunties, Uncles come and go,
Made much harder in the wind and snow.
Lighter nights are on the way,
Feeling better every day.
Won't be long till I'm in Ull,
Life in Yorkshire's never dull.

Working on Crossrail in 2015/16

THE POETIC HOOLIGAN

The mini tunnels ranged from 1M to 1.3M high. This operation would take place by firstly sinking a shaft approximately thirty foot down by thirty foot across. A tunnelling rig would then be lowered into the shaft bottom and set up with lasers to connect to other shafts the same and then the rig would be set off cutting its way through the earth. It was basically like a large tin can with the ends missing from each end about twelve - foot long, an inch thick and up to 1.3M high. There were six hydraulic rams attached to the inside that were powered by an air over hydraulic power pack. As the hydraulics were operated the rams would extend and push the outer casing - the shield into the ground. Then as the rams were retracted the miners would place the semi-circular concrete segments behind the rig and the whole process would begin again. After each movement the miners at the face would dig out and fill skips behind them laid out on a small track like a coal train wagon. They would then be driven out to the end of the tunnel and lifted up by the crane and emptied into a skip. This procedure was a highly dangerous method of laying tunnels working in unbelievably dirty and strenuous conditions but with very effective results and minimum disruption to the general public who did not realise what was going on under their feet.

The first tunnel job I ever experienced was at Bridlington in 1984 to replace a hundred year old, hand built brick culvert that was the main public toilet sewage pipe situated in the middle of the road near the Harbour Lights Club. The tunnel was approximately two to three hundred yards long and was constantly running in live sewage from the toilets above. When I first looked down the shaft it was first thing on a Monday morning and the pumps had been broken down all weekend so the sewage had risen to about ten

Working on Crossrail in 2015/16

feet up the shaft walls. It was an awful sight, not to mention the smell.

It was like a cauldron full of 'blind eels', sanitary towels, toilet paper and condoms, not a nice way to start a day, and really stomach churning. The site foreman was Frank, one of the maddest men you could ever meet. Outside of work or in the pub he was great and one of the lads. But as soon as he got back to work he'd sack any of them as soon as look at them if they upset him or did something wrong quoting his favourite saying, "I think it's time you took a bit of gardening leave."

When I looked down into the shaft it resembled the wall of death at Hull Fair but made of concrete.

I said to Frank, "There's no way I can go down there," to which he replied, "Don't worry, I will pump it out and spray it with Jeyes fluid."

Once they'd finished I set off down with a handful of tools and wearing my wader boots as worn by fishermen. I got down on my hands and knees and set off up the tunnel towards the small light at the end of the tunnel where the miner was digging out, I could hear the power pack pumping away which got louder as I approached. As I got half way up the tunnel it was completely dark as there was no light from either end, but I could feel the slime of the mud on my hands, or that's what I thought until I got to the face where Rich from York was digging out. Then I saw it wasn't mud but human shite and toilet roll all over me. I couldn't eat solid food for the next three days but as with anything like that you eventually get used to it until it becomes the norm. And only a day or two later I would sit in the tunnel when I was really busy and have a steak sandwich in bacofoil sent down with a milk bottle full of tea to wash it down.

When you came out of the tunnel there was a

Working on Crossrail in 2015/16 with my workmate James

washing bowl of cold water with a thick scum on top to wash your hands in. It was the same with the toilet block and showers, which were portacabins with a few sinks and toilets inside. In the summer it was okay, but come winter the water would freeze so your wash would be from a 45-gallon drum where you would have to break the ice off to swill your face. The toilets never had showers so the lads would just have a strip down wash in a sink that had a Sadia water heater between two sinks. The lads used to take the piss out of me because I made a shower from a piece of rubber hose. I attached it to the chrome spout that came out of the water heater and fixed the other end to the support that ran across the top of the toilet door. I then removed the centre pipe from a gas mantle from one of the old lights in the caravan, which had an end on it and fixed the pipe onto it, which sprayed water out when it was turned on. I timed it so that the water did not get too hot and then hosed the mud off the floor to have my shower while the lads were having a wash. They used to laugh and call me 'a fucking puff!' but it ended up being popular with a few of them who also used it. The majority of them just had a 'Stepney shower', that was a face and neck wash, finished off with a spray of deodorant under the arms and feet. You could see the black tide marks around their necks when we went for a beer.

Frank would get at the men so much at times so whenever they got the chance they would take revenge. Before the days of mobile phones there was an invention called pagers that anyone in their twenties would laugh at now. We used to carry one with us which was linked to a national call centre, and when someone wanted you they would ring a number and leave a message. The call centre would then activate your pager, which sounded like a pedestrian crossing bleeper. You would then ring the call centre and receive the message to ring whoever wanted you. This became a source of entertainment for the lads at Bridlington as there was a crossing near the site and one of them would press the crossing button and then shout, "Frank, your bleeper's going off." He'd go running to a phone box and come back five minutes later shaking his head and calling hell out of the bleepers and saying how useless they were.

One of the funniest things the lads ever did to him was again at Bridlington. Frank had got a rash around his bollocks and arse, there's no wonder when you think of the conditions that we had to work in, especially Frank. I remember the lads telling me of how he visited the site one weekend whilst he was out with his wife and kids. When he got there they had a problem up the tunnel so Frank being so hands on and impatient went diving down the shaft with his best gear on, including an expensive leather coat that got ruined. There was no wonder he developed a 'knacker rash'. He visited his doctor and got some powder that he had to apply at regular intervals. You would then see him running off to his office, dropping his trousers as he went through the door and returning a few minutes later with a look of relief on his face. That was until somebody thought it would be good fun to add a little something to the powder, which was either bicarbonate of soda or caustic soda. Whatever it was it had the desired effect as the next time he went to put some on he came running out with his trousers around his ankles screaming, "Bejesus!" as he ran to the hose pipe to cool his tackle off. I asked who did it, but no one seemed to know. However, Tommy and Jimmy Brown had big smiles on their faces. He should maybe have used a saying that an old bloke at Westies used to say about "Max Factor knacker lacquer, adds lustre to your cluster, and perfection to your erection!"

THE POETIC HOOLIGAN

JIMMY BROWN

Jimmy Brown, Oh what a man,
His friends may call him Desperate Dan
With a smile as wide as the Cheddar Gorge,
You'd think his friendship was only yours.

Born in Mexborough, strong and kind,
Came to Hull and left his youth behind
The man with two birthdays, so famous in Hull,
Life with Brownie was never dull.

He met young Kath, the love of his life,
Who made him complete by becoming his wife.
They soon had a son and life was dandy,
A lad like his dad who they named Andy.

He worked down the tunnels for many a year,
After a long hard shift he enjoyed a beer
Everybody's friend with a glint in his eye,
Oh what a man, oh what a guy.

Jimmy Brown always lived just a few hundred yards from me so every Monday morning I used to give him a lift up to Monkseaton near Whitley Bay. Although Jim was not Irish like the majority of the lads you would have thought he was having worked with them for so long and his structure was the opposite, they were all about 5ft 6" with chests like barrels and strong arms through working the pneumatic hammers (bull workers) at the face. Jim is a big man who was always laughing, he's always reminded me of Tommy Cooper and was too big to work in the tunnels so he was a crane driver, wagon driver and Pitt top man. On a Monday I would drive around to his home at 4.30 am and throw his big old brown suitcase - Mr Bean style - in the back of my little Y-reg Mk 3 Escort van. I took him up to Monkseaton one Monday morning and got straight on with welding a fence post with my electric welder alongside a pathway that lead to a school where all the mothers would walk their kids to school. Jim's job was to stand with an 8x4' sheet of plywood to shield the welding rays from their eyes. As I was welding with my full face mask on Jim said, "It's just as well you've got that mask on you ugly bastard or you'd frighten the kids with a face like that."

Later that day he got a cardboard box and cut holes in it for my eyes and nose to put over my head for when I was working near the pathway. It's still a standing joke now when I see him.

My duties were to maintain all the sites in the north of England from Whitley Bay, Peebles near Edinburgh, Workington, Cumbria, Widnes and Stourton, Leeds. I could be called to any of these sites at any time of the day or night to repair anything from a Coles 6t iron fairy crane, KL33 or KL66 crane, compressor, water pump, car or wagon. If it moved, I fixed it.

When they were working at Leeds and had a heavy night on the pop on a Friday, I would get an early morning call telling me they did not want the van to start and make something up so it wouldn't be running by eight o'clock knowing that Frank would stand the job down until Monday. I have seen a dozen pints of Guinness lined up on the bar at 8am as the landlord could make as much out of that lot by opening time as most would take on a Saturday night.

CHAPTER 20
HAVE BED,
WILL TRAVEL

The first time I had to stay overnight on a tunnel's site in a caravan was in 1984, up in Percy Main, near Newcastle. The repair I' been sent to carry out was on Danny Richardson's crane.

Danny was always the entertainer and would stand on the runner boards of his crane singing to the residents of the high-rise flats. He said that Errol Brown of Hot Chocolate had alledgedly stolen his image, including his bald head and moustache. Danny looked just like Errol and also insisted that he had fronted a band called Cool Coffee long before Hot Chocolate hit the headlines. Whilst we were on site however, someone committed suicide and I blamed Danny's singing for it.

The work on Danny's RB22 couldn't be done in one day so the lads offered me a bed for the night. But when I looked in the caravan at the room I was supposed to stay in I noticed there was no mattress on the bed. And when I asked where it was they pointed at the fence outside and said, "It's drying out, it should be okay by tonight."

Evidently some of the lads would get that drunk that they would piss the bed and this was the norm to hang it out to dry. In the winter they would prop the mattress up and turn the calor gas heaters on full to dry them. When you opened the caravan door at the end of a shift the smell of ammonia would nearly knock you over. Not for me I'm afraid! I went to a local shop and bought a camping bed and a sleeping bag. I then emptied out the

Ernie Chapman looking into
shaft at Monkseaton.
1985 with Coles crane.

A typical kitchen

bathroom, which obviously was never going to be used including the bath. I then cleaned the floor and made this my bedroom for when I stayed over. I used to carry my bed around to different sites, ' Have bed, will travel'.

The state of most of the beds was disgusting as some of the lads would sleep in their work gear having finished at 7pm, they would head off straight to the pub without a wash and have a dozen pints of Guinness and then stagger back to the caravan eating fish and chips, fall on the bed as drunk as a skunk and not even take their clothes off, even when some of them had damped down as they called it, pissed the bed in other words and then hang the mattress out again and change their work gear for some they'd dried out the night before.

My main base was Whitley Bay where I shared a caravan with Jimmy Brown, Maurice Walsh and Ernie Chapman (Lobster) as he was affectionately known because of his red face, Maurice was known as the boxer because of his fighting days. All three were the best you could wish to share with, I had known Ernie all my life and even our dads were workmates.

The first night I stayed over in Whitley Bay we had done a twelve-hour shift that finished at seven. Maurice had already started tea and as I walked past the window the smell was beautiful. That was until I walked in the caravan and saw it. There was a huge cooking pot on the gas stove with a lid on. As it simmered away, there was a mucky grey froth running down the side of the pot and onto the gas rings that were filthy. Our places were set at the breakfast bar tops, which again were disgusting. They were blathered in old food and grease with tab ends and matches buried into it. The knives and forks looked like they'd been used to dig the garden, with all the old food between the blades of the forks. I had to scald and wash mine before I could use them.

They all laughed at me and said, "You'll soon get

used to it".

The meal was one of two popular dishes that were served. This one consisted of a large lump of ham the size of a man's head with a thick side of fat that was half-cooked and then cut into four - and a full cabbage that had the outer leaves taken off, cut in four and thrown in. Spuds were unwashed and cut in half as were the carrots, they went in whole. The lot burbled away and then was dished out with a large ladle. It did taste gorgeous apart from the pieces of grit from the tatties and carrots, which had gone in the pan covered in mud.

The next night I finished early and went and bought some cleaning stuffs, knives and forks, tea towels etc., plus plenty of bleach and had a good clean up. I had to literally scrape the layer of fat from the worktops, after that the other lads on site would try and get a bed in our van if anyone had to go to another site. The other meal they did was basically the same as the first but done in a large baking tray. The lump of ham or beef would be dropped in the tray and surrounded with tatties, carrots and parsnips, then left to cook in half a block of lard and covered in bacofoil. This meal got me out of cooking for the rest of my life at home as I cooked it for my wife and kids one weekend when I came home. I was given the freedom of the kitchen and when I served them the meal they all went a funny shade of green. It got me out of cooking from that day on. I was dead proud thinking how well I'd done.

On returning to Whitley Bay from Peebles one hot summer's night at about eight o'clock, I found that the lads had gone into town. I was still in my work gear of jeans, tee shirt, rigger boots and was covered in oil but I decided to join them rather than go back to the local we used. They were all in a club called The Rex, which was as rough a club as you'd find anywhere, even the women shaved, a bit like how Tower in Hull used to be.

THE POETIC HOOLIGAN

There were about twenty of the lads out and welcomed by all the pubs due to the amount of beer they went through. It was always a good night with the likes of muscular Tony from Bradford who wasn't big at all but introduced himself as that, and then followed by studying tunnel technology, along with Spud from Hull who was another character.

We'd been in there before and never had a problem getting served. On this particular night however the service was terrible with only one barmaid on who kept disappearing, much to the annoyance of everyone.

It was a sure way to stir unrest among a thirsty gang of miners and one of the lads, Paul McDonnagh said to me, "Fuck this for a lark Rich, they aren't serving very fast are they?"

We decided to take matters into our own hands and I said to him, "Do you fancy giving me a hand as a barman?" and we jumped over the bar and started pulling pints and handing them out to the boys. After a few minutes the frumpy little barmaid came back behind the bar and started screaming at us to get out from behind her bar. I was laughing my cock off with the rest of the lads but Paul never even cracked his face as he looked at her in disgust and said, "Shut up you ugly, fat, little bastard! The only way anyone could fuck you is if they were too lazy to have a wank." She ran from behind the bar as everyone nearly choked on their beer. The bouncers saw the funny side of it and politely asked us to come from behind the bar as they knew what good customers we were.

I used to often take my mate Harry Dooley up with me if we were just going for the day, as with a lot of apprentices they are often at the butt end of a prank as we've all experienced for generations. It seems that the tradesmen, usually the younger ones who have not long been qualified themselves, feel it is an initiation ceremony that they have to pass on in retribution for what they endured. Although I have never been a bully and was brought up by my Dad never to fight anyone you know you can beat and always stand up for the underdog, Harry and me did on one occasion unintentionally overstep the mark at Stepneys with Paul Fearn. I was twenty-three and Paul was about ten years older and was Works Manager. We were all stood around a Wickham Pump as Harry and me were fitting new diaphragms to it when I picked up the rubber diaphragms and said to Harry it looked like a big fanny and pulled it over his head with Paul, not realising that as it went over his head the hole was slightly smaller than his neck and he started choking. We quickly pulled it back off and apologised profusely. He said it was worth the pain to see the look of panic on our faces.

I used to take Harry all over the country with me and we were forever winding each other up. We had to go up to a place called Crawcrook near Newcastle one day to remove a gearbox from a Jones KL33 crane.

We had been up a few days earlier to start the job and he had found it highly amusing that I burnt myself with a piece of hot slag that spat back at me whilst burning as I was jammed into an awkward position and landed nicely on my knob end and I just had to sit and endure the pain until it cooled.

I got my revenge by asking him to climb up onto the top of the gearbox which was about six feet long and tapered down at one end. He had to put his head over the top of the box and one arm, then slide it down so he couldn't pull it back out, as to be able to hold some bolts as I unfastened the nuts. At this point his face was looking over the top of the site hoardings onto a public footpath, I then lifted his trouser leg and started pulling the hairs from his legs, he was hurling abuse at me as women were taking their kids to school. They could not see me so he was getting a telling off from the Geordie lasses. We would often leave home at the crack of dawn and not get home until late. I went up to Crawcrook to fit a extension onto the front cutting edge of the shield so the miners could work at the face without being hurt from the falling loose rocks as they were digging in loose sandy earth however, I was the one who had to work outside the safety of the shield to tap out about fifty 16mm holes that secured the extension on. I was working with an Irish man called John who was one of the fittest miners you'd ever come across, he didn't drink and would go for a run up the hills at break time.

While I was tapping out he said "I just need to pop to the shops, I won't be long," and left me working alone, which wouldn't happen today with all the 'health and safety'.

He hadn't been gone long when a large rock fell from the earth that had been shook loose by a wagon passing overhead on the main road. It landed on my leg and had me trapped for over an hour until John got back, when he saw me he couldn't apologise enough knowing he shouldn't have left me alone. On the way home that day I saw my dad driving his John Tutty Volvo wagon on the other side of the dual carriage way from the Metro centre, a memory I'll treasure for the rest of my life. Another one of our trips took us up to Middlesbrough, working close to the railway station. I'll never forget that trip as on the way up we heard on the radio that John Lennon had been murdered, or assassinated depending on your political views. It was December 8th 1980, which may have been the warmest day on record in New York but that news sent a chill down the spine of every Beatles fan throughout the world. We had gone there to remove the gearbox from a Jones KL66 crane which is no mean feat even in a workshop, it was literally open heart surgery as everything revolved around it. We had to remove all the clutch plate assemblies, brake bands that held the cable drums steady, there was also several propeller shafts that in turn turned other auxiliaries. What made it worse was that it was freezing cold and windy as is normally the case when you have a big job on, they never breakdown on a hot day. Then just to make it interesting we had to work from the top of a ladder ten feet from the floor.

We removed everything and in doing so I nearly removed my thumb. As I was levering the main shaft out that everything run off, as I levered with a six foot crow bar it slipped and trapped my thumb between the bar and the frame. The pain was excruciating and my thumb ended up throbbing and swollen. When I did eventually release the shaft everything free-wheeled. Harry was on top of the ladder leaning inside the engine compartment as the wind blew the jib like a large weather vane and slewing the crane, which took the ladder from under him. I managed to make a grab for him and pulled him into the engine bay. I then had to remove all the gears and selectors from the shaft and lay them out in order in the engine bay, ready for the new shaft to be fitted when it arrived.

The next day I went to Beverley Westwood Hospital to have my thumb looked at having been kept awake all night with a throbbing under my right armpit. My nail was black and swollen. The doctor got a paper clip and straightened it out and then heated it up to a cherry red, then as he put the end onto my nail to burn a hole through I looked the other way expecting a lot of pain as it went through the nail. Instead I suddenly felt the pain disappear, and as I looked there was a jet of blood squirting six-foot in the air. It was the best relief I'd ever had. I've since helped a few other people by doing the same or drilling a small hole.

CHAPTER 21
HAPPY DAYS

A lot of jobs used to be done on a weekend to save downtime during the week. And as every outside job was on a building site you had to improvise if the weather was bad. We would often set up a temporary cover over a job if it rained. Harry and I had an engine to overall on a Winget dumper with a twin cylinder Petter engine. It was on the Queens Road site in Hull, which was a hundred yards from Harry's home, where he lived with his brother Tim and his Mam and Dad; Sheila and Billy and was very handy for cups of tea and sandwiches.

We set up some scaffold tubes over the dumper and lashed on some tarpaulin sheets to make what was to become affectionately known as our den. We spent the whole day Saturday removing cylinder heads, barrels, inspection plates from the engine block to remove the big ends and then pulled out the pistons and con rods, we then fitted new big end shells and rebuilt it with new pistons and barrels. It pissed down all day but it didn't dampen our spirits. We often reminisce and look back on those days with very happy memories.

I had another experience on that site that wasn't as happy whilst working on a digger. I was stood on the bonnet of a Hymac 370 fitting a windscreen when a horrible little bastard site labourer was waiting for the digger to move something for him.

He was constantly badgering me to the point that I said to him, "If you fuck off and leave me alone the job will get done much quicker."

RICHARD HALDENBY

He shouted to me, "Get down here and say that," which I did. I dived off the bonnet smacking him in the face as I came down. The momentum took us both flying and we ended up rolling about in the thick mud in the bucket of the digger with me laid on top of him with my back on his front like a spooning position. He had his hands in my face trying to gouge my eyes and his fingers in my mouth pulling at my lips trying to split them. I was biting his fingers and back head butting him in the face as well as elbowing the little bastard in the ribs. This went on for a while until we were pulled apart.

I've had a few run-ins on site, the last one only a few years ago when a good mate who was a digger driver came into the workshop shouting and bawling. Being a mate I grabbed him by his leg as he walked by to lighten the situation, thinking he'd start laughing but instead he got hold of me and started pulling me about. I thought he was skylarking and carried on wrestling with him until the point he said, "You've bit off more than you can chew old boy haven't you?" as he was twenty-seven and I was in my fifties. But I've always kept fit and with that I saw red and grabbed him by the balls and collar then put him on his back. I knelt on his chest holding his neck with one hand and with the other raised ready to punch his face in, when he realised he'd made a mistake and apologised. The next day I saw him and he said he'd seen some of the Orchard Park lads on site including Hoss and Fozzy and told them he'd had a run in with Haldenby to which they replied, "I bet you came off second best?"

I was on the way back from Middlesbrough one night after another long day at work. It was around midnight when I came through York on the A1079 near Pocklington.

THE POETIC HOOLIGAN

There are two pubs on the left heading towards Hull between the A64 roundabout and Pocklington. As I approached the second one, which has a car park at the front, I saw what I thought was a very large dog walking across the car park. My lights were shining on its side as it walked with its head facing me. It was a fair distance away but I thought that dog looks strange. As I got closer I realised its eyes were a different colour to a dog and as it walked its head was hung low and stayed level with its shoulders, rolling from side to side. I then noticed its tail went nearly down to the floor and then curled up. I then realised it wasn't a dog at all. It was a huge cat. Its back was level with the bonnet of the cars as it passed them. Having no mobile phone in them days I rang the police when I got home expecting them to laugh. But he asked where I had seen it and put me through to a police station near to where the sighting had been. They said it had been reported many times over the years. The story goes that some rock star had bought some big cats and later let them go when they couldn't control them, much like Christian the Lion that was bought from Harrods in the early seventies by two Australian students living in London.

Looking back on the hours I used to work I don't know how I managed it. There were times I have left home at 4.30 on a Monday morning and drove up to Whitley Bay and gone straight underground to strip out a rig that had been distorted and then fit a new one. Then after twelve hours underground and looking forward to my tea, I've then had to jump in my van and drive up to Peebles near Edinburgh to do the same again, eating fish and chips on the way and getting on site at 11pm and going straight underground again. I then came out at 10am the next day, making it nearly thirty hours. From there I went straight down to Widnes to repair another rig, coming out of the ground late afternoon and then up to Workington to remove the gearbox from a Coles' 6t crane and fit a new set of lay shaft bearings, finishing at midnight and then driving back home. I arrived home at 5am on Wednesday, making a total of 48 hours non-stop!

I left Peebles late one afternoon to head back to Whitley Bay in the snow through open countryside with hardly another vehicle on the road. I drove through the hills and large Scott's pines that all looked beautiful covered in snow as the darkness drew in. I had been driving about an hour when I saw hazard lights in the distance and thought, Oh shit, this could be trouble and hoped it would be snowploughs. As I got closer it certainly was trouble. It was my good friend Harold Corner, our low loader driver. He had left Peebles earlier in the day with a machine on board and his brakes had frozen on. I pulled up behind him and knocked on his cab door. When he saw me he was like a dog with two tails. I've never seen anyone so pleased to see me. It was 1985 and he had no way to make contact with the outside world. He said he thought he was a 'goner' having been there for hours already.

I got a shovel out of my van and had to dig a tunnel under the wagon to get at each of his brakes to free them off. The snow and ice had packed around the air pots and actuating arms. I dug them free and sprayed everything in antifreeze. He tested them and set off home and I stayed behind him until he reached the main roads near Newcastle.

I went to see him recently at Bempton near Flamborough and he told his brother how I had saved his life twice. The first time had been that night when he could have frozen in the snow and the other time when we were working at the Widnes site and Harold delivered some concrete segments that were used for building the tunnels. They were laid out on the back of

THE POETIC HOOLIGAN

a forty-foot flatbed trailer and should have been lifted off by the crane with a special segment frame. However on this site they did not have one or could not be bothered to set it up, as it was a slower method of unloading. The crane driver used a wire strop to go through the holes in the top of the segment and then put a round bar through the eye of the strop to lift three at a time. This was normally okay but not ideal as the crane's wire rope had a rider in it, which meant it had a kink in the wire and would jump instead of levelling off as he winched in. Harold was bent down attaching the strop when the crane driver lifted the load over Harold without him knowing.

At this point the wire jumped and jolted the segments making them break and drop onto the back of Harold's head. Luckily he had a safety helmet on which prevented further injury but they still crushed the back of his skull. It was touch and go if he pulled through as he was in a coma and we were told that if he didn't gain consciousness within seventy-two hours he might not survive.

I went to the hospital on the third day just in time to see him come round. It took a lot of years for his claim to go through the courts. I think there was a deadline of about ten years but some of the lads were afraid to give statements in fear of losing their jobs. I gave one statement that was cocked up by his solicitor, and Harold asked me for another with just a few months to the deadline. I went to Bridlington and gave one to another solicitor that secured his claim and won him a good payout. That is what he calls 'saving his life'.

Stourton near Leeds was a site we spent a fair bit of time at, as there were a few shafts and a lot of gear. Harry and me turned up on site one day and were told to keep out of Scouse's way as he was in a foul mood. We were safe with Scouse as Harry's dad Billy got on well with him due to them both coming from Liverpool and Scouse looked up to him like a father figure. You couldn't help but like Billy, he was a great bloke. The lads told us that Scouse and Charlie Chang, Mike really, the site fitter had had an almighty argument. Charlie came with a big reputation of being a tunnels' specialist who had worked on a big project in Hong Kong. I was suspicious of him when I saw his toolbox that consisted of a hammer, a chisel, an adjustable spanner and a hacksaw. Scouse never rated him from day one and being of Irish descent his temper was fiery. He was built like a brick shithouse and fit as a fiddle. When he was sober he was great but if he'd had a bad day and got on the beer he was best left alone. He was always fighting the locals wherever we worked and he was said to have been in one of the special services. Scouse had asked Charlie on the night shift to do something for him and he refused. So Scouse picked up a pair of 24" stiltsons and chased him around the floor of the shaft screaming, "Stand still you little bastard while I hit you!" as Charlie jumped onto the ladder and shot up the shaft like a rat up a pipe.

I could have swung for him myself one weekend at Stourton as we had a new gearbox to fit to a Bedford TK tipper. I had done all the hard work on the Friday by removing the box and collecting a second-hand one from a scrapyard in Leeds. On the Saturday I transferred all the ancillaries over and laid sheets of plywood on the rough land so that we could wheel the trolley jack into place. On the Sunday we lifted it into place and started connecting everything up from prop shaft, P.T.O etc.

I lined up the selectors in the box and said to Charlie, "Will you just pop the gearbox lid on and make sure you slot the gear stick into the selectors while I finish off underneath?"

After a few minutes I heard a loud crack and asked

what it was to which he replied, "Nothing, nothing." But as I laid underneath oil started dripping and when I looked I noticed a large crack in the side of the box. He had not entered the stick into the selectors and nipped it up. When I told him what he'd done he burst into tears screaming, "Oh fucky fucky!"

I said we would have to take the box back out to get a head start for the Monday, which he refused to do and threw his tools down and went home, leaving it to me to strip the box out alone. He didn't reign long after that. Like I said Harry and me got on well with Scouse. So when we arrived at Stourton one freezing Saturday morning, to remove an engine from a KL 33 crane that had been damaged by vandals overnight, he decided to light a fire for us. He piled up a load of old wood and pallets near the crane and poured some diesel on it to get it going. Then as we worked throughout the day he kept bringing more wood to stoke up the fire and poured a bit more diesel on it. We finished removing the engine and tootled off home, only to find out on the Monday morning that there had been another break in at the site. This time vandals had set fire to a brand new compressor that had been stood on the other side of a pile of pea gravel.

In reality what had happened was the diesel that Scouse had been pouring on the fire had run under the pea gravel and ignited underneath without him knowing.

Arthur's Coventry Climax. 60DA.

CHAPTER 22
RETURN TO GOOLE DOCKS

I left Stepneys in 1986 and returned to Malcolm West's who had won the Goole docks contract back and asked me to go on site to look after the twenty-two trucks. I had always loved working at Goole having first gone there as a fifteen year old apprentice and had done a two year contract there from 1982 to 1984, where I made some lifelong friends. We had twenty-four forklifts ranging from four ton to thirteen ton. I had an office in one of the sheds on Bridge Street where the cement plant is now.

I used to service one truck every morning and whatever repairs were needed after lunch, then by the time I'd finished the last one it was time to start again with the first. If the weather was nice I would do them outside, or if it was bad I'd put the truck inside the shed next to my office.

Harry had been made redundant from Stepneys when he came out of his apprenticeship and was unemployed for a few months. I used to take him out on jobs with me and let him help to keep him occupied. During this period I saw a job advertised for a funeral directors' assistant and applied for the job using Harry's name. It was a very well written letter expressing his desire to have always wanted to get into this line of work having worked on fork lift trucks at a coffin factory in Beverley which we gave the nickname of Willy Wonka's Coffin Factory. They were so impressed that they offered him the job without an interview. When he rang and told me of the offer I said the name of the company and he called me all the bastards under the sun.

I got Harry to a job with me at Westies and would take him with me for a couple of weeks to get to know the job. We were working in the corner of a shed one day on Goole docks when we noticed a couple of HM customs officers back into the shed in a little blue Metro van. They sat there all afternoon watching a ship across the dock with a pair of binoculars, totally unaware that we were behind them. When it came to going home time I always pulled the big doors together and locked up. But knowing they had not seen us working away behind them, I walked across the dimly lit shed and banged on their van window and I asked them if they were going to lock up. They both nearly died of fright and must have thought their days were up, as there were lots of Russian and Polish ships there at the time with contraband being sold all over the dock and rumours of gangsters carrying guns.

Goole docks as with any other docks in the country, were made up of a hardy bunch of men not dissimilar to the North Sea fishermen who were hardened to anything that life could throw at them. Injuries and death were all too common in those days before we'd heard of Health & Safety, RAMS (Risk Assessment and Method Statements) along with relevant insurance which is what it's all about, offloading the blame so companies don't have to pay out. In their day the job had to be done no matter what and if you did not want to do it there were fifty men waiting to take your place. The old dockers told me of how life used to be in the fifties and sixties when work was hard to find and hundreds of dockers would gather in the poolroom, hoping they would be offered work. They would hold their book in the air hoping their face would fit and they'd be selected. If not, they were sent home and they went hungry as there was no social security or tax credits back then.

Many of the men in the Goole area were from a farming background and were used to low wages and hard work, all of which developed their characters to be as dry as a bone and so funny. They would suddenly come out with a one liner that would have you crying with laughter, as they remained poker-faced.

I've seen men sustain disabling injuries and even die at work. I remember a docker I was friendly with who lost his life in the early eighties working on a ship. He climbed up some steps and through a hatch hole about two-foot square and was cut in half by the hatchway's mechanical concertina doors. Some of the Goole dockers were the nicest men you'd ever meet, different to Hull dockers who were more 'Jack the lads', as you'd expect living in a big city.

The Goole men, the likes of Cyril Fielder, Jimmy Clements, Alan Rogers, and Arthur and Frank Harrison, always seemed more gentlemanly. I was going to say Des Wales, but as good a friend as he was I wouldn't put him in the country gentleman category. He was a big hard case of a man who was more suited to the Hull docks, a proper piss-taker who ribbed everybody, but a good friend of mine.

In 1986 I lost my driving license for drink driving. The day after I'd been done I was stood with Des in the queue getting our dinner, feeling thoroughly depressed and miles away. I had put a plate of dinner and a dish of sweet on my tray and went to put my gravy on my dinner and custard on my sweet, but instead I did it the wrong way around. Anyone else would have had a little chuckle, but not Des. He made it known to everyone what I'd done and never let me forget it.

Arthur Harrison had been a professional football referee in his day and took charge of some big games.

RICHARD HALDENBY

He was a very funny man and worked alongside my good friend Cyril Fielder in 25 shed. Cyril and I hit it off straight away as he also raced pigeons. I used to always pop and see them both first thing for a cuppa in their little wooden shed. Arthur always had a long drawn out joke to tell you with a corny punch line. I went in one morning and said to Arthur, "Morning Arthur. Are you well?"

He replied, "I am now Rick, I've just got back from the doctors."

I knew I was being reeled in but asked him why and then sat back for the next five minutes and listened to his story. He explained to the doctor that he was having a problem with his sex life. The doctor checked him over and asked how long it took to reach a climax, to which Arthur replied, "It depends which end of the shed it's at Doc."

To those of you unfamiliar, a Coventry Climax used to be a type of forklift popular in those days.

Arthur had a brother called Frank who also was a comedian. He had a weggy eye that made it look like he was looking anywhere but at you, 'one eye up the chimney' as they say.

They used to have a little boat they would take on the river Ouse after work to catch eels. They would take a yard of wool and thread it through a needle and then thread it through a load of worms so they had a yard of worms and then tie the ends and double over and over until they had a ball of worms. They'd then tie it to a fishing line and drop it over the side of the boat. Apparently eels teeth face backwards so as they bite into something they can't let go. They'd leave it for a while then lift it out and hold it over a drum and shake the rod to release the eels into the drum. They would fill a forty-five gallon drum and then drive them down to London to sell as jellied eels. They reckoned they made a fortune.

Whilst I was at Westies in 1987, I organised a Christmas night out in town with some of the lads from Westies and MFI, including Mike Kerman from MFI Howden, commonly known as Ted legs because of his tight jeans that resembled Teddy boy's.

On the day of the do I had been working at B Line Industries, which was a part of the Blind Institute on Beverley Road. I noticed a white collapsible stick as used by the blind that had been thrown away, so I thought I'd take it out on the night for a bit of fun. A bit further down Beverley Road on the corner of Sculcoates Lane there used to be a sex shop where the tax shop is now, so Tony and I went in and bought a vibrator to take out with us on the night as well.

We met in 'Star of the West' which used to be where the entrance to Prospect Centre is now.

As we all stood around the bar I put the vibe down my shirt with the bell end stuck out of my collar and said to the lads, "I'll stand between a group of women at the bar to order a drink."

As I stood waiting to get served one of them noticed it and started laughing. I kept a straight face and asked what was she laughing at? She replied, "That thing sticking out your collar."

I looked down and said, "Oh shit I haven't got a hard on again have I?" much to their amusement and fits of laughter. We left there and set off to Hull Cheese on Paragon Street. I lead the way with the vibe stuck out my fly hole and the white stick in my hand, followed by all the lads with their hands on each other's shoulder forming a long line of about a dozen. As we passed a bus stop in front of what is now Waterstones there was a crowd of women who had just left Bingo, and at that precise moment the vibe fell on the floor.

I shouted, "Stop, my knob's fell off!"

The old ladies said, "Give it here, we'll give it a good home," – the dirty old buggers.

We carried on to Cheese, cock in place and as we got to the doors the bouncers were about to stop us going in. I gave one of them a tap on the bollocks with the stick and said, "Can you show me to the bar pal?" Luckily he saw the funny side of it and let us in. We went from there to the Bali Hai nightclub, which is now Laser Quest. We had a few laughs in there with it until I put it on one of the DJs spinning discs.

He was embarrassed and said, "If someone takes this off I'll give them a T-shirt."

A blonde girl walked up and took it off and then walked straight out the door, not even collecting the T-shirt. I just hope she gave it a good home and looked after it well.

CHAPTER 23

MY MATE MAURICE

There are not as many characters around today as there used to be in years gone by. One of the first and undoubtedly the most memorable that I met was Maurice Coggin.

Where do you begin with Mo? I knew Maurice for 37 years so I feel more than qualified to give a life and times assessment of him. I first met him in 1971 and he had an immediate impact on me. How many of your friends can you say you remember the exact time when you met!

I was a fifteen-year-old apprentice at West Plant Hire when he and his newly formed business partner of C&C Engineering walked through the workshop whistling away as usual. I shall always remember that first meeting. He never changed, whether he was old looking then or young looking when he was older I don't know!

I know what Mauriati would say, "Look at my profile son. I've got the rugged good looks of Antonio Bandaros, people often mistake me for him on holiday you know."

He had more aliases than Smith and Jones, including the whistler, Mad Mo, Moz, Mo, The Ninja Mauriati and Hurricane because he used to be in and out and gone before you knew what had hit you. There were a few choice descriptions of him, which I can't repeat, the most famous one being Black Adder! We could meet at 7am and by 30 seconds past he would be covered in oil!

Everyone knew Maurice Coggin, just the mention of his name made people laugh. Companies who we got parts from would say, "I think I saw Mo today."

When you asked what did they mean by, 'think I saw' they would reply, "Well it was that quick I might have imagined it. The doors burst open, he walked round the counter and grabbed the parts he needed, hurled a load of abuse at us, said for us to pull our fingers out, pinched a fag, then vanished in a flash."

They then usually described how he disappeared, leaving a trail of oil and grease all over the counter and oily footprints all over the carpet to the echo of, "Haven't got time to give an order number my mate, I'll ring it through later," which he rarely did but I had to!

Over the thirty-seven years I knew Mo our relationship had several guises.

For four days in 1979 he was my boss whilst he had C&C Engineering.

We met again in 1987 when he was practising one of his many trades as a taxi driver for his brother Jeff. He gave me a lift home from a pigeon presentation one night and I found out he too had racing pigeons, or should I say he kept homing pigeons. He took me down to the bottom of his garden at midnight with the loft lights on showed me his stock. He probably charged me for the extra time on his fare too. His bird's rarely collected top prizes but always got home no matter how hard the race.

Everyone knew that the pigeons were just an excuse to have a few beers with the lads and greet the birds home from a race whilst having a barbecue and a few tinnies! On one occasion though the birds excelled in the penultimate race of the season - The 500 Miler - the race that most people wanted to win! This race was exceptionally hard with lots of losses but Mo's birds were fantastic and claimed eight of the ten prizes. His first bird got home half an hour before everyone else's. Maurice shot, or should I say staggered, into the loft and clocked it in and then had another tinnie. He went back into the loft a short time later to give it a kiss and a cuddle only to find it still had its rubber race ring on. He then realised what he had done as he had clocked one of the birds that hadn't been in the race but one that had come back late from the week before. He promptly clocked the right bird but was beaten into second place by a few minutes by club mate Stan Monahan.

In 1990 our paths crossed again whilst working at Barek Lift trucks when we decided we'd had enough of working for other people as we had both previously had our own companies. We started trading as Wide Range Repairs, a company I had started in 1984. We were partners for eleven years until we sold out to Initial Metals. Mo carried on working for them until he died in 2008.

Mauriati was never a technician, he was more of a magician, as what he lacked in technical ability he made up for with his true grit and determination.

I remember John Altiss, the founder of I.M.E. saying to me after Mo had got him out of the mire one Friday night when his main fork truck had broken down and queues of wagons were trailing out of the gate, "There is no finer sight than Maurice's oily arse sticking out of a fork truck when you desperately need it up and running."

He always managed somehow to get it working by hook or by crook, even if it meant getting on the phone to ask advice, as he would often say when posed with a problem, "I don't know what's wrong with it my mate but I know a man who does."

The Ninja Mauriatti was the kind of soldier you would want with you on the front line when your tank had broken down.He had that Normandy attitude, a proper British bulldog with that streetwise experience and survival instinct that always got him through! His knowledge for the whereabouts of a part, be it new or second-hand, when you could not get one was amazing. He would pull out his little black book full of the contact names he had built up over the years.

He would often say, "I am the oldest man in the world and know everybody" although he was only two weeks short of sixty when he died.

If you asked him where he had got something from he would give a cheeky grin and a laugh, then pull his woolly hat down over his eyes and say, "If I told you my mate I would have to kill you," whilst bouncing about doing a Ninja Mauriatti movement! His exploits in the field were legendary and you could make a film about him but people would think the stories were too far-fetched and he had to be a fictional character.

Maurice lived life in the fast lane and everything had to be done yesterday, which often resulted in him knocking a bit of bark off his head or hands. On one occasion his over eagerness resulted in him losing two finger ends, which happened whilst we were fitting new leaf springs to a Douglas Tug Master for Nippress Cold Stores. We had brought the tug into the workshop and set about stripping it. We jacked it high enough to raise the front wheels off the floor and enable us to remove the front wheels and then securely placed the machine on axle stands, all of which was too slow and drawn out for Maurice.

He just wanted to stack some blocks of wood for speed and said, "That'll do my mate."

I stood my ground and made sure it was done properly, there was no way I was putting my life in Maurice's hands! We started to strip it down by removing the front wheels and slackening off the front and rear leaf spring anchor plates and swinging shackles. We then supported the front axle using a forklift and removed the pivot pins. At this point I said

THE POETIC HOOLIGAN

to Maurice, "When we refit the new springs remember to leave the anchor plates loose so we can get the pins back in easier." But when the new springs arrived, he thought he would impress me by putting it back together on his own.

He came into work early the next morning but instead of lifting the truck up a bit higher to allow for the extra curve of the new springs, again he 'didn't have time' and thought he could cut corners.

He placed a hydraulic jack between the flat chassis and the curve of the spring to fit the pin. Not only did he compromise safety but he also tightened the anchor plates, which I had told him to leave loose to enable easier fitting of the pins into the holes. When he could not get the pins started he decided to put his middle finger of one hand and the index finger of the other into the holes to feel if it was lined up. Just as he did that the jack holding the spring apart decided to jump out releasing tons of pressure, which sliced his finger ends off like a carrot, midway between the nail and the first joint.

I received a call at 7.40am from him sounding like Rolf Harris making a lot of "Ooh" and "Ahhh" noises and asking, "How long you gonna be my mate?"

I replied, "About twenty minutes, why?"

There was a slight pause then he answered, "I've chopped two of my fucking fingers off."

I paused expecting him to laugh, as he'd wound me up so many times before! But when I realised he was serious I replied, "Please don't tell me you've been working on that tug."

I had warned him not to and even sent a fax to the office from home in large letters saying,

DO NOT WORK BY YOURSELF

But he had carried on regardless and when I asked him had he lined the holes up with his fingers he

243

answered "Don't be fucking daft, I'm not that stupid. I don't know what happened the jack just slipped."

Upon arrival at the workshop I carried out my forensic fitter inspection, and found it was evident he was that daft!

I got out of my van and could see blood all over the office roller shutters. I opened the shutters and followed the trail of blood, which was all over the desk and telephone and led to the tug. I knelt on the floor and looked under the machine for his fingers but could not see them anywhere. Then as I looked up right in front of my nose was a finger-end inside the leaf spring eye with the other finger-end in the opposite side. I got a plastic beaker from the drinks machine and filled it with water and dropped the finger ends in it. I rang him and by this time he was in an ambulance being moved from one hospital to another for further treatment. I asked him if he wanted the finger ends, thinking they may be able to stitch them back on but he said, "No, it's too late my mate, they've cauterised the ends now."

I replied, "No, I didn't mean to stitch them back onto your fingers. I thought they might graft them onto your cock to give it a bit of length for a change," which made him laugh!

When Tony came into the workshop I told him what had happened and showed him the grizzly trail to the machine. I then asked him if he fancied one of our new soups and passed him the beaker with the two finger-ends bobbing around, and he was nearly sick! As a reminder for Maurice we bought two joke shop finger ends and made a glass fronted frame and mounted on the wall of the workshop to encourage him to work more safely in the future. But he never did! Another of my countless funny memories of predictable 'Mauriati mishaps' was whilst we were removing an engine from a tug on Queen Elizabeth Dock. I noticed the bonnet support was missing as Maurice had already buried himself in the engine compartment with just a thin stick propping up the heavy six-foot long bonnet. I could see what was going to happen and tried warning him of the inevitable accident that was about to occur. I suggested he tied the bonnet up more securely with a piece of rope. He replied with his usual answer, "Alright my mate, I'll do it in a minute, I haven't got time."

I walked away into 18 Shed but returned to see he had knocked the stick out with his oily arse, which made it look like he had been half eaten by the machine. There was one arm and one leg stuck out from under the bonnet. Having already taken the radiator out his face was pushed up against the radiator grill inside the engine compartment and there was blood pouring from a cut on his forehead! It looked like a crocodile had him in its mouth. I promptly ran back into the shed to get a few of the dockers to come and assist me. Fortunately it ended well and with a lot of laughter. And the more Maurice hurled abuse at us the more we laughed, as he shouted, "Never mind stood grinning like a load of Cheshire cats, get me out of here you daft bastards."

Another time he was performing in front of an audience of dockers whilst mimicking someone we had worked with. I again saw an accident waiting to happen and warned him to move a footplate, which he had put on the back of a Henley 26/48 fork lift counter weight which was at head height.

Again he said, "In a minute my mate." And then bang, "Aagh" and again the claret poured from yet another wound on his head!

He should have had another nickname as I think back about him, 'Staffordshire Bull Terrier' as he was about 5ft 9in and stocky with short hair, which showed all the scars on his head like a fighting dog.

He was famous for his early starts so that he could

Maurice with his burnt body warmer.

get away early enough to be able to nip into the pub on the way home for a couple of beers thinking that Carol wouldn't know! I was occasionally cajoled into joining him for a beer after work, which was never really my scene to go in the pub straight from work. It always amazed me that he was never caught for drink-driving as when I was with him, he only had two beers then I would say, "Lets be off," to which he always replied, "I'll just have another swift half my mate."

That was usually followed by another swift half with the excuse he'd had a 'grueller' – a hard day - as he slumped over the bar blathered in oil telling the barmaid how hard he had worked. Yet when you were pushed to finish a job he would not let you down, if you asked him for help unless it was a bank holiday weekend. Then you had no chance of help as he'd always start a bank holiday with a 'poets day' (Piss Off Early, Tomorrow's Saturday) in readiness for his booze and barbecue. We had a mutual understanding though when either of us were struggling with a job, which was "Do you want a bit of moral support my mate?" and vice versa.

Even when I left Wide Range I would ring him if I was having a bad day and needed cheering up. Just hearing his voice and having a laugh with him perked you up. He would answer the phone with, "Hello my boy, how are you doing my mate?"

I'd reply, "Struggling Mo, how about you?"

To which he'd answer "Ahh fair to crap but you can't let the bastards get you down, you've got to fight the good fight, onward and upward."

He was frightened of no man but he didn't have to be. He was never a fighter, he just won people over with his cheek. Occasionally if he came across a nasty customer he would just laugh and say, "They'll pay for it son" and they did. He would hit them where it hurts, in the pocket! Anyone who hadn't met him would ask what's Maurice like? I could only describe him as a mixture of Del Boy and Dennis from Auf Wiedersehen Pet. Oh yeah, and Antonio Banderas as he would keep reminding me. Whilst on holiday people actually did stop him and ask if he was Dennis! Working away with Maurice was always an adventure, like the first time we ever went to Liverpool in 2002 having just sold Wide Range Lift Trucks to Initial Metals who had just won a contract to maintain a fleet of container handling trucks on Seaforth Docks. I was dreading going as being a United supporter I had developed a hatred for Liverpool F.C., which had passed onto Scousers even though I had never actually met anyone from there. When I arrived there I proudly displayed my United players strip in the window of my van, as I got out of my van to meet the lads on site I was greeted with, "Oh no, not a fucking Mancy pants."

That was fighting talk to me and I was ready for a battle but how wrong I was. Within minutes they made me feel like I had known them all my life and had me laughing my tits off. It turned out to be one of the best six months of my working life and I became best friends with a stacker truck driver called John, who I won over shortly after I'd arrived when one of the up and over hydraulic pipes came off his Valmet container stacker. There were about eight pipes that ran over a wheel with grooves in for the pipes to run on at the top of the mast. Unfortunately one came off and got snagged with the others and the only way to release them was to lift the mast to the top and prise them back into place. I had to stand on the spreader beam, which was only about twelve inches wide so my boots just fitted on. I climbed on whilst it was on the floor and had John lift me up to the top whilst it was blowing a gale and snowing. I then levered them back into place, all the time only having the flexy, hydraulic pipes to hold onto. This is where my

Lockwood Street dare devil antics came into use.

When I came back down some wagon drivers who had been waiting to be loaded came over to me and said, "You must be fucking crazy! We've never seen anything like it."

When I arrived in Liverpool I was supposed to be staying at the Campanile Hotel but I had to first visit the site, and as I pulled onto the docks there was a security gate I had to book in at. I parked across the road from security outside a rough looking pub and wondered if a lifelong friend, Ernie Chapman, who I'd worked the mini tunnels with was still working in Liverpool, as he'd told me a few months earlier that he was working for Global Shipping, loading cocoa beans. I rang him and asked where he was working and he told me Liverpool and he was staying in a pub on Seaforth Docks called 'The Rubber Duck'.

He said, "It's a rough little pub like the Earl De Grey in Hull," (in other words a knocking shop). When he told me the real name of the pub I couldn't believe it. I was stood outside it. I carried on talking to him as I walked into the pub much to their surprise. I paid my £12 for the night and stayed with them in the doss house. The next day the Scouse lads on site couldn't believe I had stayed there. I worked by myself for a week and then the Ninja Mauriati joined me. We were there from the October through to the end of March, the full winter! Every night after work we would go back to the Campanile Hotel and have half a gallon of beer before we went for a shower, then back down to the bar for another half a gallon and our meal. However, once a week on a Thursday we would go for a thirty-two ounce steak at a restaurant in the town centre that Mo had tracked down called JR's. They served a fantastic steak, which Maurice liked so rare he would say, "All they've done is break it's horns off, wipe it's arse and stuck it on a plate so as you stick your fork in, the bastard squealed."

Maurice was always an embarrassment when you went for a meal but he didn't give a shit. Every time we went for a steak he would pester the poor waitress for sachets of mustard, English of course none of your French soft shite and would then stash them in his jacket pocket. He also had the nerve to ask for a bag to put more in, and he'd even walk by the empty tables and pinch some more. He'd then cheekily beg a ciggie off the young waitress on the way out.

When I asked him why he needed so many mustard sachets he said, "Cos I take them on holiday with me my mate."

"What?" I replied, never knowing whether or not to believe him. It turned out that whenever he went on holiday he would not pack his case with normal things like you and me, such as clothes and sun cream. He would firstly make space for his barbecue stuff including a piece of wire mesh so he could build a barby on the beach. He then packed his best steaks on top. When I asked him why he didn't buy steaks over there he said, "Nah, theirs are shite and too expensive!"

I warned him if he got caught he would be in trouble for taking meat out of the country but he just laughed and said, "Fuck 'em my mate, they've got to catch me first."

He was the original barbecue king and would often fire the barby up in mid winter in a blizzard of snow. I wish he could have shown as much finesse in his work as he did in his barbecue preparation. He would often disappear on a Friday to select the best meats and king prawns from his favourite butchers and then marinate them for the weekend! I'd ask him just for fun where he'd been as I'd tried ringing him and he'd come out with little white lies, not that it mattered, after all he was a partner!

After we'd been working in Liverpool for a couple of months we were joined by John Liversedge of J.K.S. Autolectrics - A.K.A Marlon Dingle to everyone in the town. He adopted the name Marlon after I called Viking F.M. in a response to a request to anyone knowing someone who looks like a TV star. A lot of dockers and local lads heard it and called him Marlon from that day on. When he arrived at the Campanile Hotel he booked in at reception to find that he was in room number one, directly next to reception which he was cock-a-hoop about. He laughed and said "Ahh well, not far for me to go to bed tonight," unbeknown to him that I had actually arranged for him to be put in the 'invalid' room. He threw his bag through the door and joined us at the bar. All night Maurice and I were making wise cracks about getting laid out in the bath and if he would require a handmaid to wash him.

We walked him to his room and wished him goodnight. But then we'd no sooner got into our rooms than the phone rang with him laughing and calling us all the bastards under the sun. He had seen the specially designed bathroom with a small bath with handrails etc but he had to stay in the room until the next day!

Another time while staying at the Campanile I was stood at the bar with Mo when the door opened and a beautiful girl walked in, or should I say her tits first followed by her. She had long blonde hair and was wearing a grey tracksuit.

I said to Mo, "Have you seen the tits on her?"

But Mo being Mo was more bothered about a nice pint than a nice bird. He'd often say, "I would rather have a good dinner than a shag."

When he looked at her however he said, "That's that bird off Brookie."

I didn't know as I'd never watched the programme,

but as she approached the bar he displayed all the charm of a bulldog chewing a wasp and barked at her, "Hey, you're that bird off Brookie aren't you? I don't like you and your husband Tim Head, or whoever he is. I like Jimmy Corkhill though."

She laughed and chatted for a while. She turned out to be Jennifer Ellison. And the next day Mo had all the lads on site believing he had scored and spent the night with her!

Another night we were sat having a meal with Marlon and Mo showed us another one of his chat up lines by calling over a waitress and politely asking, "Sweetness, could I have some more of your wonderful bread?"

When she delivered it he thanked her by saying, "Thanks darling, you're a little minger," to which she replied, "I beg your pardon, who are you calling a minger?"

Mo had a look of bemusement on his face realising he had upset her. When we'd stopped laughing and asked him if he knew what a minger was, he replied, "Yes, it's just like a little darling."

Bless his little oily socks.

CHAPTER 24

MEN BEHAVING BADLY

Mauriati got the nickname Black Adder due to always being dirty, so once I thought I would give him the clean and easy part of an engine removal to do, renewing a fibre drive ring between the engine and transmission. Seeing as it was my job I let him work up on top whilst I went under the Valmet twenty-eight ton lift truck to undo the engine mountings and bell housing bolts etc. The engine had not been out from new and was about twenty years old and looked like it had never been steam cleaned. It was absolutely covered with thick black sludgy oil and as the truck had been pushed into a dark corner of 13 Shed on King George Dock there was no way it could be cleaned. Mo was laughing all the time in response to me complaining of being laid on my back and feeling clumps of crusty oil dropping on to my face. He kept saying "You'll be as black as me when you come out of there my mate."

When I finally crawled from under the machine I thought, he is going to be proud of me looking as black as him as I'd been saying to him "I'm going to look like a grease monkey when I get out of here Moz." Yet when I surfaced he looked at me and said, "You've done your usual Teflon trick," as not a speck of oil had stuck to me but when I looked at him he was blathered in it. When we had finished on the dock we had to go do a quick job in Brocklesby's Scrap Yard where he buried himself in the bowels of the earth as he would put it, or in other words the centre of the car crusher. When finishing work I always remove my overalls and boots and wash my hands and face to look quite presentable. Not Maurice though, he would get into his van blathered in oil and grease from head to toe. I would never get into his van without my overalls and gloves on as his seats and steering wheel were dripping in oil!

That night as we finished work we decided to go to the Goodfellowship Inn for a beer as it had been a hot day and as usual Maurice felt he'd had a grueller! Goodfellowship is a beautiful Tudor style pub come restaurant on Cottingham Road and definitely not your average working man's pub but that didn't bother Maurice. I looked at the state of him and said, "We can't go in there with you looking like that," but he laughed and said, "Bollocks to them my mate, my money's as good as anyone's." When we arrived at Goodfellowship Mo led the way to the bar as per usual, like a greyhound after a rabbit! And as we walked through the doors and across the coconut mat he left the biggest black oily footprints on the mat and carpet.

I was horrified and said to him, "Maurice, look at the mess you've made on the carpet." He looked behind, laughed and said, "Fuck 'em my mate, c'mon lets get a beer, I'm gagging."

A few nights later we went back in but I made sure he cleaned his boots first. We were met at the door by an old gentleman in a traditional commissioner's uniform. You could see that someone had been trying to clean the footprints off the floor but they were still evident.

Maurice looked at the carpet and said to him, "Bah! There's some mucky bastards about my mate," then trudged to the bar and sprawled all over it telling yet another barmaid how much he deserved this pint having had another grueller! He'd then get on the phone to the office and say, "Resume for the day my mate," and give a blow by blow account of what he'd done for the day.

THE POETIC HOOLIGAN

Maurice always had a story to tell the barmaids, usually a bag of lies to wind them up. One of his aliases that he used when chatting to a barmaid was Mauriatti Cogginnini, which was a name I gave him after we'd had some business cards printed and his had an extra 'ini' at the end of his name. He'd say, "You may have guessed I am related to the underworld. You know it's not just a coincidence that I have these rugged good looks. I am actually related to the Mafia but it's something I don't like to talk about, if I do I'll have to kill you."

He'd then say, "I've got nerves of steel me, you know, nerves of steel," showing you one hand, steady in front of him, then lifting his other hand that was shaking like a leaf and add, "Unfortunately this is my drinking hand."

However, his nerves of steel failed him one day whilst he was laid under a big truck, carrying out a repair at Initial Metals. Somebody turned over a twenty-foot steel container with another forklift next to where Maurice was working without giving him a warning. There was an almighty bang and a massive cloud of dust, like what you see when a building is demolished, which rolled under the truck where Maurice was laid.

You can imagine the shock he felt as he came scurrying from under the truck screaming, "You stupid bastards!" with his face black with dust and just the whites of his eyes showing with another cut and a bump on his head from when he jumped up in fright!

Another time he was left battered and dusted was when we rented a workshop from John Blythe at Lord and Midgley's scrapyard. Our then partner Tony Fairburn had pulled into the entrance of the yard and couldn't get through as a wagon was parked in the way. So in a temper he slammed it in reverse, looked in his mirror and reversed at speed. He then heard someone shouting so slammed his brakes on and looked in his mirrors again. He waited a few seconds but didn't see anything so set off again. Someone came running out of the office alongside him waving their arms and telling him to stop and pointing at the back of his van. He got out and rushed to the back of the van to find Maurice laid on the floor groaning.

It transpired that Maurice had ran out of the office and behind the van as Tony had first pulled up. Then as Tony set off, the first shout was from Maurice, which stopped Tony. But then when he hadn't heard or seen anything he set off again and hit Maurice a second time just as he was getting to his feet. What made it funnier was the 'Tom and Jerry' type dirty imprint of Maurice on the back doors of the van.

Two lads who used to work with Maurice and I at Barek Lift trucks were Rob and Karl who now own R and K Motors on Hedon Road. They told me a story about Mo which beggers belief to anyone with any amount of common sense. As I said earlier, every job that Maurice did had to be done yesterday, even if it wasn't urgent. On this occasion Karl and Mo had removed a six cylinder 2700 series Ford Diesel engine from a Henley 26/48 lift truck and were about to lift it back in. But unbeknown to Karl, Maurice had suspended the engine with one-inch straps and aluminium locking mechanisms, basically luggage straps, which have no lift bearing capacity at all. They were later to be known by everyone as the lifting cottons instead of straps! Karl had already climbed into the engine bay and sat down, legs akimbo, not realising Maurice was lifting the engine overhead. As the engine was directly above, the straps snapped, plummeting the engine approximately six-feet, miraculously landing in between Karl's legs without giving him a scratch and only causing a slight bit of damage to the engine.

THE POETIC HOOLIGAN

I was always very wary working alongside Maurice, as there was always an accident waiting to happen either to him or somebody else. This was the case whilst working in the yard on Alexandra Dock, which always reminds me of a scene from the film Roxanne with Steve Martin when the fireman hilariously sets fire to himself. Maurice was using a nine-inch angle grinder and again breaking all health and safety regulations by letting the shower of sparks hit him on his right hip area. As usual with Maurice, his overalls were thick oil and grease making them highly flammable, and the inevitable soon happened and one of the lads shouted, "Maurice, you're on fire!"

Everyone in the yard heard this and started shouting at him but he could not hear anyone due to the noise from the grinder. We could see the flames getting bigger and bigger but he still didn't notice them until he stopped grinding.

When he heard us all shouting, he turned to us and shouted, "You what my mate, what's up?"

By then the flames were lapping up at his chest. Before he realised, a couple of lads had ran across the yard and helped to douse the flames whilst the rest of us creased up with laughter.

Only Mo could barbecue himself and not know. When we went over to him the full right-hand side of his overalls from his hip to his armpit was gone and had even burned through his body warmer, which was under his overalls. However, he carried on wearing that body warmer for God knows how long after the event!

We went one further than his self-inflicted barbecue by putting him on top of a fire at Marlon's bonfire party. Fortunately for Mo it was an effigy of him, consisting of a pair of overalls stuffed with newspapers, complete with his trademark woolly hat and boots, and finished off with a pair of gloves minus the two fingers he'd lost in the accident.

He was never allowed to forget that incident and was constantly reminded wherever he went. And so that he never forgot, Tony and I went to a joke shop and bought some imitation severed fingers and made a wooden frame and mounted them inside it with the date and a few words to explain what had happened.

We finished it off with a glass front to make it look like a proper display case and mounted it on the workshop wall for all to see.

The strange thing about that accident was that after a while his fingers grew back completely including his nails. And we said it proved what I always thought - he was an alien!

I was having a 'Men Behaving Badly,' type conversation with Mo one day somewhere between how pert Kylie's bum was and how he would rather have a hot dinner than his leg over, when the subject somehow got onto razor blades and how often you change them. My answer was about once a month on my Gillette M3. Maurice being the greedy git he was said, "Nah, that's throwing money away my mate. I wait till it's ripping my skin off before I change mine." He would have used a cut-throat razor to save money if he hadn't been so clumsy and would have cut his own throat.

The company, Thermos, must have made more money out of Maurice than anyone. He would either drop his flask or more often crush it behind the seat of his little Escort van. I had seen him crush two in one day behind his seat. He would open the door and slide the seat forward, sit down, then slide it back and crush the flask. I said one day as he put yet another brand new one behind his seat, "Be careful Mo, slide it back slowly."

"Ok my mate, I will," he replied.

Then wham, bang, crash, another new flask

knackered! He even damaged a stainless steel one, the same type as the one I had used most days for the last twenty-three years. I suggested he fix a stop on the rail so he couldn't slide the seat back and he said, "I will my mate, when I get time."

Maurice being tighter than a duck's arse got great pleasure from begging a ciggie off someone. His trick was to carry two packs of ten cigarettes, one in each of the top pockets of his overalls. One pack that no-one ever got to see was full and the other always had just one in. He would get the nearly empty pack out wherever he went and plead poverty, "Giz a fag my mate, I've only got one left." Then he'd wink and give me that cheeky grin as he turned to walk out with his little prize, it really made his day!

I constantly bollocked him about the state of his van. Every time I got in it he'd say, "It's an anti theft device my mate, no one will ever want to pinch this when they see inside." and that's exactly what happened one night when someone broke into his little grey van. The scumbags broke in the front and must have had second thoughts about sitting in it but then broke into the back and stole his toolbox and ran off down the street with it. But when they got under a street light a hundred yards away they must have seen all the oil and grease on themselves, so then dropped it and did a runner. Whilst working at Barek Lift Trucks with Maurice in 1990, Rob Adams, Karl and me used to have a competition to see who could make Maurice whistle the most tunes by starting to whistle or sing a song, knowing that he would join in and whistle along to it.

Barek was a great place to work in the early 90s, you were always guaranteed a laugh usually at Mo's expense. Saturday mornings were an experience after everyone had been on the beer on a Friday night. Mauriati always went over the top and how he never got done for drink driving, I'll never know. If you asked him how he was feeling you'd get the answer, "Rough as a bear's arse, my mate, got a mouth like an Arab's armpit, arrgh!" Then with a shake of his head and his tongue flicking from one side of his mouth to the other he would make an awful noise like something from the Exorcist, which we would imitate by saying, "Laddle ladle, devil fuck the beer."

He had a way with words and some unusual quotes that could turn a quite normal question into a 'Mauriatti Esq. saying' that would never cease to amaze you and have the room erupting with laughter. For example, if we were ever faced with a challenging job we'd say to him, "This is going to be a bastard of a job Mo." He would reply with his version of 'a faint heart never won a fair maid' by saying, "We'll be alright my mate, a faint heart never fucked a pig!" Where did he get it from?

Another time whilst working at Barek Karl had read in the Hull Mail under the 'Personal Ads' that a gay man had listed one of his hobbies as being a pigeon fancier and thought it would be a laugh to reply using Mo's name and address. The two things about that which have often made me laugh are, what was Karl doing looking in the 'men seeking men' column, - and the look on Maurice's face if he'd had a reply!

Another character that I will always remember was Graham (Welly) Beadham who I first worked with at Westies. Graham was known as Welly because he never took his wellies and wooly hat off, even in mid-summer with his overalls tucked into his wellies. He was one of the quirkiest people you'd ever meet. He was known as the mad inventor, and also for his storytelling, most of which he actually believed were true.

A few of us including Dave and Andy went round to his house one night for a few beers. Graham was married to Jeanie at the time who put a few sandwiches on. We sat in the living room while Jeanie was in the kitchen. Graham told us of the days they lived in South Africa, which was true and he put a video on of a lion killing a Springbok, which was superb and obviously professionally made.

He then looked over his shoulder to see where Jeanie was and then said, "I took that video from up a tree at the bottom of our garden. I waited three days for that shot from a hide I'd built in the tree."

At that point Jeanie shouted from the kitchen, "Graham! You lying bastard!"

The three of us fell about laughing. Graham was a clever man who could make all sorts of things like an electric welder out of an old forklift battery charger. One of his less conventional inventions was a cannon he made from a piece of steel tube that he welded to a steel plate at a 45-degree angle like a rocket launcher. He rammed a rag half way down it and put a handful of nuts and bolts in the top. He then drilled a hole at the bottom and filled it with oxy/acetylene and ignited it when some crows came down for some bread, blowing them out of the sky.

Wilky used to play hell with him for some of the rough handed things he did like the day he was stripping an engine that had wet liners, which are what the pistons slide up and down. We had a special tool that went over the end of the liner to be drawn out, but Graham thought he could do it quicker by using a hydraulic road breaker to knock them out, just as Wilky walked into the workshop, earning himself a right bollocking.

I left Westies and got a job with an oil rig company Aaronite, who were fire proofing specialists that sprayed the legs of the rig with a fireproofing cement and stopped them from buckling in case of a fire.

I only did two trips up to Middlesborough partly

because of me being young, but mainly due to some of the bastards I worked with. They were all a lot older than me and were bullies who thought it was funny to constantly wind you up by playing tricks. These included putting fibre glass down the back of your overalls or putting plastic bags in the cement mix, or when we went back to the digs they'd piss in your rigger boots, or when you went to bed, there would be a leg off your bed. The last of these tricks was the last straw and I grabbed hold of two of them and threatened them and said if anything else happened I'd batter them. But the next morning they had told the others who then threatened me that if I hit these two I'd have all of them to deal with.

I never returned and passed the job onto Graham and even though he was in his thirties and a bit more streetwise than I was they did the same to him. One of the things they did was to set fire to his socks whilst he slept. He did however stick it out and ended up working all over the world, which ultimately cost him his marriage. I heard that Graham did make a very clever invention that saved the company a fortune by making some kind of a timer mechanism on a machine. He sadly died recently whilst working in Dubai.

CHAPTER 25
A GOOD CATCH

One hot summer's day a few of us decided to go fishing off Flamborough Head near Scarborough.

We set sail from a small, beached cove called Danes Dyke, in a little twelve-foot boat with a seven horsepower engine that plodded away like a tiny sewing machine. The crew were John (Crewie) Glen, Alan and Mike.

The sea was a bit rough with heavy waves breaking on the beach which made it hard to launch, so three of us sat on board to steady it down a bit, as the other two pushed it into the waves and jumped in. As we did one of us pulled the petrol pipe off the engine, which we quickly popped back on before sailing out into the white riders.

We only got a few hundred yards out when the engine cut out and we couldn't get it started again. As we tried in vain, all the time we were getting washed closer and closer to the three hundred-foot sheer rock face of Flamborough Head. We had run out of beach and were about fifty feet from the cliff face and about a hundred yards from being washed around the point of the head where we would have been smashed against the cliffs. I used my boat rod to see how deep the water was and found it was only about five-foot deep. A few of us jumped over the side and faced the nose of the boat onto the waves and started walking back towards the beach. But as we did Crewie slipped and went under the water, and as he did he banged his head on the side of the boat, knocking himself out. We lost sight of him for a few seconds but then I saw him floating on the bottom and pulled him out unceremoniously by his hair and threw him on board. We finally got back to the beach by which time he'd gained consciousness. We got the engine started and set off again for a good day's fishing.

After about eight hours fishing on a red hot day and only catching mackerel we decided to set off back in but with it being so hot we thought we'd stop off for a beer in Bridlington harbour. We picked our spot to moor up under the walkway where the fish and chip bars and ice cream parlours are and tied off and went for a well deserved beer with everything shipshape and Bristol fashion. However the one beer became a few as the hours ticked by and we eventually returned to find the tide had gone out and left our little coggy boat trapped under two twenty-footers.

Bearing in mind it was a hot day, the harbour was packed with people directly above where the pedestrian walkway goes over the Gypsey race. As the tide had gone out the two boats on either side had folded on top of ours. All the boats along the harbour wall were sat on a mud flat with the water about fifty-foot away. Four of us had wader boots on but Glen had shoes on so we climbed down the steel ladders and told him to go to the end of the pier to wait for us and then climb down the ladders onto the boat. We got down to the boat and positioned ourselves so our backs were against the hull of one of the boats. By then the day trippers above had started to gather and to look at what we were doing, but luckily there were no video cameras or mobile phones as this was the late eighties. As we all pushed, the boat slowly went over the point of the keel and landed with some force on the other side, splashing the sloppy mud all over the boat moored next to it and causing some laughter above. Next we repeated the process on the other boat with the same effect, creating more laughter. We then had the small matter of getting our boat down to the small stream of water that runs through the harbour at low tide known as the Gypsey race, which I think is the feed from Barmston drain. We started to push our boat towards the stream, but as you can imagine it was well embedded in the mud. After several attempts it started moving and then as we gave another big push it took off as the air got under it and it aquaplaned. Mike didn't manage to balance himself and ended up face down in the mud with everyone above and all of us in tears of laughter. He looked like Al Jolson as he stood up and waved to the crowd.

We got her down to the stream and started the engine, then we sailed her to the end of the harbour where Glen was waiting for us. As we waited at the bottom of the ladders Glen set off down just as the Yorkshire Bell pleasure cruiser rounded the pier blowing its horn and with the captain waving his hands and telling us to get out the way, which we did rather promptly. But poor Glen nearly got smeared up the side of the quay as he scampered back up the ladder to safety. We came back for Glen and set off back to Danes Dyke, arriving home at about eleven at night and being in trouble for not letting our wives know what time we'd be home.

Another time Mike and I went on a fishing trip up to Whitby in my Triumph Stag, pulling a little old boat we'd just got. It was twelve feet long and had a little seven and a half horsepower Honda engine in it. When we got there the sea was really rough, so much so that even the local fishermen weren't going out. We decided to take our chances and set off out, receiving abuse from the fishermen for doing so. The waves were so big that they were completely submerging the pier. Our thinking was that if we got far enough out to sea, it would be

Me with Stag and boat.

A good catch.

THE POETIC HOOLIGAN

calmer. But it wasn't. It was mountainous!

One minute you were looking up a mountain of water to the sky. The next you were looking down into a valley of water and hanging onto your seat, almost vertical, like being on a ride at Alton Towers, thinking you were going to be tipped over. Luckily we came out okay but never caught a fish.

It's a wonder we're still alive when I look back on some of the crazy things we did when we were younger. Like going eight or ten miles into the commercial traffic lanes of main shipping and being so engrossed in our fishing that we'd suddenly hear a horn blowing and turn round to see a great big tanker steaming towards us.

One of the funniest days we ever had fishing was when we went out with a friend of Mike's who had just bought himself a twenty-one foot Shetland with two eighty horsepower Johnsons on it. At least I think they were eighty. They may have been smaller but whatever they were, it was still unbelievably fast. We set off from Whitby and had a good day's fishing and again like the Bridlington episode we were left high and dry. Well not so high this time as when we came to moor up next to the pedestrian walkway we set off from, we were about six feet away and could not find anywhere closer to moor up. But again there was a mud flat between us and terafirma which wasn't a problem for the three of us men, but the boat owners wife who looked like Olive from 'On The Buses, was panicking. We assured her that it was okay to jump, which each of us did with ease. She finally plucked up courage and leapt for the walkway, but failed miserably landing face down in the sloppy mud. When she stood up and took her glasses off me and Mike nearly collapsed with laughter as her husband tried to console her as she stood there crying, which made it even funnier.

RICHARD HALDENBY

We were invited to Donnington Moto GP a few years ago by Mike who had the contract for site maintenance to cover the weekend in case of flooding etc. My son Jonathan and I got there on the Saturday lunch on a hot summer's day with Andy and his son Jamie who I'd just sold my business to. Mike and his lads had been there since the Friday and were all set up in a newish looking warehouse that incorporated offices, which were to be our bedrooms for the night as we'd took our sleeping bags. These weekends often resulted in a lot of sitting around and tinkering about, on this occasion though Mike had kindly supplied lots of T-bone steaks and a pile of BBQ meats from a local farmer, along with copious amounts of alcohol.

We started off nice and steady having a few beers in the sun but as the sun got hotter we blew the froth off a few more beers resulting in a full-blown piss up. The steaks were on the BBQ and by teatime I'd had about half a dozen beers and a bottle of red wine that no one wanted. When we finished our tea we drove to the onsite pub where we didn't have to venture onto the public roads and carried on drinking until midnight. Then we set off back to the warehouse, which was only a few minutes away in our cars and vans. I'd jumped into the back of a van and our Jonathan went back in one of the cars. I arrived back before him, but after five minutes I became worried about his whereabouts and decided to go looking for him on one of Mike's little twist and go motorbikes that he used for bombing around the site.

As I was about to set off Mike said, "Be careful when you get to the end of the concrete road and it meets with a gravel track as it is dangerous."

"I'll be alright," I arrogantly replied as I set off in a short sleeved T-shirt and no helmet. But as they say, 'When drinks in, wit's out.'

THE POETIC HOOLIGAN

I set off at full throttle, which was surprisingly nippy for a little bike and came a cropper at the spot he had warned me of. To come off any bike at thirty miles an hour with no protective clothing is probably equivalent to coming off at sixty with your leathers on. The next thing I remember was waking up the next morning with a terrible hangover lying on an office desk with Jonathan on another desk looking at me a bit strangely. We both went down stairs into the kitchen area where everyone was having breakfast. As we walked in they were all wincing and taking the piss out of my Evel Knievel impersonation. I did not know what they were talking about until I saw a pile of blooded paper towelling and asked, "What happened there?"

They replied, "Can't you remember? Look in the mirror."

I got the shock of my life when I did and I saw the full right-hand side of my face was skinned, grazed and cut from above my right eyebrow or what was left of it. My right cheek had a one and a half-inch gash to the bone. My nose had two slits in it. My top lip had three holes right the way through the size of peas where pieces of gravel had gone straight through and stuck in my gum. The rest of the right side of my face was one mass of bare flesh and small pieces of gravel which kept me busy for the next few days picking them out with tweezers, along with those in my knuckles, forearms and hip.

I still have no recollection of the accident but was told how lucky I was not to have broken my neck as they found me unconscious lying partly under a parked car with my head next to one of the tyres. Andy said how much of a wuss I was, squealing like a pig as they pulled the gravel out of my gums with tweezers and cleaned off the bits of grit from my face and cuts with baby wipes and swarfega cloths.

RICHARD HALDENBY

I didn't go to hospital as I usually do home repairs of cuts and breaks with my homemade butterfly stitches. However, I often think I should have done as I get sharp stabbing pains in my lip where I think I must still have a piece of grit imbedded. The rugged scar on my cheek is a stark reminder, which makes me see sense at times of attempting something foolish again whilst under the influence.

The next day as we walked around the track watching the races, people would look at my injuries and Andy would make out that I was one of the riders who had dropped a bike when training and got gravel rash. Andy said that my biggest concern on the night of the accident was my new shirt that Jackie had just bought me had been ripped and torn and I was worried that she'd be upset that I'd ruined it. But he just said, "I don't think she'll worry much about the shirt when she sees the state of your face."

Fishing and shooting were always a big part of my life when I was younger, unlike now, I can't kill anything. I used to spend a lot of time going out early morning fishing on a weekend or late at night rabbiting and then bring them home to clean them on the draining board. My lovely Grandad showed me a lot of my 'life skills' including how to fillet a fish and gut a rabbit.

I spent a lot of my twenties with one of my best mates from school, Terry, getting into some right scrapes when we worked on the doors of Concorde Club on Orchard Park as bouncers. Every night was manic as we regularly had to sort out five or six fights. One night in particular was a bit rough when a fight broke out on the dance floor and we went in to sort it. We never went in fists flying and always separated them and gave them a warning, which usually worked, as most of the lads knew each other. On this night though a gang of strangers came in looking for trouble and kicked off on the dance floor. As usual we stepped in and separated them but as I was dealing with one lad I saw a punch coming from the side but couldn't do anything to avoid it. The last thing I remember was being laid on the floor with the sole of a boot coming down on my face. The next thing I knew was being stood at the bar with Terry's brother Joe as they carried three blokes out with their faces smashed up.

I said to him, "Fuck me Joe, what happened to them?"

He looked at me strangely and replied, "You're joking aren't you? You did it."

Apparently as I was laid on the floor and this lad's boot was coming down, I got hold of the boot and upended him, then nutted him and his two mates about ten times each in the face before following them down to the floor still nutting them.

He said, "I've never seen anybody move so fast."

It actually frightened me to think I could do something like that and have no recollection of it.

For a lot of years now if I'm faced with trouble I try and talk my way out of it or smile and walk away. I've brought my son up to be the opposite to how I was, and even though he's a big lad and could look after himself if he had to, he never puts himself into those situations. We used to work in Concorde on a Friday and Saturday night but if ever we didn't work a Saturday we would go fishing early on Sunday morning.

We went off Holmpton one night and were 'fishing the tide up' for three hours and then down for three hours. On this occasion it was a cold winter's night and we were fishing and talking away, concentrating on watching the end of our rods. Without realising it though, we had been backing up onto a sand bank and as we picked up our gear to move back up the beach a bit more, we noticed the tide had come in further along the beach and filled a large hollow behind us. We started to wade through the water with our wader boots on but within no time at all the water was rising very quickly and was up to our chests. We had to abandon our gear and swim for our lives.

Another good night's fishing started by going out with Terry to dig some lug worms and then fish the tide up and down again at Spurn Point, which is at the mouth of the River Humber. I had told Jackie I'd be home in the early hours of the morning before she woke. We started fishing after tea on the sea side of the Spurn peninsula, but the wind was blowing a strong Northeast, which made it impossible to fish. We decided to fish the Humber side of Spurn that was very calm, so much so that we stood up to our knees with our lines reeled right in and dangling the bait in the water at rod length. Terry got the first bite, a three-pound cod, then another, then another. I couldn't believe it! This carried on until it was five-nil to him and the tide had gone out. By this time it was the early hours and we decided to move down to the tip of Spurn Point to 'fish the tide up' as the wind had dropped. As soon as we cast in I got a bite and pulled in a beautiful silver blue codling, a pound in weight. I cast in again and instantly caught another. This went on for the next hour or so until I had caught sixteen codling all exactly the same and Terry didn't catch one. This proved to me that the old fisherman's tale, 'once a fish has nibbled your hook they leave a scent for the others' couldn't be far from the truth.

When we got home we got yet another fisherman's wife's bollocking for not letting them know that we'd be late, as they were just about to ring the Police thinking we'd drowned.

CHAPTER 26
GOODBYE
MR CHIPS

In 1986 I decided to restart with pigeons having got rid of them ten years earlier when I got married. I spent some time looking into who had the best pigeons as I wanted to do it properly and hit the ground running. I read all the pigeon magazines and was undecided who to buy from. Then I spoke to my Mam who told me about a big loft that our life-long family friend, Freddie Billham, had built. He was the brother of Lucy, who had been my Mam's best friend from being very young.

I rang Freddie and got the number of Eddie Wright and Norman Barrett who had just gone into business together as Fountainhead Lofts in 1985, after meeting ten years earlier whilst racing in the Hornsea Racing Pigeon Club.

Fountainhead Racing Pigeon Stud became arguably the world's top breeding and racing stud with the belief that a good apple never falls far from the tree and only selling birds that were direct children or grandchildren of the champion racers. They were so confident in their policy that they introduced a replacement guarantee that if matched pairs were not successful they would replace one or both of the birds. The highlight of this venture was to breed and race Virgo which won the N.F.C. young bird national in 1986.

When I first went to meet Eddie and Norman at Balkholme near Howden I was instantly won over by their complete honesty in how the breeding programme was conducted and by the healthy and open environment that was provided for the birds.

RICHARD HALDENBY

I immediately took to 'Steady' with his infectious enthusiasm. Nothing was too much bother as he showed me around the aviaries and what impressed me most was how the breeding programme was logged for all to see. You could pick a bird of your choice from the aviary and look up the ring number in the main breeding book, which told you the strain and pair number.

They had thirteen families of birds and each one had their own run with outside access to large aviaries. Each pair had a list of ring numbers of youngsters they'd bred with colours and aviary numbers so when you wanted one from a particular pair you could easily select them. As I looked through the principle pairs one pigeon stood out like I'd never seen before. It was love at first sight when I saw De 16, the finest specimen I'd ever set eyes on. I ended up buying a son and daughter from him and a son of Blauwe Orleans and a daughter of Asduif Witpen. I spent £1,000 on them, which was a lot of money then.

The following year I bred from them and developed my own very successful family that took me to the top within a few years. When I finished racing and decided to withdraw from the sport ten years later due to business commitments, I gave my best four cocks to Eddie and Norman which were all long distance champions including Lionheart, Norsea, Richard and Jonathan. My claim to fame was when Eddie rang one day and said, "You'll never guess who has just rang and ordered one from Lionheart and Norsea?"

So I jokingly said, "Oh I don't know, the King of Dubai?"

He went quiet and then said, "Who told you?"

It transpired that it wasn't the King himself who had rang but his loft manager. But that was good enough for me.

In 1988 I went to work at Fountainhead and loved it,

particularly in the first year to eighteen months as I got to meet lots of visitors who came from all over the world. I would show them around the lofts and do the away day sales with Eddie, Danny or Gary Rush. We would select sixty birds from the aviaries, a selection of young birds and mature matched pairs of each family. We would set off on a Friday afternoon and travel all over the country and set up our pens in a clubhouse run by different pigeon clubs. I have conducted sales from as far afield as Edinburgh down to Poole in Dorset, and all over Wales and in Dublin. I even travelled with Norman to Belgium in his car to visit Internationally recognised fanciers and to watch them clock their birds in from the extreme distance races of over six to seven hundred miles. These fanciers were the ones we owned direct champions from.

When I first started I studied each of the champions' catalogues and their performances until I knew every pigeon's racing history along with its ring number.

Coachloads of fanciers would come on a weekend from all over the country and I would show them round. They would point at a pigeon and ask what it was called and I would tell them and reel off its performances and ring number while they looked in the brochure of that family along with its mate and children saying, "He's right."

It became a novelty, and people would write into the magazines that they'd been to Fountainhead and couldn't believe that I knew all the details. But unfortunately the more successful I got in the advertising side of the business, the more office based my job became. And eventually, just sitting at a desk all day writing adverts and letters started to drive me mad…

There are not many days go by that I don't still think

275

about Eddie. Like most of our friends that we lose it's hard to accept that they are no longer with us, especially a larger than life character like Eddie. There are still times I automatically think I shall just ring 'Edwardo', especially on a Saturday when the football is on, then immediately realise that I can't.

Eddie was born in Hornsea, a small village on the east-coast near Bridlington. He was a very good footballer in his younger days, known as Chopper Wright, although he was a striker. If I remember rightly he held the record for the most goals scored in the season and had the trophy proudly on display to prove it. He went on to become a pig farmer and had his own farm near Hornsea for a number of years.

Eddie was football mad especially as a Manchester United supporter. We both used to go watch United regularly where he would often get into arguments with people standing up in front of him. He would dig them in the back and tell them to sit down.

He was never afraid to voice his opinion which some people did not like but with Eddie you got what you saw and he said what he thought, like it or not and usually with a few expletives thrown in.

The one thing he lacked was etiquette, he thought that was a place in France!

Everyone who knew him was aware of his love of chips. No matter where we ate he always demanded a large portion!

I remember one year going to the N.E.C. Show and stopping over in a big flash hotel, The Metropol, which had a fantastic restaurant but it was only good for Steady Eddie if they served lashings of his beloved chips. On this occasion we all sat down with our wives and ordered our meals and Eddie asked for a few baskets of chips to keep us going until our meals arrived.

THE POETIC HOOLIGAN

The waiter replied in his best brummie accent, "Sorry sir, we don't do chips," much to Eddie's horror and a massive argument broke out between him and the waiter. With that Eddie said "Come on, we're off," and we had to go to another restaurant which did serve chips.

Another time we were doing The Blackpool Show and stayed at the top hotel in Lytham St Annes, which was like a stately home. When we returned back to the hotel after a long day at the stands we sat down in the restaurant and ordered our meal. The clientele spoke with a plum in their mouths but they soon received a culture shock when our al-a-carte food was served, which was very attractive with little squiggles of decorations etc. but not very filling.

Again the starter was accepted by Eddie with not much fuss but when the main course was delivered it was not much bigger than the starter and he shouted, "Oy mush! what's the idea of serving up two (bleep) starters? We want summat proper to eat."

The waiter said, "Sorry sir, that is the main course, it is a la carte."

Eddie said, "Sorry? You want to be sorry, and you know what you can do with your 'cart', get me some chips." But as before the waiter replied, "I'm sorry sir we don't serve chips."

Eddie said, "You'd better get some (bleep) chips or you won't be getting paid." And considering there were about twelve of us the waiters soon arrived with some big plates of chips.

Outwardly Eddie was always laughing and happy with everyone and was a source of inspiration and ready with some advice when you had a problem. Even though he had his own demons you could always ring and ask, "Are you alright Edwardo?" to which he would always laugh and say, "Aye" in that distinctive country voice, which still makes me smile when I think of him.

He was ever the joker and would often wind someone up with one of his tricks like the time a joiner from Hornsea, Bernard Clark, was working at the lofts.

Bernard was about to go home one Friday night, but as usual, before he left, he told us how he'd clean his van out on the Saturday morning.

On this particular Friday night however Eddie had caught a wild cat in a humane trap. He told Danny and I to put it in a bag and place it in the back of Bernard's van, knowing that on Saturday morning he would open the back of his van and look in the bag and get the shock of his life when the cat jumped out. Unfortunately though the plan slightly backfired with near dire consequences.

After work, Bernard drove home in his little Astra van with the back of the seats boarded out apart from a square hole cut out for lengths of wood to pop through.

As he drove through the open countryside in the dark he could hear a rustling noise coming from the back of the van but he could not make out what it was. Then as he went down a dark country lane a car came towards him with its headlights on. With that, the cat, which had clawed its way out of the bag, jumped through the hole and onto his dashboard. He screamed and swerved in panic narrowly missing the oncoming car, which went off the road and onto the grass verge. He ran over to the car to find a woman and kids screaming and crying.

The woman shouted, "What the hell were you doing?"

He explained that a cat had jumped onto the dashboard and made him swerve.

She asked, "How could a cat just appear on your dashboard?"

They walked back to his van and opened the door and the cat leapt out and over his shoulder onto the woman, sending her into another screaming fit!

When Bernard came into work on the Monday morning he chased Danny Murray and me with a hammer threatening to kill us, whilst we ran away in tears of laughter!

Another one of Eddie's wind-ups led to Danny Murray leaving a hotel in Blackpool in the early hours of the morning with no trousers or boots. This happened after a crowd of us had been out after the show and ended up drinking in a large hotel. When it was time to go we could not wake Danny, so Eddie said with a cheeky grin, " Whip his kegs off that'll wake him."

So I carefully took off his boots expecting him to wake up and crack me round the ear but he still didn't. I then proceeded to remove his pants, again expecting a clip but still he remained fast asleep. So I gave the boots and pants to one of the lads we knew who was staying in another hotel and told him to bring them to the stand the next morning.

When we finally woke up Danny he looked down and asked where his gear was. He then had to endure the embarrassment of standing in a taxi queue in just his suit jacket, boxers and socks at 5am on a cold January morning. And then he had to travel to the show the next day with no boots until his gear was delivered.

Alan Bridges, who had become a very close friend of Eddie after buying some pigeons from him, told me another story about him.

He said that whilst over in Germany at the Kassel Show they met up with Peter Hall of Petron Lofts and as was customary after a show a few of them went out for a drink on the night. Whether it was the strong German beer or the travelling that got to him they don't know but Peter ended up in bed feeling the worse for wear. Eddie and Alan stayed out for a few more beers, Eddie being the beer monster he was, always last to

RICHARD HALDENBY

Stripogramme - We wish you a Happy Birthday Dick

finish. On the way back to the hotel they saw a 6ft plastic penguin advertising something, and Eddie being Eddie, the oldest teenager in town and the bird lover that he was, thought it would be a good idea to give the bird a bed for the night.

You can imagine Peter's face when he woke in the morning with a 6ft penguin beside him and receiving flack from Eddie and Alan that it was the only bird that he was likely to pull.

Another set up that Eddie arranged was on my birthday when he, Norman, Danny, Christine and Vanessa came for a drink with me in the Rose and Crown near Howden. We were stood at the bar which was empty apart from us when I heard the door open and turned to see a beautiful girl walk in wearing an all red outfit including a red shawl, short skirt, stockings and stilettos.

I turned to Eddie and said, "Bloody hell! Have you seen her!"

With that I felt a tap on my shoulder and turned to see the girl, now in just a basque and suspenders. She sat on my knee and read a poem that Christine and Vanessa had written that went along the lines of:

We wish you a Happy Birthday Dick,
And trust this bird will do the trick.
We know you study all types of bird,
Feathered or not or so we've heard.
You think you'd make a good stud cock,
Norman could retain you at stock.
We'd send the brochure across the nation,
To see Dick's outstanding confirmation.
But we couldn't make you wait till then,
So we organised this wonderhen.
Like a Jansen cock you're ever ready,
Up to racing speed, then hold it steady.

With Lisa and Jonathan and trophies won as top prize winner. 1993. Inc, Yorkshire middle route channel averages.

With Romain Legeist outside my loft.

THE POETIC HOOLIGAN

Your Damm Jackie thinks that you're the leader,
And certainly no racer breeder.
Always doing well at amalgamation,
And not too bad in the Federation.
So Happy Birthday from Norm and Ed,
Chris and Vanessa at Fountainhead.

In 1989 whilst working at Foutainhead I had a frightening and 'near death' experience as I sat in my office, which looked out across Norman's horse paddock. I felt the windows and room start to shake and vibrate like there was an earthquake. And as I sat thinking my days were up I saw a Chinook twin blade helicopter flying out of control about fifty yards away from my window. It was on an angle, with the rear blade actually hitting the ground and digging up grass sods, which were flying up and hitting my window.

I could see the pilot as plain as day. He was a young lad in his mid twenties looking straight at me, with his eyes nearly popping out of his head and with a look of fear that I will never forget. I pushed myself back in my chair as far as I could until I was up against the wall equally as fearful as he was. The few seconds it took from first seeing the helicopter to it disappearing over the roof seemed like an eternity. It came so close to the window at one point belly first that I thought it was going to take the roof off. I could see every rivet as it cleared the roof blowing several tiles off as it passed. The poor horses in the paddock were petrified and scattered all over.

A minute later Eddie came bursting into my office saying, "What the fuck was that?"

I was still frozen in my chair and told him what had happened as he was at the front of the house and never saw it but had felt the vibrations throughout the building. We went out onto the paddock to calm the horses down and realised how lucky we'd been when we saw the divots in the grass. Luckily we'd had a wet period and the ground was water logged. Another inch or so further down and the blades would have buckled. When I see a Chinook now I always wonder if that pilot remembers the look of shock on my face as I do his.

CHAPTER 27
A DREAM COME TRUE

In January 1990 I started the New Year at Barlow World based on Queen Elizabeth Dock, working continental shifts of three twelve -hour days on, then three days off. That was the best working hours I've ever done as if you wanted a week's holiday you only had to use three days to get nine off. It was here that I met my great friend Steve Wise who now lives in Melbourne. I was fortunately matched up with Steve, with George and Mike on the opposing shift.

We were given the old battery shed opposite 12 Shed that's now Titan Cement. The battery shed was where the electric forklifts were put on charge. When we walked in it was piled high with rubbish and we spent weeks cleaning it and fitting it out with steel conduit pipes all round the workshop and fitting in a compressor and oil tanks etc to make it a fully functioning workshop.

Steve had been a car mechanic and never worked on a diesel or even seen a forklift but was obviously a clever lad as he had been a foreman. I took him under my wing and taught him all I could. He picked it up quickly and yet nearly got sacked after a short while as people complained he was no good. I was called in to speak to the management who said they were thinking of letting him go and asked what I thought. I told them I thought he had a lot of potential and had a young family and if he went, so would I.

They kept him on and he became one of the top engineers in the company. He did get some stick from

Jimmy Shires though, but who didn't? Jim was a big, loud-mouthed docker who was always noisy and brash but really funny once you got to know him. The first time I met him he came bursting through the doors with his mate Trevor Deyes who is the dead opposite to him and who I still keep in touch with now.

He started shouting at me about a truck being broken down, to which I met fire with fire and shouted back, "Who do you think you're fucking shouting at? Talk to me like that again and you won't get it at all." He wound his neck in and we got on great after that. As I got to know him I realised it was just his way and he did it for the craic.

He used to come in and say to Steve, "I don't want you working on my truck, you're only good at making tea, get the fucking kettle on."

Then he would lace into Mick and say, "I don't want you working on my truck Salman Rushie," as Mick had dark skin and a tash, the same as Salman Rushdie who was in the news at the time.

He'd say, "You're just working here to keep out of the media." Sadly Jim died a few years ago and is sadly missed by everyone.

When it was our turn to work a weekend and me and Steve had been out clubbing the night before, we'd take turns at one of us getting there early to open up at seven and the other come in an hour later. Our hangovers used to kick in at different times, which was handy as I would be okay early doors and feel rough at lunch. So Steve would get laid out in the Transit van for a couple of hours in the morning, then come dinnertime as I started to wilt, Steve would take over and I'd get my head down.

We all had to go to the main depot at Leeds for a forklift driver training course. Even though I had driven forklifts all my working life George and Steve hadn't, so we all did our test under a gobby, arrogant instructor. At one point I was sat operating a truck with another truck next to me being driven by someone else when the instructor shouted something to me. I couldn't hear him and asked him to repeat himself, and he bawled something back to me. I saw red and shot across to him and warned him if he raised his voice at me again I'd knock him out.

He said, "For that you won't get a pass", which he had to give me although I got the lowest points of us all.

The rest of the lads took the piss, until a few weeks later when an A-frame lifting rig came all parcelled up in kit form. When one of them unloaded it off the wagon they had to get a twenty foot long load through a ten foot workshop door. They tried and tried while I stood and laughed. But they eventually had to ask me how to do it. I swung one end in first and then changed lock and swung the other end in and then got my revenge by taking the piss out of them.

Barlow's ordered a brand new fleet of Hyster trucks to be made in Holland, which were mainly H7s, these were a seven ton lifter and two specially designed RoRo 21 ton trucks with compact masts for going on the ferries. We were fortunate enough to go to Nijmegan in Holland for a week's training course at the Hyster plant. It was educational but also entertaining as we would go out on the night around Nijmegen and get pissed and then the next day we would be shown around the factory and see the trucks getting built and ask questions. Then in the afternoon we would sit in a classroom and do theory, which was okay until they put the slide films on and turned the lights off. I would go straight to sleep and have Wisey nudging me to keep me awake.

Nijmegen was next to the Bridge at Arnhem that was featured in the film a bridge too far, the true story of

RICHARD HALDENBY

Operation Market Garden, a failed attempt by the allied forces to secure several bridges to outflank the Germans. We visited the bridge and paused for a thought for all the soldiers who died there. We spent seven nights in Nijmegen and then made our way back to Schipol airport by train.

When we got to the airport and got on the taxi bus to our plane, we saw an old plane that looked like it was part of an historic air day, that was until we pulled alongside. It was a 1958 Viscount twin propeller job, we couldn't stop laughing, that was until we took off and crossed the North Sea with gale force side winds.

I don't exaggerate when I say there was masking tape around the windows to keep the draughts out and the hostess spoke into a large wire mesh type microphone. I say micro but it was anything but micro, it was huge. We flew so low that fishermen and oil rig workers were waving at us and as we looked out of the port hole windows you could see the plane fighting against the strong wind as it had the tail end being blown to put us in a crab movement. Mike had never flown before and had his head between his knees panicking. I tried to get him to look at the wing tips that were lifting up and down about twelve inches in a flapping motion like a bird. When we eventually landed at Humberside Airport we were queuing to get into the terminal when a girl next to me said, "That was terrifying. I've never had a flight like it."

A voice behind us said, "Neither have I, we too were worried." I turned and saw that it was the pilot.

I left Barlow's after two years when my son Jonathan had reached twelve months old and was absolutely wearing us out. We were often working sixteen-hour days in the back end of 1991, from seven in a morning until eleven at night by the time we'd done our paperwork. When I got home Jonathan would be awake playing, as he never slept. We'd go to bed and he would lay there gurgling away, although he never cried he just wore us out.

Jonathan was born on November 12th 1990 and was a dream come true. I'd always yearned for a son and carried a vision of a blonde haired, blue-eyed boy. We had Sarah and Lisa and Jackie had been on the pill for about twelve years and started feeling unwell. She went to the doctors and he said, "You need to come off the pill first," which she did.

This coincided with me just having started work at Barlow World and I had to work a month in hand and then a month in hand overtime, which meant my first full month's wages with overtime was due in March. We agreed that I would have 'the snip' or vasectomy being the correct terminology. However, it never went to plan as Jackie came off the pill at the beginning of January and we went to Blackpool three weeks later for the annual racing pigeon weekend for the Blackpool show with Fountainhead Lofts. I was still helping out Eddie and Norman with the show and the weekend was one massive piss up from the moment we got there on the Friday. Having had a good night we awoke on the Saturday morning and Jackie was saying how nice the night before had been. I couldn't remember making love as I'd been so drunk but I started to worry a little as Jackie was no longer on the pill.

But then I thought, no, it will be okay, you have to come off the pill months before you conceive. Yet three weeks later I came home from work and as I walked in I looked at Jackie and said, "You're pregnant!" to which she replied, "Don't be daft, I've only just come off the pill."

But there was something about her that was different…

RICHARD HALDENBY

When he was born we had no idea what sex the baby was going to be and yet as soon as he was born exactly on time it was like I'd known him all my life. He was completely blue as the umbilical cord was wrapped around his neck and was choking him. But he was quickly sorted out and was dry as though he'd been rubbed down with a towel. He had blonde hair and bum fluff around his face with big blue eyes as I'd always wished. Jackie was crying with joy too and said, "Rich, you've got the son you always wanted."

Prior to that I would often get upset if I saw a man playing with his young son and I was like a broody hen.

By this time I was offered a job at Barek Lift Trucks by Mike Leak as a service engineer with a view to becoming manager. One the customers I had been asked to go and try and win over was John Drury of JD Handling. Mike had wanted a chance to put things right by letting me go to service his trucks, as Maurice had done one of his 'bodge' jobs and upset John. The first time I ever went there Mike said to me, "Will you go and see this customer JD? He's very abrupt and hard to deal with, but whatever you do don't lose your rag and smack him one. He's a queer bastard but just keep calm."

I arrived on site full of anticipation as to how he was going to be. We exchanged pleasantries and he showed me which trucks needed servicing explaining they had been serviced a few months previously by Maurice but still had lots of problems. All the time I was thinking, don't start getting clever with me. I started the servicing and he left me alone but I could feel him watching my every move from his portacabin office up in the corner of his warehouse, which was based on Freightliner Road under the umbrella of MAT transport. I spent the full day there and serviced three trucks, which were all container spec trucks commonly known as 'stuffer'

THE POETIC HOOLIGAN

trucks. The one exception was his heavy lifter that he affectionately referred to as 'Bertha'. I filled in my service sheets and nervously walked up the steps into his office. As soon as I walked in the first thing that hit me was that the walls were adorned with page 3 girls and pictures of Lady Di and Kylie. There was also lots of aphorisms stating the obvious aimed at his employees, such as 'never assume', 'always double check!' and 'check twice, load once'. I stepped up to his desk and put the service sheets on it. He read through them carefully without saying a word and then asked about some recommended repairs I'd noted. He gave me a blank, emotionless look that many a good businessman has learnt to use, like a good poker player. He then picked the phone up and rang Mike Leak.

His first words were, "I thought you said this bloke was good?"

I started to boil up thinking, You bastard, you're going to get both barrels when you get off that phone.

After a response from Mike saying, "He is John, why what's the problem?" John said "He's not good, he's fucking brilliant. Don't send anybody but him again."

From that day on we've never had a crossed word which takes some doing with John as he falls out with people as soon as look at them if they let him down. His philosophy is he doesn't do anyone any wrong but if you let him down you're off his list. The only time we ever argue is about him supporting the wrong team in red. He's a Liverpool fan and I'm of course United.

I gave him a list of jobs that day which totalled £1,700.00, a lot of money in 1991. He gave me the go ahead to do the work but argued with Mike how so much had been missed by the previous fitters.

One day John was playing hell about the pigeons that were nesting in the overhang roof section on the front of his warehouse and shitting all over some export machinery. He complained that he had to clean all the machinery before it could be loaded into his wagons and said, "If I had a gun I'd shoot them."

So I offered to take my gun in from home and get rid of them for him, and the next day I appeared with my Weirach air rifle competition gun and set my sights up. I've always been a good shot but even by my standards I excelled that day. At the end of the overhang was a pair of pigeons nesting with two squeakers in the nest. Even though I love pigeons these were being a nuisance and if they'd been left they would have multiplied. The only angle I could see them in the nest was from about a hundred yards away, where there was a two-inch gap and I could see a head bobbing from side to side every two seconds. I lined up my sights and kept counting two seconds, then fired as the head appeared.

John laughed and said, "You've missed!"

I said, "I never, just wait." And a few seconds later it fell out of the nest with a hole through its head. I did the same with the second one and then with the parents. Four shots. Four hits.

One of John's employees was an ex-docker called Jack, a typical docker who'd seen and done it all. Nothing seemed to faze him and he never showed any emotion, so you never knew if he was happy or sad, but you couldn't help but like him. He was the type of grandad anyone would be proud of, made in the same mould as my own father-in-law, John Precious, who was an ex-North Sea fisherman and took everything life could throw at him and still soldiered on without complaining.

Some of the things Jack would say to JD were always without a smile, like the night they were finishing off loading a trailer late on a cold wet Friday night. They were just lacing up a tilt trailer, ie: running the security cord through the brackets that secure the curtain-sider, when Jack asked JD, "What time is it boss?"

JD replied, "About ten o'clock."

A few minutes went by and Jack asked, "Have we got any more trailers coming in boss?"

JD replied, "No, why?"

Jack said, "I've got to be back in Withernsea soon to turn the lighthouse on," then carried on without cracking a smile as JD nearly fell off the forklift laughing.

Another time they were loading a trailer when JD answered the phone and shouted, "Jack, it's your lass for you."

Jack walked into his office and said, "It'll be about the car, it's in the newspaper for sale." He stood in the office and kept saying to his wife, "Yep, yep, yep, okay then, see you later," and put the phone down and turned around to walk out saying, "Thanks boss."

JD asked, "Well, did she sell it?"

"No," he replied, "They nicked it." And then explained that someone came to look at it and his wife let them have the keys to test drive it and they never came back.

JD said, "You must be fuming Jack?"

He just replied, "Nah, what do you expect? That's the story of my life."

JD could always rely on Jack to be there and never let him down. However he was prone to the odd lack in concentration and would sometimes load a pallet onto a wrong trailer, resulting in the pallet being delivered to the wrong side of Europe and then costing JD to have it retrieved and sent to the correct address.

When Jack decided to hang up his keys and take early retirement, they were sadly working the last day and ultimately loading the last pallet on the last trailer.

JD said, "Jack, you can have the honour of loading the last pallet and when you're halfway up the loading ramp, stop and I'll take your photograph," which he did.

When JD got the photos developed he took a copy round to Jack and said, "There you go Jack, you can put it on your mantelpiece."

Jack looked at it and again without a smile said, "Was it the right pallet boss?"

CHAPTER 28

I'D BE
A MILLIONAIRE

When I started the business with Maurice on November 18th 1991, one of our biggest customers was Global Shipping based at 6 Shed on Alexandra Dock. I was introduced to the manager Peter Ward, a surprisingly very young man in his early twenties, by a friend of mine Glynn, who was a tyre-fitter for Industrial Tyres. I think Peter was about twenty-one at the time but a very clever lad and well ahead of his years. We are still good friends now and he's never changed. Most companies I have worked for or been associated with tend to reflect the man at the top down to the lads on the workshop floor. Companies with a bad man at the top always have a big turnover of men with a dog eat dog attitude. I have worked for a company like that with men who'd stab you in the back as soon as look at you. One in particular had a bloke nicknamed by everyone as 'Toenails', as that was the only thing you could see of him as he was that far up the gaffer's arse. I called him 'Kipper' because he was two-faced and had no guts.

Global's men were mostly lifers and proper men who were raised when men were men and women were grateful. It was always a pleasure going to Global and I soon became part of the team even though I didn't work for them I spent so much time there it felt like I did. I remember one of the old men, John nearly killing me one hot summer's day back of 13 Shed on King George Dock. I had been working exceptionally long hours for months without a day off sometimes working from seven in a morning until midnight or even later. On this occasion I was doing the head gaskets on a Volvo Fl10 shunt wagon as well as a big fabricating job making large glass case platforms. John backed a forty-foot trailer through the doorway alongside me using a Douglas tug master and asked if I'd look at the brakes on the trailer.

Normally I would always put safety first and block the trailer wheels if I was going to go under to work on it. On this day though I was under a lot of pressure and wasn't thinking properly. I went to the cab where John was sitting and said to him "I'm just going under to check the air pots are working so press the pedal when I say." Ian was stood alongside him and witnessed what I said. I went to the back of the trailer and crawled between both axles to see the operation of the air pots and shouted "John, press the brakes!"

The next thing I knew was my head was being pushed into the floor and my ribs were being crushed as the trailer rolled forward. What had happened was John had misunderstood me and thought I meant to set off and press the brake. The two things that saved me were, firstly he'd forgotten to flick the hydraulic switch that operated the fifth wheel locking jaws that engage onto the kingpin of the trailer. If it had been a shunter that he was driving I'd have been dead as the jaws lock on automatically and have to be manually released. And secondly the trailer wasn't loaded with steel. My head and back acted as a wedge and allowed the tug to slide from under the fifth wheel and drop on its knees.

I ran to the cab and screamed at him, "You stupid bastard, what where you playing at?"

He apologised, not realising I'd been underneath and then casually said, "Luckily for you, I'm a useless bastard."

John like most of the dockers had learnt his trade in

the fifties and sixties when times were hard. He was tall and gangly with glasses and dry as a bone with a sense of humour that seems unique to the old dockers. They were the type of men that if you said, "Your lass has pissed off with another bloke," he'd reply "What a bastard! That means I'll have to do me own tea."

Another time I got a call to shoot down to North Gap on King George Dock to have a look at a tug that John had wrapped around a lamp post. Apparently the steering had just failed. I was panicking a bit as I'd just serviced it, however as I got there and saw John was the driver I asked him what had really happened and he told me "the steering had just failed". The near side front wheel was wrapped around the lamp post and had snapped track rod ends etc. I had a quiet word and asked if it really had failed or was it driver error, and told him if it was an accident I would not tell anyone but it would help me a lot not having to look for a problem that did not exist. He answered with a wry grin, "Well it might not have failed," with a wink and apologised saying, "It's always me that causes you problems."

I said "John, I wish Global had more drivers like you, if they did I'd be a millionaire."

One of the other lads that had a great sense of humour and always had everyone laughing was Lambo. I got a call from my then business partner Tony saying, "You'd best get yourself back to the office quick, I need to talk to you about something personal."

When I got there I asked what was wrong and he said a bloke had just come bursting into the office and screamed, "Where's Haldenby? He's been shagging my Mrs," and that he was going to kill me when he found me.

I said, "My conscience is clear," and then asked what the bloke looked like. When he said he was rough looking with a broken tooth I knew it would be Lambo.

RICHARD HALDENBY

The night I met David Beckham at Old Trafford when he asked,
'Are you Richard Haldenby? Can I have your autograph?'

THE POETIC HOOLIGAN

I rung his number and said, "Are you looking for me?" He burst out laughing and asked how I knew it was him. Every day was a play day there. I met some good people through the business, some of who I still keep in touch with now.

My ex-partner and I took some colleagues to Old Trafford one night in the Executive Suite to see United versus Everton for the first home game of the season four days after David Beckham had scored the 'halfway goal' against Wimbledon on August 17th 1996.

We were sat at our table with a United legend Norman Whiteside, when the Entertainments Manager announced that one of the first team players would be coming on stage for photos. As I looked to my right I saw David stood in a side room doorway waiting to come on stage. I took my programme to him and asked if he would sign it for my son and he politely did so. I congratulated him on the great goal he'd scored against Wimbledon and he quite shyly thanked me and asked if I'd liked it. When I asked if I could get my camera, pre-mobile phone days and have a photo with him he said, "I'm going on stage any second", which he did. They announced that due to the popularity of David they were only allowing woman and children on stage. I said to a mate, "Get ready with my camera as when they say you can go on, I am."

He said, "You can't do that," to which I replied, "Just watch me."

When they announced, 'Women and children only please,' I pushed my way through saying, "Excuse me."

I stood next to David and he laughed and said, "You were determined weren't you?"

I said, "I'm sorry David but I'll never see these people again but my six-year-old son will thank me forever."

RICHARD HALDENBY

How I imagine my mate Maurice as a reincarnated pigeon.

Good Luck Richard...

Testimonials

Mike Butler - CEO Clearway Environmental

Richard and I have been best friends for sixty years. We first met as infants down Lockwood Street when I lived in the Engineer's Arms down Bridlington Avenue and Richard lived down Lockwood Terrace. Our Dads were workmates and were good friends too.

We lost touch for a few years when the houses were demolished in 1967 but we met up again and have stayed great friends since.

We've had some hair-raising experiences and cheated death a few times on some of our fishing trips whilst going out into the North Sea in a small boat which looking back was hardly fit enough to sail in East Park boating lake.

I wish Richard all the best with the book as I know it is something he's wanted to do for a lot of years to keep the memory of our childhood and his family alive.

Mike Butler

Mike Krebs – Ferriby Recycling

I first met Richard back in 1978, we were both working for the same company, just two young lads we hit it off instantly and I got to know Rich well over the following six years we worked together and over that period we forged a friendship which is still good to this day forty-two years on. Richard became involved in football hooliganism and followed Mancheser United all over the country and got himself involved in the tribal mania that was sweeping the football world in the late seventies. He attracted the wrong kind of reputation and unfortunately the reputation stuck. But Rich

RICHARD HALDENBY

being the decent person he is deep down he turned his life around and although he was a football hooligan he has removed himself from that dark period in his life and...
Well, the rest is history.
He's a good honest person whom I have grown to trust and respect.
Regards,
Mike Krebs

Danny Murray - Proprietor, Moderation Bar, Hull
I've known Richard for thirty years since we worked together at Fountainhead racing stud when I was not long out of school. We had some great times there, especially when we pulled a prank on the joiner involving a cat that backfired on us with near fatal consequences. Another memorable night was when we were at Blackpool for the British Homing World annual pigeon show which involved a lot of drinking. I woke up in the early hours of the morning in a hotel bar minus my boots and trousers thanks to Richard and didn't get them back until the next day. Both stories are contained within this book in detail. My dad Kenny has been a friend of Richard's family for nigh on fifty years. Richard or should I say Clint, due to his remarkable likeness to Mr Eastwood often pops into my bar and has a natter.
Wishing you every success with the book Richard, I know it will be straight from the heart, warts n all.
Regards,
Danny Murray

Malcolm West
Richard joined my company back in 1971 as an apprentice engineer, in fact he was classed as a bound apprentice, which in effect tied him to the company until the age of 21 whereby he hopefully became qualified, he attended both day & night school to become a certified engineer.
A number of years earlier I did a similar course myself to become a bricklayer, my duties included digging holes in the

THE POETIC HOOLIGAN

ground on building sites, nailing 4 doors together to provide for a toilet, brewing tea and washing up after the lads in the lobby. I didn't even lay a brick for around two years, anyway back to Richard.

One of my earliest recollections was with Richard coming to see me one morning after he had watched an old Errol Flynn Pirate movie, he informed me that he had decided his life was going to be on the ocean waves and he was going to hand in his notice, I pointed out to Richard that he was a bound employee and that he must finish his apprenticeship which of course didn't go down too well and he was very upset, he got over this disappointment and fulfilled his obligation to become without doubt one of the best mechanical engineers I have personally ever known.

Over the years Richard has moved around the industry but always managed to make his way back to our company on numerous occasions, I was delighted when I found out that Richard was back with us and he had decided to finish his working career where it started, all I would say is I hope he doesn't watch too many navel movies, and get the urge!!

Good luck to you Richard and all the very best,
Malcolm West

Nick West

I started work with my father back in 1981/1982 and after a few weeks of sweeping the floors my father decided to send me out with an Engineer in an attempt to teach me a bit about engineering, Richard Haldenby' was his first choice.

Richard, take this useless little bugger out and teach him something about our industry will you said my father, so on my little 50cc moped every morning down to his home on Orchard Park ready for a 7.30am start I went, what Richard taught me some 39 years ago still stays with me to date, always polite, always charming, not bad at tinkering with a few spanners, and always very clean?

I could never work out how Richard managed to stay so clean, he always did the job well but always looked so clean and tidy, after all who else do you know who used to keep

RICHARD HALDENBY

aftershave in his van glovebox (just for emergencies he used to say)

Richard went on to do the same with my younger brother so needless to say he has always been someone that the full family has always looked up to. So I was very happy when Richard rang me a couple of years ago saying he would like to come back and work for the family once again. He was very open saying this would probably be his last job before his retirement and needless to say we welcomed Richard back for the fourth time I think.

I guess I have known Richard for nearly 40 years now, I cannot think of a better engineer, colleague and friend so when it does eventually happen, enjoy your retirement as I reckon you may have earnt it.

Regards,
Nick West